FOUR WAYS ON1

Christian Journeying Illustrated by the Histories of
Iulia de Beausobre, Dag Hammarskjöld,
Martin Luther King and Angelo Roncalli

David Goodacre

Published by
LEIGHTON COUNSELLING SERVICES

First published in Great Britain June 2006
Leighton Counselling Services,
9 Wilmington Close,
Newcastle upon Tyne, NE3 2SF
© David Goodacre

The right of David Goodacre to be identified as author of this work has been asserted in
accordance with Section 77 of the Copyright, Design and Patents Act 1988

*This book is sold subject to the condition that it shall not, by way of trade or otherwise,
be lent, resold, hired out or otherwise circulated without the publisher's prior consent in
any form or binding or cover that that in which it is published and without a similar
condition including this condition being imposed on the subsequent purchaser.*

British Library Cataloguing in Publication Data
A catalogue record for this book is available from the British Library

ISBN 0-9552546-0-4

978-0-9552546-0-4

Typeset by Leighton Counselling Services
Printed by Alphagraphics Ltd.,
19-21 Collingwood Street, Newcastle upon Tyne, NE1 1JE
Bound by 24/7

ACKNOWLEDGEMENTS

The publisher has tried to trace all copyright holders and apologizes if there is any inadvertent breach of copyright. This will be put right in any future edition. The publisher is grateful to those listed below and all who have given permission for material to be reprinted:

The scripture quotations are from the New Revised Standard Version of the Bible, Anglicized Edition, copyright © 1989 by the National Council of the Churches of Christ in the United States of America. Used by permission. All rights reserved.

Extracts from the Covenant Service are © TMCP and are used by permission of the Methodist Publishing House.

Extracts from 'The Woman who could not die' by Iulia de Beausobre (Victor Gollancz Ltd.), a division of the Orion Publishing Group are reprinted by permission

4 quotes from pp 131, 261, 314, 320 from "Lewis Namier: a biography" by Namier, J (1971) by permission of Oxford University Press.

Material from 'the Observer' is © Guardian Newspapers Limited 1983.

Quotations from *Markings,* © Faber and Faber are reprinted by permission.

Extracts from *Bearing the Cross* by David Garrow published by Jonathan Cape are reprinted by permission of The Random House Group Ltd.

Material from *A Testament of Hope* is reprinted by arrangement with the Estate of Martin Luther King Jr, c/o Writers House as agent for the proprietor, New York, NY, USA. © 1968 Martin Luther King, Jr, copyright renewed 1996 Coretta Scott King.

Extracts from *Stride Towards Freedom* are reprinted by arrangement with the Estate of Martin Luther King Jr, c/o Writers House as agent for the proprietor, New York, NY, USA. © 1958 Martin Luther King, Jr. copyright renewed 1986 Coretta Scott King

Extracts from *Strength to Love* are reprinted by arrangement with the Estate of Martin Luther King Jr, c/o Writers House as agent for the proprietor, New York, NY, USA. © 1963 Martin Luther King, Jr., copyright renewed 1991 Coretta Scott King.

Extracts from *My life with Martin Luther King, Jr.* are reprinted by permission of Writers House, New York, NY, USA © 1969 Coretta Scott King.

The copyright for *Let the Trumpet Sound* by Stephen B Oates, published by Search Press is administered by © the Continuum International Publishing Group Ltd.

The copyright for the diaries and letters of Angelo Roncalli, (Pope John XXIII), *Journal of a Soul, My Bishop, a portrait of Mgr Giacomo Maria Radini Tedeschi, Mission to France 1945-1953*, and *Letters to his Family 1901-1963*, each published by Geoffrey Chapman, is administered by © the Continuum International Publishing Group Ltd.

The copyright for *John XXIII, Pope of the Council* by Peter Hebblethwaite, published by Geoffrey Chapman is administered by © the Continuum International Publishing Group Ltd.

The extract from the Tablet – Website address http://www.thetablet.co.uk - of November 7th, 1992 is reprinted by permission.

The extract from © Kenelm Foster & Mary John Ronayne *I Catherine* 1980 is reprinted by permission of Harper Collins Publishers Ltd.

In memory of
JOY
1939-1998
who gave such encouragement and shared so much in the preparation
of this study

CONTENTS

The Front Cover illustration is of the River Tyne at Wylam, where the tide meets the river. Further illustrations are of the meeting of the waters on page 78 and of the mouth of the Tyne on page 160. Photos: author. A map is on page 17. A figure illustrating the Spiritual Dynamic is on page 12. Inside cover photo: Marie Goodacre

... there is a basic distinction between religion and politics: 'Religion means goal and way, politics implies end and means.' The political end can be recognized visibly by what the world considers 'success': whereas even in the highest experiences of mankind the religious goal remains 'that which simply provides direction'.

Encounter with Martin Buber – Aubrey Hodes (Penguin 1972) 187.

PREFACE

This study is of the spiritual journey in relatedness to God, illustrated by the histories of four Christians - Dag Hammarskjöld, Angelo Roncalli, Iulia de Beausobre and Martin Luther King - who balanced a life of prayer with active and genuine social concern. There are also, because inevitably such a study is a reflection on my own formation as a Christian in the latter half of the 20th century, some personal illustrations.

Dag Hammarskjöld
Dag Hammarskjöld was the second Secretary General of the United Nations, serving from 1953 until his death in Zambia in 1961. He was Swedish, born in 1905, the youngest son of a father who became Prime Minister of Sweden during the First World War. He was a man of precocious brilliance who after education in Uppsala rose rapidly in the Civil Service, serving in France as well as in Sweden, until his election to the United Nations Office. He kept a personal 'White Book' as he called it of his spiritual reflections.

It so happened that my wife Joy had a relation who came from Uppsala and indeed went to school with Hammarskjöld. She was Ulla Quarles van Ufford, who remembered him as rather shy and retiring. She showed us where he was buried in Uppsala. At a later date we visited the Dag Hammarskjöld memorial library, part of the Mindolo Ecumenical Institute in Kitwe, Zambia, near where he died. Ulla's friend Ulf Zandren, a pastor of the Swedish Lutheran Church arranged meetings for me with friends of Hammarskjöld and Joy and I met Karl Gierow, Secretary of the Swedish Academy, which awards the Nobel prize for literature, He also introduced us to Uno Willers, Director of the Swedish Royal Library - who showed me books from Hammarskjöld's library, especially his beautiful edition of the Book of Common Prayer - and Per Lind, a colleague from the Swedish Foreign service. Per Lind very kindly entertained me to a meal in a Stockholm restaurant. Both Joy and I were most grateful for the kindness of everyone in Sweden.

Angelo Roncalli (Pope John XXIII)
Angelo Roncalli became Pope John XXIII, the Pope of the Second Vatican Council, in 1959 He was Italian, born of peasant stock in 1881 in a small village in the North near to Bergamo where he was largely educated. He served in Bergamo as a priest until 1921 when he was moved to Rome. He was consecrated bishop in 1925 and thereafter until his appointment as Patriarch of Venice worked in the Vatican diplomatic service in Bulgaria, Turkey and France. He was Pope for four years and died in 1963. He also kept a journal of his spiritual way.

In preparing for this study, Joy, our older daughter Christine aged about 4 at the time and I, visited the scattered village of Sotto il Monte in the late Sixties. On a later journey we hoped to meet Loris Capovilla, who was then Archbishop of Loreto, but the slowness of the Italian post meant that my letter took too long to reach him. He kindly asked a friend to visit us where we were staying in Spello. The late Archbishop Bruno Heim, one of Roncalli's staff in Paris who later became Apostolic Nuncio to the United Kingdom, invited me to lunch at the Nunciature and regaled me with happy stories about Roncalli. As I left he gave me a picture of himself in cassock and apron baking a cake. My thanks to them.

Iulia de Beausobre
Iulia de Beausobre was born in St Petersburg in 1893. She married young, during the Kerensky period and after a brief time together in England returned to join her husband in Moscow where they were caught up in the Stalinist Terror of the Thirties. She and her husband were both imprisoned in the Gulag, only Iulia surviving. Eventually she sought asylum in England. Shortly after the war she married the historian Lewis Namier. She wrote about her experiences in Russia and also a number of spiritual works. She died in 1977.

Iulia de Beausobre had a great influence on a close friend of mine, Brian Frost, and it was through him that I came to know about her. He wrote a poem about her, which is in one of his collections.[1] I went on pilgrimage to Shepherd's Bush to see her flat, a pure example of Art Deco near the Tube station and again to Edinburgh for a delightful meeting with Irina Prehn, a Russian friend who knew both Nicolay and the Brunis. I am grateful to Brian, Irina and also to Una Kroll for their contribution to the study.

Martin Luther King Jr.
Martin Luther King Jr hardly needs an introduction. He was born in Atlanta, Georgia in the United States in 1929, trained as a minister in the Southern Baptist Church and a year after beginning in his first charge was elected to chair the Montgomery Improvement Association which organized the bus boycott and inaugurated the Human Rights movement. He was assassinated in Memphis on April 4th, 1988. His writings and sermons are collected in James Washington's study, *A Testament of Hope.*[2]

Joy and I with our younger daughter Marie visited Georgia and Alabama in 1988 and through the kind offices of John Patton, chairman of the International Association for Pastoral Care at the time, and his wife Helen were introduced to Ebenezer Church and its then pastor, the Revd Joe Roberts. Southern Baptist worship is an electrifying celebration of music, prayer and preaching and when we attended worship the woman next to our daughter was so exhilarated by the preacher that she became concerned lest her enthusiasm might alarm Marie. "Am I frightening you, l'il girl? She asked. Marie with 8 year old consideration assured her that it was "OK!" From Atlanta we headed off on pilgrimage to Birmingham, Selma and finally Montgomery - where the curator of the museum deplored 'all that marching about' - before returning to Atlanta. In visiting this small corner of the States, we had travelled as far as if we had travelled around England in its entirety. My thanks to all who made this possible.

Why these four?
The idea for two of them came shortly after I was ordained when I was working in my first parish in Stockton-on-Tees. I can still remember seeing the bold lettering on the billboard, 'Hammarskjöld dead' and the shock it was to so many of us then. This was the man who in the previous few years had made the United Nations such a potent tool for peace and had come to represent for many a new hope in a world recovering from the Second World War. The other, Pope John XXIII, was a similar symbol of hope. At the time Hammarskjöld died, Pope John had been in Rome some two years and the Vatican Council was to begin in the following year, 1962. As the Council progressed and in particular as the new Secretariat for Christian Unity was beginning to have an impact, our Stockton Church decided to attend Mass at the local Catholic Church during the week of prayer for Christian Unity. Hardly a matter for comment now, but then an almost revolutionary development and it brought the vicar, Trevor Beeson[3] an avalanche of letters, many of them decidedly hostile. It also brought smiles in the street from fellow Christians who until that point had studiously looked away whenever one of us clergy had happened to walk by. I felt inspired by both Hammarskjöld and Roncalli and wanted to know more about them and the way they lived. Not long after they died, their journals were published, *Markings* in 1964[4] and *Journal of a Soul* in 1965.[5] These gave me what I was looking for, examples of people whose prayerfulness could be studied as seriously as their social and political activities.

I completed an early draft studying these two alone in the 1970s and John Bowden of SCM advised me to expand the book to include a woman and someone who was married. This was when Iulia de Beausobre and Martin Luther King were added. Both had been married; so my quartet was complete. This process of evolution accounts for the imbalance of gender caused by having three men, two of them single and only one a woman. But in other ways they are a fascinating mix. They represent four Churches, none of them as it happens Anglican, four different aspects of Western culture, four nationalities, different races and attitudes, all in all a grouping which has evolved and made for a fascinating study.

Purpose of the study
Primarily this book is a phenomenological study of the spiritual journey illustrated by four completed spiritual journeys lived by actual persons. It considers in particular the balance of holiness and righteousness in their lives. It examines further what happened, the hazards, the challenges, the stages, the transitions which occur on the way, and learns from the four how they journeyed through them.

The histories were originally written as continuous narratives and only on completion were they spread around the chapters to illustrate the journey. Readers who would prefer to string the sections together so that they can read the histories as a whole should refer to the 'Further Reading' section at the end which gives the page numbers and the order. Names are highlighted in bold in the different chapters so that it is easier to see where each section begins.

Inevitably there are interpretations; where I have placed their transitions for example, what their experiences might have meant to them. It would be normal practice to check any such interpretations with the persons being interpreted but in the circumstances this is impossible. Interpretations where they occur should be read as considered reflections rather than as absolute statements.

I hope the book will be helpful to individual readers reflecting on their own pilgrimage, but also to those who find themselves asked by others to help them on their way. I have in mind also those who are counsellors, who wonder what spiritual matters might have to add to their counselling expertise. I remember well a Relate counsellor in a group in which we were both participating, responding to some observation I had made about this, asking me, "what does spirituality add to our work?" There was a suspicion in her tone that psychological talk was probably enough, but a question nonetheless whether there might be something. This book is partly a meditation on her question. The wider aim is to be of general help to all who look to follow Christ in this modern age as we journey towards the goal.

Structure of the book
The book begins with an introductory chapter, which outlines the underlying patterns and models, in particular the ideas of 'relatedness to God' and 'journey'. It also introduces the river Tyne as an extended metaphor of the spiritual way. The mountain metaphor for the chapter headings is also explained. There then follows a portion of St Mark's gospel and, apart from the first and in a different way the third,

an illustration of the journey from each of the four biographies – not always in the same order. Biographical sections in the later chapters are introduced by a summary to orientate readers who have forgotten where they were in the story. Each chapter then ends with some general reflections highlighting the significant points on the journey so far and either a concluding application or an illustration.

Chapters 2 to 8 follow the spiritual journey from birth until death beginning with childhood and adolescence in chapter 2 until it's ending at the moment or transition to young adulthood. This is the first transition to the Galilee/Wilderness way, which is the subject of the next two chapters. Chapter 3 is about the disciplines of the way, chapter 4 about the Galilee/Wilderness journey itself. The pivotal chapter, chapter 5, is about the Caesarea Philippi transition from early Christian life to the adult way of the cross. Chapter 6 describes this way of holiness and righteousness. Chapter 7 is about the transition to the more transparent living in the Spirit of the anointed way and the final chapter is on passion and dying. A final epilogue gives a short meditation on the role of the spiritual companion. A glossary of some of the words used - 'soul', 'spirit', 'person', 'bodiliness' etc. and some of the psychodynamic terms - is included with the end section.

*   *   *

It has taken me almost all of my ministry to write this book so there are many to thank in addition to those I have already mentioned: my late parents, Norman and Ruth Goodacre, who taught me to pray, my teachers at King's College, London, the late Jack Churchill and Sydney Evans and tutors Fr Benedict Green CR and Ulrich Simon and also the Warden of St Boniface, Warminster John Townroe. My first Vicar, Trevor Beeson has been a continuing influence, so many of the things learnt in those early years of ministry preparing me for all I have been able to do since. I owe much too to Bill Wright and Peter Kaim-Caudle and their teaching about social and political issues. For five years I worked with the late Bill Portsmouth[6], author of *Healing Prayer* and during the time continued learning psychology and theology under Frank Lake[7] and his colleagues and had psychotherapy from Harry Guntrip.[8] Bob Lambourne, Michael Wilson [9] and James Mathers guided me through the Birmingham University Diploma in Pastoral Studies' course. These mentors made me realize how each of the disciplines they represented, the life of prayer, ministry, political and social concerns, counselling, health and healing, pastoral care were all necessary components of any spiritual care that might be offered. I am deeply grateful to all of them.

In addition I would like to thank those who helped me write the book, especially Dr Callan Slipper. I would like to thank also Michael Perry and the late Alexander Hamilton and Malcolm Sweeting who read the first draft and Alec Graham and Peter Selby and the late Fr Aelred Stubbs who read and commented on a later one. Fr John Dale, Dorothy Heard, Robert Innes and Christine Smith were part of a group who considered a chapter of the book and Alan Bartlett, Judy Hirst, John Pritchard and Alison White were a continual support when I was using some of the material for lectures at Cranmer Hall in Durham. Thanks also to the many others, too many to list, who made their comments on the final draft.

My late wife Joy, to whose beloved memory the book is dedicated, lived with the study throughout our married life as have our two daughters, Christine and Marie. One or the other of them accompanied us to a number of the places associated with the four subjects of the study. .

David Goodacre
Newcastle upon Tyne
June 2006

FOUR WAYS ONE GOAL

*Christian Journeying Illustrated by the Histories of
Iulia de Beausobre, Dag Hammarskjöld,
Martin Luther King and Angelo Roncalli.*

CHAPTER 1

SUMMONS TO THE WAY

Relatedness and Journey

'See, I am sending my messenger ahead of you, who will prepare your way;'
(Mark 1, 2b)

At the end of an Ignatian Thirty Day Retreat at St Beuno's in North Wales, the participants are given a much needed four-day break. One Spiritual Director advised her group of retreatants to be alert to casual people they might meet on the holiday who might want to tell them their story. "At the end of such a long time of silence," she explained, "people will respond to your stillness and see in you a person to whom they can talk." A skilled Spiritual Director was sharing her discernment that as praying Christians they might be called upon to listen. People do intuitively discern the kind of person to whom they can talk about such intimate matters, which means that those who are asked to do the work need themselves to be personally on the way.

While I do not subscribe in any way to the idea that Spiritual counsellors can manage without knowing how to listen or learning a more than basic knowledge about human growth and development – spiritual direction is brought into disrepute when it fails to acquire such skills – they are of secondary importance beside the vital necessity of developing a prayerful relationship with God, however weak they might judge this to be. Just as counsellors or psychotherapists are of little value if they pay no attention to their own relationships, so spiritual counsellors need first of all to be in relationship with God. St Paul could not have urged the Galatians to 'bear one another's burdens'[1] if he had not recognized that it is praying and journeying Christians who are the best people to support praying and journeying Christians. So while taking for granted the importance of developing the necessary skills this first chapter is about these basics, introducing models of the relationship with and the journey towards God.

*   *   *

Relatedness to God
In the second section of each chapter, a portion of St Mark's Gospel [2] is considered. The reflection begins with the prologue and continues through the chapters until the first ending at chapter 16, verse 8. The reading is personal, a meditation on the way of the Christian who desires to follow Christ.

The dynamic of relatedness to God is taken from the prologue, not simply as a description of the beginning of the way but as a model of response in each and every transition of the way – address, baptismal celebration, engagement in discipleship. St Mark plunges straight into the first part, the preaching of St John, moves from there to the baptism of Jesus and completes the cycle with a description of Jesus's time of trial in the wilderness. The same cycle is in St Matthew and St Luke and in a different way in St John, but it is most explicit in St Mark. It begins with an address from God, a relationship which is mediated through the Baptist. It continues with Jesus's response in allowing himself to be baptized, and is completed by his engagement with all that opposes him as he enters the wilderness; three stages: First address and response, secondly baptism, thirdly disciplined engagement.[3]

Analysing this more closely, St Mark describes John the Baptist as a herald, who like Isaiah tells the people of a new way for which they must prepare by penitence and baptism and at the same time he points to another who will follow him and baptize with the Holy Spirit. In the Church's calendar, John is remembered in the Advent season as a type of minister, who invites people to turn to God. He is an intermediary who speaks on God's behalf, inviting souls to take a new and creative step towards their future by trying not only for something higher than before but to relate to someone who is higher than anyone they have known before. John then represents all those who urge us in whatever way they may to take a new direction in life. Persons may sometimes be hardly aware of such a summons, but they will know in their hearts that they have been nudged towards a new and creative choice, that they have been asked to take on a more demanding and fulfilling life in a new relationship to God.

There are two reasons why the address, however powerful it may feel, comes in this slightly slant and un-pressured way. The first is because it is in the nature of Love to require a free response and the second because unless persons themselves do respond freely they will be unable to muster the energy to follow. The address must both reach the heart and at the same time – even if couched in the most persuasive terms – allow the person the freedom to reject it. (Mark 1, 1-8)

The second part is baptism. In St Mark Jesus is baptized by John in the Jordan, the Son rising from the water, anointed by the Holy Spirit to the delight of the Father who declares, "You are my son, the Beloved." The Trinity celebrates, each Person of the one God delighting in this eternal moment of mystery, which identifies Jesus as the Spirit-filled self or person who is rooted in God. Like so many such important spiritual occasions it is a remarkably brief event.

In the first part John, or whoever, is pointing to Jesus. In this second, the person having heeded the call and having decided to follow needs to mark the response in some celebratory moment of baptismal quality. At its most basic persons have died to what they have rejected in order to embrace a new future. In terms of the journey, they have specifically decided to turn from the way they were going to a take a new route. In so doing they have implicitly accepted an ultimate commitment to die and to rise with Christ, marking the decision by some ritual event which is not just a personal response but one made in association with the whole community of the disciples. (Mark 1, 9-11)

In the third part, Jesus is compelled by the Spirit to go into the wilderness. Mark says little about his time there, simply that it was long, that he was with the wild animals and that angels attended him. The text does not actually say that he fasted, but it does emphasize that he had no choice but to go there. Once his decision in the first part had been celebrated in the second then he was required to confront and battle with everything that was lesser and ultimately evil in the third. His followers are similarly called to engage in life in their own wilderness, not simply as a moratorium, a space for taking stock, but in a full commitment to discipleship.

Morna Hooker points out that St Mark refers both to wilderness and the presence of the Holy Spirit in each of the three parts[4]. John preaches in the wilderness and looks to the one who will baptize with the Holy Spirit. Jesus is baptized in the Jordan, which runs through the wilderness and the Spirit descends upon him. As he enters the wilderness he is driven there by the Holy Spirit. Later in the chapter, I pick up this theme of wilderness, symbolizing as it does the harsh environment of the world in which disciples, energized by the Holy Spirit, are to follow. In this part the emphasis is on discipleship in the presence of Christ whatever the difficult surroundings. Mark[5] makes constant allusions to presence in the wilderness in his early chapters. One example is the odd story of Jesus and his disciples eating grain on the Sabbath. Jesus draws his critics' attention to the story of David and Abiathar[6], when David asked for bread before starting his journey with his companions into the wilderness. Moses similarly led his people through the 'baptismal' waters of the Red Sea into the wilderness where God was to sustain them on the way with food and drink. Each of the allusions in fact includes a feeding so that as they journey Mark is assuring them that they will be sustained. In St John[7] where his dynamic lacks this symbol of the wilderness, he nonetheless talks of discipleship. The ones who are following Jesus are invited to come and be with him that they might engage with the way. (Mark 1, 12-13)

As persons we are called by God, we are baptized into the death and resurrection of Christ and if we are to engage with the problems we will encounter we will only succeed if we know ourselves accompanied, if we are fed with the bread of life and have the strength of the Holy Spirit for the journey.

Put visually the threefold cycle of response might look like this: address first, celebration/baptism second, discipleship/engagement third.

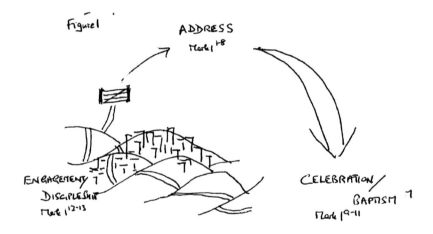

The gate refers to the divide between one experience and the next. In this chapter and indeed in much of the book there are special moments of transition when the passage through the dynamic is sharp and clear, but it is equally applicable to the 'lesser' day to day spiritual encounters in which persons hear the call, celebrate the event in the Eucharist and daily, weekly, monthly set out once again on the way. This is the spiritual dynamic, the energy which comes from responding to the call of God to journey after Christ on the way. This is the first part of the model, the relational the proper responding to the day today spiritual call from God to follow.

The Journey
The second part is the journey itself. 'Journey' is of course only one of the metaphors used of the spiritual life and one friend commented, hardly appropriate for the disabled. But why not? Often when taking retreats I ask the participants to take one of the days to go off on a pilgrimage. They are given sandwiches, asked to be aware of walking with Christ as they travel and however they go, and to return by a given time. One elderly nun, I remember, walked to the gate of the retreat house and whiled away her day by sitting in a nearby bus-shelter talking to an old man who had joined her - much banter among the other religious when she recounted the tale at the end of the retreat. Journeying does not necessarily require great movement. Even this short journey had a beginning, the walk to the gate, a middle which in this case she spent in spiritual companionship, and an end when she walked back to the retreat house. Not much movement certainly, but enough. Even if there had been none, there would still have been interior movement.

What is particularly useful in taking 'journey' as a metaphor is that St Mark sets his narrative within a journey. Some commentators[8] insist that geography is not important to him. Nonetheless, after the initial introduction Jesus is living in Capernaum beside the lake. In the following chapters, until the middle of Chapter 8, he and his disciples cross and re-cross the lake, as if his boat were marking a cross on the font of the lake, as he visits the whole area. There is one journey to the Decapolis and round by Tyre, but for the most part he remains in Galilee. A turning point is the scene set in Caesarea Philippi, a town not otherwise mentioned, which is to the North of Bethsaida. After that signal point, the recognition by the disciples through Peter of Christ's identity, Jesus turns to the South and heads for Jerusalem, the site of the transfiguration being taken as Mount Tabor, a prominent hill which rears up out of Galilee and was a high point not far from Nazareth which may long have been of significance to Jesus. He then continues his way to Jerusalem, to the place which was to be the physical and spiritual goal of his journey. This is also the journey his disciples are to take after him.

Iulia de Beausobre tells a story of St Serafim of Sarov[9] at the time of his emergence from long years of contemplative stillness. He had begun to receive visits from Princess Xenia of a nearby convent, who was a rigorous and not over-wise lady who wished to encourage her dilatory nuns to walk in the footsteps of Christ. She would soliloquise in Serafim's cell on the matter and once implored him, "If I could I'd put every one of them through every single step of our dear Lord's agony; then they'd begin to understand." Serafim was roused to break his silence. He heard the Virgin Mary interiorly telling him to say, "My Son's life on earth was his alone. Not theirs, not hers. My Son's servants do follow his path; but they follow it in spirit, not in the flesh. Bethlehem, Nazareth, Jerusalem, Gethsemane, Calvary, all men can live them in their own souls. But no other feet can tread my Son's way."

Each person then has his or her own personal way which if it is a path following the Lord in spirit still remains his or her own. It is in each case also a journey with stopping places, stations on the way or 'markings' to use Hammarskjöld's metaphor, piles of stones on a mountain path, where they stopped to do particular pieces of work. Moving house is a real sign of an identifiable change in the circumstances of most, each home being like a cairn, and nowadays, when people move a great deal, an objective marker of some, usually significant change in life; of some spiritual deepening in the relationship with God also. The various moves of the four are highlighted in bold in the histories. The markings provide a link between the journey and the relationship, an outward sign of what is happening interiorly.

In the course of the journey, the relationship with God, powered by the spiritual dynamic of address, celebration and discipleship, deepens and three main stages on the journey will be identified. Whether 'stage' is quite the right word is uncertain, perhaps a change in consciousness or in the discernment of God and life might be better. For example, the counselling theorist John Rowan[10] speaks of instrumental, authentic and transpersonal stages, the first to do with the healing of problems, the second with personal maturity and the third – only possible he argues for those who practice some spiritual discipline – with the development of heart and soul in relationship with the Divine.

Something similar can be identified in St Mark. It will become clearer as the journey progresses but the stages are the Galilee ministry (1.14 – 8,26), which comes to a climax at Caesarea Philippi (8.27 – 9,1). The second stage is the way of the cross to Jerusalem. (9.2 – 12,end). The final stage after a transition (13) is the Passion (14,1 – 15,end). The same three-fold way appears again and again in the spiritual literature. One of the first to speak of it was Pseudo-Dionysius the Areopagite[11], writing in about 500. He described the first stage as a purgative way, a cleansing of all that separates from God – very similar to what Rowan is speaking about -, the second as an illuminative way, an inner enlightenment as to the identity of Christ and a time of active following and a third stage as the unitive or perfect way when God brings the soul into a new closeness and unity with himself.

Dionysius's study of this was in connection with ministry and the sacraments to which he compared these ways. He looked at purgation together with baptism, illumination with the Eucharist and the final stage, the unitive with anointing. I was tempted to use these sacraments as names for the spiritual stages but in the end decided against it for the first two. Baptism is indeed the sacrament of purging and cleansing and begins the way, but it is not confined to that stage. The same is even more true of the Eucharist, which sustains the traveller from beginning to end. Anointing, of the three, is perhaps most particularly suited to the unitive way and I have used this term in preference to unitive, but the same applies. Persons are anointed with the Holy Spirit from the start. This is how it is in all of the spiritual way, but people do draw closer to God on the spiritual journey so that while it is possible to speak of people facing any of the dilemmas of life at any stage there is also identifiable movement which begins at birth, passes through the whole of life and comes to a final end in the baptism of death.

The developing relationship can be compared to the love of a couple for each other. Initially they fall in love and settle into a loving relationship, which they then have to work at on both sides as each learns to recognize the other, coming to see how different each is from what they first thought they were. Rows, times of misery, forgiveness and healing and acceptance follow until slowly but surely the couple come to see each other in a new light. Their life then has a new joy and they face fresh and perhaps greater difficulties as they progress in their relationship. But they have still not reached the end. Love continues to grow until it reaches the point where communion has become instant, where they are so emotionally, physically and spiritually one that they appear to be a unity, each a person in themselves but more than that, a couple whose joint being radiates their love. They as it were first become a couple, then in the second stage they are a couple and finally they are in love. This is what each of the analogies is trying to say, that the relationship of the soul with God grows as they journey together, the beloved one's love for the One who loves deepening and growing throughout.

Another description of this progress is in Antony Bloom's meditation on the Lord's Prayer.[12]   He began with the petitions which speak of penitence and trial and the threat of evil.

> Forgive us our sins, as we forgive those who sin against us,
> Lead us not into temptation (or 'time of trial' in another translation)
> But deliver us from evil.

The main thrust of the spiritual life, the way of the cross, is in the middle section.

> Your kingdom come,
> Your will be done, on earth as in heaven.
> Give us today our daily bread

Perhaps the quotidian petition links them both.   The final unitive way is in the opening contemplative words.

> Our Father in heaven,

Hallowed be your name.

It is a telling reversal, which illustrates both the deepening of the communion with God and also that the contemplative yearning is there from the beginning. The soul longs to behold the face of God, perhaps from the moment it first catches an earnest of it in the countenance of the mother at the beginning of life.

The words I will use to name the three stages are Galilee/Wilderness or Purgative way for the first, the Way of the Cross or Illuminative way for the second and the Anointed way for the third. Galilee and Wilderness symbolize the paradox, that Christians at the beginning experience both light and darkness. I can remember once presenting these ideas to a group and talking about the wilderness as an appropriate symbol for the first stage of the way and the comment of one of them: "Surely for many people, all of life is in a constant wilderness." Yes it can be, and this is symbolized by the way of the cross of the next stage and by the anointed way with its familiarity with affliction and passion. But her anger was not simply about my limited presentation, it was also about wretchedness. There was a depressive, even masochistic edge to what she said, which needed healing. The spiritual way may be hard but it is not miserable. It is real and meaningful, enhanced by the health and vigour of the first stage, the exhilaration of vocation in the second, and increasing joy in the final stages.

These are the stages of the journey. The transitions between them will be in terms of the spiritual dynamic of relatedness described above (address, celebration, engagement) The dynamic is a daily constant of the way - life as a continual responding to the address of God – as persons move through the transitions to an ever-deepening encounter with God.

Two extended metaphors are used in the book to illustrate both this deepening and the character of the transitions. The first one, which comes in the chapter headings, is from Dag Hammarskjöld's comparison of the spiritual journey with a mountain ascent. The soul marks his or her passage by adding to 'markings' on the way.

The second one is of the river Tyne.[13] as an allegory both of the whole way and in particular of the Caesarea Philippi moment and the transitions to the anointed way and passion which follow. There is the briefest of allusions to it at the beginning of the first chapter but primarily it is used as an illustration of these later stages of the way. In the 7th and 8th centuries the Tyne was at the heart of European civilization and it was at the same time that Christianity first came to the North. Oswald, the King of Northumbria, invited the Scottish speaking St Aidan of Iona to preach the gospel at different points beside the river, the king travelling around with Aidan acting as his interpreter. Many of the churches founded at that time are still standing and are like 'markings' on the way to the coast.

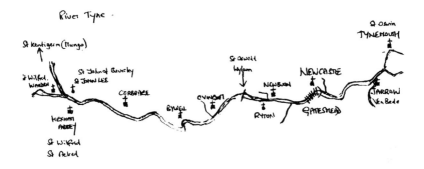

Figure 2 – the Lower Reaches of the Tyne

This chapter has been first about the underlying dynamics of the journey, the initial call, baptismal celebration and engagement which is to be repeated again and again throughout life and especially at the points of transition. Secondly, it has been about the spiritual journey of the Galilee/Wilderness way, the way of the cross and the anointed way and the various stations or markings that are likely to be passed on such a journey. Persons may find it helpful whether as readers or companions to reflect upon their own experience of address, their own prayerful relationship with God and their discipleship and perhaps also – as they think of their journey - the significance of their current home and what previous markings they have passed.

In the chapters which follow, this journey in relatedness with God is illustrated by what happened in the lives of Iulia de Beausobre, Dag Hammarskjöld, Martin Luther King and Angelo Roncalli, who empowered by the Holy Spirit trod their ways in Christ. The way begins in the following chapter at the very beginning of life, at the earliest point of the address of God, even before the celebratory moment of birth and the tentative beginnings of the spiritual way. The chapter explores the spiritual development through childhood and adolescence until the moment of transition to young adulthood at a climax on a Jordan Day.

CHAPTER 2

THE CHILD ADDRESSED

Childhood, Adolescence and Call

'In those days Jesus came from Nazareth of Galilee and was baptized by John in the Jordan. And just as he was coming up out of the water he saw the heavens torn apart and the Spirit descending like a dove upon him. And a voice came from heaven, "You are my son, the Beloved; with you I am well pleased.' (Mark 1, 9-11)

It is difficult nowadays to say exactly when life can be said to begin. Is it at 14 days or 24 weeks as some ethical opinions imply or is it rather as procreators in their love for each other feel within themselves, at the moment of conception? The Chinese apparently date the beginning of life from conception and certainly the Church dates the story of redemption from the annunciation which is celebrated nine months before Christmas on March 25th; in past history appropriately enough New Year's Day. Even before the physical event of conception the child has been conceived as an idea within the dreams and prayers of the parents, especially the mother, as a kind of annunciation that she hopes to bear a child.

The presence of a new being in the womb, like a trickle of water at the source of a great river, is assured when the infinitely small cells begin to duplicate after the implantation of the sperm in the ovum. As the psalmist says to God, 'you knitted me together in my mother's womb' and I 'was intricately woven in the depths of the earth,' where 'your eyes beheld my unformed substance.'[1] As the foetus is known to God so also it is known to the mother. Winnicott suggests that the child in the womb is able to sense something of its mother's feelings whether she is in anguish or distressed, a finding which is supported by an increasing body of research.[2] On the completion of gestation the first great journey of life begins. The distance to be travelled is not great, just the length of the vagina, but it is the first adventure, a journey from the comparative safety of the womb to the entirely different and separate existence which is outside.

It is worth dwelling on this process of birth because it is so central in Christian symbolism. Both dominical sacraments, perhaps the experience of crisis in general, reflect this first crisis, the casting out from the womb into the rigours of a new form of life. When the second stage of labour is reached and as, let us say for the sake of simplicity, an infant girl is about to be born, her head – usually the head – is positioned firmly at the cervical exit. She awaits the rhythmic waves of the contracting uterus to impel her insistently towards the outside world. The baby cooperates a little by moving her feet against the vagina wall, like a bargee walking a barge through a canal tunnel, but it is the contractions which impel her to birth, her cooperation being her 'yes' to new life which awaits her when her unfilled lungs, flaccid like an unused balloon until that point, are inflated by the breath of God so that she cries out in surprise. In her mother's arms she searches for the breast, the movement to suckle an instinct for survival to which her mother responds by helping her to find the nipple. Like the birth of the infant Jesus celebrated in St Luke's narrative by choirs of angels singing

Glory to God in the highest heaven.

Parents feel the same delight and rejoice similarly in their hearts.

Life outside the womb has thus begun. The first section of this chapter is a short account of the human development of the child and adolescent based on the analyst cum sociologist Erik Erikson's[3] study of the interrelated physical and psychological growth of persons from this point until old age and death. He calls it an epigenetic cycle of eight ages. Each stage, he argues, presents persons with a choice between a negative and a positive option, which they have to resolve. How they do so affects their understanding of what happened before and everything which is to occur subsequently. The first three stages are in psychoanalytic parlance the oral, anal and genital phases up to the age of 5, then there are the latency and adolescent phases up to young adulthood where this chapter ends. The three adult stages are young adulthood, adulthood and old age. Interestingly to the Christian reader he identifies a virtue which he thinks is particularly developed in each of the ages.

In 1981, James Fowler[4] and his team of researchers, building on Erikson's work, published a study of how faith develops. Fowler posits seven stages (one preliminary stage and 6 more). Later in the book I will be referring to the American Buddhist philosopher and psychologist, Ken Wilber[5] on the development of consciousness. Everyone passes through Erikson's ages, only some through all of Fowler's and Wilber's.

Erikson begins his description of the growth of the person at the moment of birth. A baby has existed within a primitive oneness of relationship with the mother in the womb. Now, in what Frank Lake used to describe as the 'womb of the spirit'[6] the infant self, although physically separate continues emotionally to remain almost as much at one. He or she is held, touched, suckled by the mother so that the baby incorporates not only her milk but also the very life substance of her bodiliness.

There is now well-supported scientific evidence[7] to show just how fundamental this early attachment between mother, or the one major person taking the role of mother, male or female, is to the child. She speaks the sweet nothings which a mother does to her infant, what one researcher, Colin Trevarthen[8] has dubbed as 'motherese;' an international parlance used by all mothers to their children everywhere. She holds her child at a natural distance, some 20 centimetres from her face, so that her child can see her. Spiritually this is a fundamental experience; she is helping her child to behold the love in her face, so that her babe may delight in her as she delights in her child.

Fowler discerns a preliminary stage in the development of faith in this primal relationship between mother and infant. As he explains, the age is largely inaccessible to the kind of empirical enquiry he and his team were able to do in the rest of their study, but he acknowledges with Erikson that this early relationship is determinative. It is the time of building through attachment to mother or her substitute, a picture of the environment as trustworthy, well symbolized by the mother cradling her infant in her arms, or the godmother when she holds her godchild before baptism, the holding being like the underlying cradling of God, the love in the face of the Lover beholding the beloved who learns to love in return. As the sociologist Peter Berger once put it, 'we become that as which we are addressed.'[9]

Through the love of the mother given physically, mentally and spiritually, the child begins to learn slowly but surely that life is safe. Alternatively, for whatever reason, that life is not safe. This is Erikson's crisis for the child of these early months. The child learns either to trust or mistrust. Even if the child's experience is very grim, enough to bring about serious mistrust, it never breeds total mistrust. There was a dreadful and unethical experiment apparently carried out by one of the Prussian kings[10] to see what would happen if children were deprived of their mothers. The finding was as stark as one would expect. They all died. They had learnt to mistrust completely. Children if they are alive have retained enough experience of love and trust in the midst of their mistrust to continue living and therefore have enough good experiences on which a lover, a carer or a therapist can build in the future. For most persons the decision to trust is made on the simple basis that they have known themselves loved

The strength which accrues from this resolution, Erikson suggests, is hope. Love awakens trust which in its turn generates hope. The life of everyone, ultimately, rests on these three fundamental virtues, the theological virtues as they are called, because they link the person to God, an experience of love, which evokes trust on the basis of which the soul hopes.

In the second age, the infant rapidly grows into a determined child, confident in being loved and ready to test the parents to find out if it is safe enough to be a person in his or her own right. This is the age when the emphasis in the bodiliness shifts from the mouth to the anus, to the good which is produced and at the same time, because it is behind and cannot be seen, to what is threatening. The child is beginning to learn how to control the muscles, what he or she can do, what hold on to, what let go. The crisis here is one of learning to assert the self against authority and become autonomous while facing the possibility that he or she might fail and as a result feel ashamed and doubtful. When, or if, the child succeeds in resolving this dilemma, the infant acquires a will of its own.

By the third age, what Erikson calls the locomotor, genital stage, little persons grow stronger in their inner conviction that they are loved and that they have an intimate relationship with their mother which they perceive to be their natural right, confident that they can do what they want. Fowler observes at this point, his first stage – which extends in his scheme until the age of 7 – that a child intuitively absorbs without question the mores, beliefs and practices of the family, accepting as axiomatic what the family understands about God and the ultimate.

A child by this time can get about with skill and confidence, a young boy feeling like a young stag prancing on the mountains ready like his father, penis proud, able to challenge all comers[11] and on the intimate level, he the rightful companion of his mother   Similarly the young girl is confident that she is the one for her father, unconsciously aware that she has a garden of lilies where her father might be happy to browse[12].   Wise parents contain these natural desires within their proper boundaries so that their children can grow in confidence and their ability to love. But the danger of abuse is real.

Children, apart from being so small, are by now surprisingly mature sexually.   It is the task of a third person, usually the father, the actual lover of the mother as the mother is of the father, to set a boundary, to convey lovingly to the child the truth of the family relationships. The father guides the child to recognize that the intimacy of infancy is at an end and that a new life beckons beyond the family. The crisis here is whether the child can continue to be a person of initiative, able to risk new things, new possibilities and relationship without being overcome by feelings of guilt for wanting to stay with Mum in the safety of infancy. The strength which comes when this is satisfactorily negotiated is a sense of purpose. The child has now become autonomous and equipped to leave the security of home and take the first steps into the unknown. "I know where I am going," the child might be imagined as saying, a self-encouragement to venture a little way from the family into the risky environment of infant and primary school.

In these first five years children have been learning the art of relationship, the human skills they need to live in intimate, supportive and companionable relationships. They have learnt in their innermost beings that they can trust and love and hope.

Now launched a little into the world, children have reached Erikson's fourth age, the latency period when the emotions are comparatively quiescent. It gives children a space for learning before the major upheavals of puberty. They learn how to make things, to be productive, to become competent, which is Erikson's virtue of this age. The crisis he identifies is the tension between industry and feeling inferior. To Fowler the period forms his second stage, when the child learns the basic myths and stories which the family and society hold to be true about life. Children of this age are moral beings, they believe an eye should be sacrificed for an eye, a tooth for a tooth, that faith is literal and true and that everyone should accept it without demur. They are faithful souls.

Such certainties are about to end. Adulthood beckons and a long and anxiety provoking time as the child proceeds through adolescence to become a mature young adult. There are three main tasks to be achieved if young persons are to become sexually and physically mature; they need a clear sense of identity, an understanding of what they believe about life and time to find the particular role they might fulfil. Adolescence, together with the childhood which precedes it, is the preparatory work of the transition to young adulthood, which will be marked at some significant and identifiable occasion on what might be called a 'Jordan' day, religious or secular, which both as it were celebrates the decisions made and marks the transition to adult status.

The onset of puberty heralding the fifth age signals a considerable change. It occurs somewhere between the ages of 10 and 16, triggered when the body reaches a certain weight by the hypothalamus which instructs the pituitary gland to circulate the growth hormones around the body. As a result the boy's body begins to change to that of a man, the girl to the body of a woman. The boy develops the secondary characteristics of facial and bodily hair and a masculine voice and he struts with the new found confidence of the youthful male as together with his friends he begin to discover his new potency. Similarly, from the onset of the menarche, the girl knows within herself that she is becoming a woman as blood passes from her during her periods. Her breasts develop, her hips broaden and she becomes womanly in line and form. Both are now capable of an adult sexual relationship, their bodies demanding that they move from the safety of total dependence on their parents to the new challenges of freedom and responsibility as young adults.

With all these changes in the bodiliness and the developing sexual maturity which accompanies them, the central task of puberty is to become secure in the identity of being a young man or woman who can relate physically with other women and men. As Erikson says[13], the task is to learn how all that they have experienced about being a person as children can be integrated into the new mature bodiliness they now are as young persons. In other words, what their identity is. Erikson considers the strength learnt in this conflict to be fidelity. The danger is that they become confused, unable to discover who they are, what faith they have, what role they should fulfil, where they should fit in and just whom they are to be and do.

In terms of identity, understanding who they are, young people usually come together in single sex groups to emphasize the qualities they find in each other for themselves. In fantasy they are being encouraged to do great things, but it is instructive how all the great myths of the hero emphasize a serious and secret vulnerability. It is as if young persons are being warned that their new found power has its limits, that much as they might think they can do what they like, they can do much but not anything. Young women also until the late 20th century adopted men as their role models, a reflection of the masculine prejudice of society but more recently and appropriately they have started looking to heroic women.[14] In either case, the inner figure based on a real person is employed as an inspirational mentor who can also be a moderating influence within as young persons search for their way.

In terms of faith, Fowler notes that the literal certainties of childhood give way now to new questions. Young adolescents can now think abstractly and logically and construct hypotheses and with the materialistic scientific world-view of the West prevailing accept the vaguely agnostic humanism influenced by residual Christianity which seems to be the dominant belief system. Young people are conventional and they accept without too much analysis these overarching beliefs and meanings held by their friends and those they value.

Now comes the climax of adolescence, the summons to autonomous adult life, which is in Erikson's scheme, the nub of the conflict of the period: autonomy versus isolation.

In the lead up to this transition a number of young people find a time away from home in what Erikson calls a moratorium[15] useful at this stage, a gap year perhaps, a course, university even, a given space in order to come to terms with the new realities which are confronting them, a retreat, a time to reflect. They are to enter into an intimate relationship or decide to remain creatively single so that they do not find themselves isolated and unable to love as they would wish. Love is Erikson's virtue of this stage. They need to discover what role they should fulfil in life, how to earn a living, how contribute to the wider world and how eventually to support a family. It may be that the role they adopt will turn out to be their vocation. Their faith, Fowler suggests, at the beginning of this stage will be clear-cut, a faith unsullied by myth or symbol, robust and solid, a black and white understanding undisturbed by too much nuance or paradox.

In these later adolescent years, indeed throughout childhood, there is a summons, a gathering address from God to grow up and become an adult. Sometimes the address comes in a direct manner, far more often through John the Baptist like figures, such as parents, important relations, school teachers and school friends, characters in books, films and on television, all the many who inspire and encourage persons to embark on the adventure of life. This is the address of the dynamic. When the three decisions, about faith, role and intimate relationships, have been made or are about to be made – sometimes one, even two, of these decisions has to be postponed, but at some point they have to be made - the second part of the dynamic beckons, the call to a new consciousness, which seems to demand some corporate celebration.

Spiritual ceremonies generally celebrate what has in fact already happened. Individual, personal decisions may have been made but they need the support and ratification of the wider corporate community of Church and Society. The ceremony if it is liturgical endows the decisions made with blessings and validation and marks the moment by the gift of the Holy Spirit for the new stage of life. The celebration recalls Jesus's baptism in the river Jordan, the baptism which inaugurated his ministry. One January Michael Haslam, at that time chaplain to the University of Newcastle, encouraged the Newcastle cathedral congregation to think of the first Sunday of the year as a 'Jordan' day and it feels an appropriate title for the liturgical or secular ceremony which marks the transition to adulthood. Such a ceremony becomes a baptismal or transforming moment which celebrates an actual change of genuine spiritual significance, a dying to the past and the beginning of a new life in Christ empowered by the Spirit to the delight of the Father. The young adult way is started.

*   *   *

The new journey begins in St Mark with his brief reference to the completion of John's ministry, his account of Jesus going to Galilee and then his succinct summary of Christ's message, that the significant moment has arrived, that the kingdom of God is near and that they must turn to God and delight in and believe the good news that God in Christ is with them. Jesus then calls four persons: Simon, Andrew, James and his brother John to follow him on the way. (Mark 1, 14-20)

St Mark says nothing about Christ's early childhood and what we have in Matthew and Luke is more a theological than an historical account. The latter gospels trace the distant roots of his coming through genealogies, St Matthew then concentrating on stories associated with Joseph, and St Luke on an interwoven narrative of the events surrounding the births of John the Baptist and Jesus. What both describe is an annunciation and after Jesus's birth some of the religious ceremonies, which marked Jesus's reception into the spiritual community at his birth, his welcome and initiation rites and in Luke's case, a kind of Bar-Mitzvah story at his puberty. Each narrative points to the activity of God at different significant points on the childhood way.

Such points are often the most that can be discovered when tracing the early spiritual histories of anyone. Sometimes there is more information, but the liturgical events, especially baptism, confirmation and the 'liturgical' occasion, whatever it is, which celebrates the transition to the young adult way are particularly important as in the short histories which follow.

The material about the four persons is rich and the stories are given in somewhat brief compass and in a fairly staccato manner in order to tell as complete a story as possible. Issues peculiar to one or other of the four illustrative histories are discussed at the end of the individual sections of biography and any points which apply generally to all of them at the end of the whole section. Each one begins with a brief description of parents and siblings and then there follows a more or less chronological account of the lives. The first is the story of Iulia de Beausobre.

Iulia de Beausobre took her surname from her first husband, who was a Russian from an originally Swiss emigré family. Much of her writing was done after he died and before she married again and it was the name she chiefly used as her by-line. She was actually born Iulia Mikhailovna Kazarin, on October 26th, 1893. Her family home was at *17 Malaya Italianskaya in St Petersburg, Russia*. In 1893 St

Petersburg was the imperial capital of Russia, its great buildings standing majestically beside the river Neva, alive with the social whirl and colour that made it such a glowing if corrupt centre of Tsarist Russia.

The Kazarin home was large, some 30 rooms, and the family was cared for by 14 servants. Mikhail, Iulia's father, held a largely honorary position as Director of Administration of the St Petersburg's Ladies Charitable Prison Commission, which entitled him to be addressed as "Excellency". Her mother, also Iulia, was the daughter of a wealthy banking family, who were patrons of the arts. Iulia was their second daughter after an older sister, Adriana (Ada) and she had a younger brother, Sergey.

Looking back on her childhood, which she did sparingly, Iulia spoke of her parents as "high-flying idle rich with too much money and not enough responsibility. She was cared for in her first year by nursery servants and then by Ada's English governess, Isobel Paxton or Pussy, as she was known to them. Pussy was with the family until Iulia was 16, an alternative mother figure during Iulia's formative years. Of the life of her parents she said. 'the whole thing was *raffish*," [16] an aristocratic life which she felt merely satisfied the social conventions.

Iulia's mother, when Iulia was still a young girl, was badly injured in a fire at Alexandrovka, their holiday home in the Urals. She thought a servant had been trapped and in her efforts to rescue him did permanent physical damage to herself. She was also unhappy in her marriage, Mikhail taking lovers, possibly from the beginning, the effect being a spiritual rupture which was on a par with the physical one. The effect on her daughter Iulia, always a sensitive child, seems to have been considerable. She counted her childhood a happy one but at the same time she had a mystifying experience of suffering, which she was too young to comprehend. This must have been a contributing factor to her many illnesses as is explored below. In these years she almost died twice, once at the age of 4 of diphtheria and again when she was 9 of scarlet fever. They must have caused great family alarm but also an unusual degree of love and affection, which may have helped her to learn how to survive them. In addition, while she may have absorbed her mother's pain, she seems also to have acquired a degree of her strength.

She was baptized and confirmed in the Russian Orthodox Church, formally no doubt but with the full rich symbolism of an Orthodox baptism, the young child stripped and dipped into the water to rise as a new born child of Christ. Naturally she could not remember it, but it is interesting that her earliest memory, when she was 2, was of her brother's baptism. She delighted in the aroma of the incense. Her baptism was to be of great significance to her.

Life in St Petersburg followed the social round dictated by Court and Church, regular worship, formal abstinence during the fasting seasons, feasting at Easter, social gatherings during the rest. Each summer they visited their estates beyond the Volga at Alexandrovka until the house was burnt down and then they went to Yalta in the Crimea. She learnt to knit and crochet, to paint and to draw and to become thoroughly accomplished in the social arts.

The death throes of Tsarist Russia were increasingly evident. She was 11 when on Bloody Sunday in January 1905[17] she could hear the shooting when unarmed factory workers were massacred by the Tsar's troops. "Things," she wrote later "were sliding in a gigantic landslide which nothing could stop."[18]

Iulia's secondary education was at the Tagentsev School, noted as an advanced school, which was the equal of the finest in Europe and she developed a love of science and literature in a disciplined atmosphere of analytic thought. She read widely in the family library, even the Koran in French, while at the same time developing the social skills she needed for coming out.

It was in these years that she developed the habit, to be so important to her later, of conversing inwardly with Leonardo da Vinci, whom she had read about in Merezhorsky's novel, *The Forerunner*. Leonardo was the thoroughly rational detached parental figure, an inner mentor giving voice to her rational self so that she could listen to his cool words calming her anxiety and monitoring her youthful exuberance.

She was formed throughout her childhood by regular attendance at the weekly liturgy of the Orthodox Church, an ongoing submersion in a tradition. During her early teens she felt called to nurse lepers and as a preparation for receiving communion went with one of the family servants on a pilgrimage to a Moscow monastery. Orthodox children receive communion until they are about 7, and then only after confession. Her experience of confession on this occasion was distressing and damaged her relationship with the Church. She felt her confessor's questions about her sex life, which she did not understand, were prurient and intrusive. She still however longed for spiritual reality, continuing to search for it in her reading. She was particularly impressed by Vyacheslav Ivanov, the Christian poet-philosopher of the Symbolist movement, who had himself been influenced by the 19th century philosopher and theologian, Vladimir Solovyov.

Iulia travelled extensively during her teens, England, Italy and Switzerland, where she once recovered from a bout of TB. She 'came out' when she was 16 and danced her way through the summer with enthusiasm. She liked things to be done well, she dressed with flair and expensively and she loved it all
.
Two years later her mother suddenly died. Adriana was already married, so Iulia and her father moved into a smaller house in *St Petersburg, 24 Kirinchanuya*. She continued to travel a good deal and was in the Austrian Tyrol when war was declared in 1914. It took her companion and herself two years to reach St Petersburg again, where she volunteered as a nurse and worked with the wounded.

She returned to a grim situation at home. Her father had become ill with what must have been General Paralysis of the Insane, one of the most serious side effects of syphilis. Iulia nursed him with difficulty, especially through the nights. He once almost burnt the house down and on another occasion mistook her for one of his mistresses. Eventually, she engineered his admission to a psychiatric hospital where a few months later he died. He was only 48.

One afternoon, shortly after her father's death, she decided to visit an aunt. A fellow visitor was a young man called Nicolay de Beausobre. He was an orphan, a few years older than Iulia, a big man as the joint portrait of the two of them by a close artist friend Lev Bruni[19] shows, and lively with a penchant for enjoying himself. In the painting he looks impatient for action with the slim fragile Iulia slightly behind him poised to follow.

She was at her 'Jordan' moment. Iulia had been expected to marry and oversee a home as a cultured and educated companion to her husband, but the death of her mother and then so recently of her father compelled her to move more quickly. She had not trained for any area of work though like many of her contemporaries and social peers, she had done some voluntary work as a nurse. She saw her likely career to be as a homemaker and mother. Her faith was, or so it seems, not much more than a conventional one but there were also signs in her of deep sensitivity and spiritual searching and in the responses she had made, they were potentially far more than this. Meeting Nicolay de Beausobre presented her with an opening to the future. Her marriage was to be into a hard world. The Tsar was to abdicate a day or two after her wedding, the country was struggling in the war with Germany, the Kerensky government was at the beginning of its brief season of power. It would be all too accurate to describe her marriage as forcing her onto a wilderness way, certainly more Wilderness than Galilee, but she embraced the challenge and she and Nicolay were married on February 3rd, 1917 when she was 23.

This occasion, as with each of the histories, marked the end of her adolescence and the beginning of her Galilee/Wilderness way. In Iulia's case, she was unable to make a complete threefold decision because she had not yet given her full personal assent to her faith. This was to come later. It will be noted too that she had been seriously ill on more than one occasion; diphtheria, scarlet fever and TB, each of them life-threatening illnesses. What made her so susceptible to this?

We do try, especially in the West at present, to think of disease as a purely physical event, assailing the body as it were inexplicably from out of the blue. But, if persons are a bodiliness, our bodies and souls integrally one as modern philosophy and psychology imply, then it has to be true that whatever happens physically must also affect them emotionally and spiritually and vice versa. What happens emotionally and spiritually also affects the body.

There are four main causes of disease: the first from some genetic flaw, something in the genes or DNA which carries the programme for a disease within the body, the second because of an accident, injuries sustained in the many accidents which occur, the third by contagion or virus or some parasitical something which invades the organism and the fourth because there is some inner problem in the person weakening the ability to resist. It could be a spiritual un-ease, some emotional or mental disturbance, which has the effect of predisposing the person to sickness. It could be said that the first three cause disease, damage to the organism, while the fourth causes sickness, the experience of being sick or ill, an inability to function. The interesting feature in this is that the fourth cause is a factor in all disease. It used to be thought that there were diseases which could be described as psycho-somatic, the fourth aspect being the dominant factor, but it is now thought more probable that spiritual and emotional factors are present whenever and however persons are sick. To take an example from Paul Tournier[20] he once described how his wife had broken her leg while in a rush to get somewhere and how when she came to reflect about what had happened she recognized that she had been trying to do too much, more in fact than she could adequately cope with. Breaking her leg had been an effective way of stopping her in her tracks. It was far more than just an accident. It had compelled her to take a much needed rest.

The understanding now is that there are greater or lesser psychological causes in almost any illness, sometimes very obviously present, at other times more subtly. In fact, because physical disease is so much easier to handle emotionally than mental disease, and earns far more sympathy, mental disturbance is commonly converted psychologically into a physical disease. The sickness then symbolizes in some way the nature of the mental disturbance, not necessarily the sick person's own disturbance alone but the disturbance of the person's friends, family, community or even nation. As the Finnish psychiatrist Martti Siirala[21] has put it, a sickness in one part of the community can bring sickness to another, a community can become sick in the person, a person in the body, a body in the organ, an organ in the cell. The African way of presenting a sufferer to a doctor with the words "I am sick in my sister" puts this very clearly.

If we take, for example Iulia's tuberculosis in her teen years, there is no doubt that while TB is a highly contagious physical disease, it also especially afflicts those who are psychologically vulnerable in some way. Rather like the diphtheria which Iulia had as an infant, it affects the breathing, consumes the body indeed as the alternative name of 'consumption' implies, and in Iulia's case accurately symbolized her predicament. She found it difficult to breathe, the TB destroying her lungs, the diphtheria causing a membrane to grow so that she could hardly breathe. They were ways of saying that she was being stifled.[22]

Well, the part which applies to Iulia's sicknesses is of course speculative, but the main argument is well enough attested. All persons are in danger of disease but for the most part their remarkable autoimmune system protects them from the vast majority of assailants – except in cases like AIDS where it is the auto-immune system itself which is damaged. The human system of mental defences is also effective in protecting persons from much mental pain, and again works well enough, except when the defence system involves converting mental pain into physical. In Iulia's case her autoimmune system must have been depressed, in itself a sign that she was probably coping with levels of anxiety beyond her comprehension and ability to manage. Why, it is not easy to be certain, though her father's infidelities, the formal relationship her parents had, perhaps symbolized by her mother's generous carelessness of her health in the Alexandrovka incident, and the emptiness of their life style, all must have contributed. Add to that the brittle times in which they all lived. Children reflect accurately their parents' alternations of mood, like finely tuned instruments responding to every nuance of feeling, which they then reflect in their behaviour, or in some other way, as here. Even with the support of a substitute mother figure in Nanny Isabel Paxton – who appears again later at a crucial stage of the story – Iulia still appears to have been particularly vulnerable.

All this was to have two very important effects; first that she found in illness a necessary moratorium to receive the tenderness and attention she needed for recovery and secondly a way of giving her bodiliness the time she required to recover her emotional equilibrium. As a general rule, if it takes a length of time to convalesce from a physical illness then it takes twice as long if not longer to recover from a mental illness. It follows that if it is taking a long time to recover from a physical disease then that is a sign that the patient is grappling with some additional inner mental turmoil. Basically, at the same time as Iulia was discovering a stratagem for coping with extreme emotional stress, she was also finding deep within her self the life giving resources of the Holy Spirit who was making her inwardly robust. .

As the young Iulia Kazarin was observing the disintegration of Tsarist Russia, a different destiny was being shaped on the other side of the Baltic. **Dag Hammarskjöld** was born in *Jönköping* at the time when his father Hjalmar was in Oslo negotiating the separation of Norway from Sweden. He was Hjalmar and Agnes Hammarskjöld's fourth son. Bo had been born in 1891 and was 14. Ake was 12 and Sten 5. As his mother used to joke, Dag was the hoped for daughter.

Hjalmar Hammarskjöld was a man of sterling purpose, conservative, dutiful. In a radio address many years later, Dag said that he inherited from his father the belief that life was giving oneself in 'selfless service ... (which) required a sacrifice of all personal interests, but likewise the courage to stand up unflinchingly for your convictions.'[23] His father was a patriarchal figure, not a person to relate to with ease.

The possibility of a daughter in so masculine a household must have seemed a delightful prospect to his mother. She was described by a family friend as "an intellectual ... (who) in many ways ... represented the emotional side of the family,"[24] a person of considerable charm and warmth, from a family of scholars and clergymen. She seems to have been a lonely soul who was close to her two younger boys, especially to Dag who appears to have instinctively understood the extent of her interior loneliness.

The custom of the Swedish Lutheran Church is that new born children are baptized soon after birth. His father revered the tradition and his mother was a woman of faith.

Shortly after Dag was born, his father had become the Swedish Government's Minister to Denmark. In 1907, he became Governor of Uppsala. The governor's residence, *Uppsala Castle*, sprawls massively above the town and Dag loved exploring its abundant space and playing in a playroom so vast that it has since been turned into a Hall of State. Sten has described how his father insisted on traditional occasions being celebrated properly; on Christmas Eve the whole household assembled for a service by the great tree led by his mother and again on New Year's Eve. The latter is noted especially in 'Markings' during his crisis years (see chapter 5)

At the beginning of the war, the family moved to *Stockholm* when Hjalmar Hammarskjöld was invited to become Prime Minister. He maintained against the drift of public opinion that Sweden should remain neutral and should work for international order. His regime was unpopular and his government fell in 1917.

Hjalmar resumed his position as Governor of Uppland province and the family returned to *Uppsala Castle*. Some years later in August 1959 Dag recalled his Uppsala childhood in five pages of short evocative poems written in the Japanese haiku form. One tells of the excitement of a film team using the castle as a backdrop, another of searching for flowers and finding an unusual buttercup. There was a darker side.

> He wasn't wanted.
> When, nonetheless, he came,
> He could only watch them play.[25]

But it was not all gloomy.

> The boy in the forest
> Throws off his best Sunday suit
> And plays naked[26]

Once at university he valued gifted friends who were interested in the arts and the Swedish countryside. With them he was cheerful and charming, though as Brian Urquhart comments, 'he tended to keep them in separate orbits.'[27]

The Hammarskjöld family were close to Nathan Söderblom, Archbishop of Uppsala from 1914 and his family. Jon Olof Söderblom and Dag were in the same class and the younger Söderblom daughter Yvonne was at university with him. In 1925 Dag was an usher at the Stockholm Universal Christian Conference on life and work, one of the first steps in the ecumenical movement of which Nathan Söderblom was a founder.

Gustaf Aulén, a Swedish bishop who wrote about Hammarskjöld, says the particular pastor who instructed Dag in the faith was an enlightened teacher, a contrast to the rigid traditionalism then dominant in Swedish Lutheranism[28]. Despite knowing Christians of evident depth and practice, faith was difficult for him throughout his youth. He found it impossible to counter Professor Axel Häggerström, the atheist intellectual who taught that since it was impossible to validate the doctrines of

Christianity against anything concrete they must be meaningless. The inner conflict, which this provoked, was the central issue in the spiritual battle he was to record in *Markings*.

In the letter to Leif Belfrage, which he attached to *Markings*, he wrote 'these entries provide the only true 'profile' that can be drawn.'[29] Mrs Söderblom had advised him to read Pascal and *Markings* has a resemblance to the *Pensées* as a collection of penetrating observations, which ruthlessly analyse every part of his soul in his search for inner truth. It apparently began in 1925. The typescript was found after his death with a covering note saying that it was a "sort of *white book* concerning my negotiations with myself – and with God."[30] The opening, and the second section, 1925-1930 are each headed by a title, which he seems to have added rather later. The first section, *Thus it was* is evidently a prologue, created from vividly remembered feelings from his past.[31] It is a statement of his early vision:

> I am being driven forward
> Into an unknown land ...

He wrote, and the image is of an ascension through steep and lofty passes towards an unknown goal drawn by a call he hears in the silence stirring him to hope. Empowered, he is prepared to commit himself to a life of service, to the point of an inevitable sacrifice.

> Tomorrow we shall meet,
> Death and I –

Meanwhile he had to overcome his deep sense of loneliness, a lack of meaning and the temptation to end his life without sacrifice in suicide. There is a telling photograph[32] of him standing alone in the emptiness of an ice-field in the Sarek Mountains of Sweden.

Dag had entered university in 1923, read the history of literature, philosophy, French and political economy in two years and then economics, completing his studies by 1930 with a "Fillalia" in law. In 1930, Hjalmar Hammarskjöld retired and the family, Dag with them, moved to **Stockholm**. As he began work and in his spare time, he continued studying for a doctorate on *The Spread of the Business Cycle;* examining the reasons for the alternations of boom and depression, which he defended before two protagonists in open debate. His work was judged 'cum laude', one under the highest grade of 'laudatur'[33]

Perhaps the graduation ceremony following this was the celebratory moment which was to mark the beginning of his Galilee/Wilderness way. Van Dusen's account of the debate shows that the result decided him against becoming an academic, so it clarified the role he was to fulfil. For the other two decisions he was still making up his mind. Faith was meaningful to him, but in a thoroughly modern way he was unable intellectually to resolve the theological issues or empirically verify his experience so that he could commit himself with any completeness to a way of Christian faith. Nonetheless he saw himself called to a serious and sacrificial spiritual quest. Partnership with another does not seem to have been something he contemplated. Brian Urquhart thought that he was uninterested in sex and many assumed that he was gay. Apart from an aesthetic delight in others, sex seems to have been of secondary importance to him He refers later to a decision not to marry. The only thing that is certain is that he preferred to remain single. So it was a tentative beginning with a number of issues which he recognized he still had to resolve.

He is completely open about the depth of his loneliness. There is much evidence to show how much Agnes Hammarskjöld loved her son and that there was an especially close bond between the two of them so he was not bereft of relationship. Loneliness sometimes stems from an early experience in the womb; from a personal awareness of loneliness that is really the mother's. Some would suggest a bad experience of the birth process itself might be a cause, the lonely and traumatic experience in the birth canal being of such an order that the infant spirit comes to despair.[34] If one of these is right it can be noted that he was born when his father was away from home in Denmark. Even when his father was home, to a small boy he must have been a fairly forbidding personage, someone to whom it was not easy to be intimate. It must have been difficult for his mother too. She was the only woman in a family of men and it would have been understandable if at times she felt bereft of female companionship and that her youngest son might experience her anguish as his own. At the least it is a possible contributing factor. Whatever the cause, there was no doubt that he was deeply lonely and coping with it was the most difficult challenge of his spiritual way.

Martin Luther King was born on January 15th, 1929 in the pastor's house in *Auburn Avenue, Atlanta*, which is now preserved as a museum. It stands some two hundred yards above Ebenezer Church, with an open veranda typical of Southern United States homes and a spacious wood-polished interior.

Martin's grandfather, Adam Daniel Williams had been the pastor of Ebenezer since 1894. He had been joined in 1926 by Michael, later Martin Luther, King, who had married his daughter Alberta and became pastor in 1931 when Adam Daniel suddenly died. Michael and Alberta had three children, Christine, Martin Luther and Alfred Daniel.

It was a joyful family but strict. Daddy King had struggled from a deprived background to become a formidable pastor and in the pulpit he was awe-inspiring. Like his father-in-law, he was a leading figure in the National Association for the Advancement of Coloured People (NAACP).

Alberta King was gentler, a humorous soul who despite a personal strength, must have been puzzled by her sexually demanding, excessively confident and righteous, patriarchal males who dominated her life in church and home yet so needed her as a woman. She perhaps needed them less. In loving Martin she gave of her physical riches without stint, inducting him into the mysteries of physical, emotional and spiritual love with generous breast and embracing heart. Her children in common with Black American practice called her "Mother dear."

Equally important was his Grandmother Williams, a warm person who told the children bible stories and joined them in the family morning and evening prayers. Freed from parental responsibility she gave herself generously to the children. Martin loved her greatly and looked to her for comfort when he was punished by his father which he was from time to time fairly severely. He would bear the beating in an almost catatonic stillness and would then rush to his grandmother for comfort. One day, thinking she had died, he flung himself from an upstairs window.

As this story suggests, Martin was a boy of powerful emotions. He was small but did not intend to be second. When his sister Christine was 6 and responded to one of Daddy King's rousing sermons by pledging herself to Jesus, in an almost comic determination not to be outdone by her, Martin aged 5 strode after her to pledge his life too. What was superficially an act of pique had become with the support of his family a true presentation of himself to God.

Every black American child, certainly in the South, eventually faces the pain of being considered inferior. For Martin it came when he was prevented from playing with a white boy. His mother counselled him to remember that "'you are as good as anyone.'"[35] He determined from that point to hate all white people. He began school locally, learning at home from his father how to be black in a segregated society. "Nobody can make a slave out of you if you don't think like a slave"; he told Martin.[36] His parents counselled further that he should not hate the white man, but love him as his Christian duty. [37]

Grandmother Williams died suddenly of a heart attack one Sunday (May 18, 1941.) Martin was devastated and again took himself to the second floor and almost killed himself by hurling himself to the ground.[38]

Shortly afterwards the family moved to a larger house in *Boulevard (Atlanta)*, Martin starting at a new High School in the following year. To his friends, he was a typical teenager, who like them boasted of his prowess with the girls and had an enviable gift for talking himself out of trouble. His teachers found him quiet and introspective.

He was determined not to follow his father, especially not his emotional fundamentalism. When he was 15 he entered Morehouse College and came under the influence of Dr Benjamin Mays, who taught him how it was possible to be Christian and socially concerned without being fundamentalist.

He had not since he was an infant met any whites and his hatred was increased when he heard himself addressed as "nigger". His feelings eased when he joined inter-racial groups from schools in Atlanta.

In the summer of 1947, when he went with a group of friends to Connecticut to pick tobacco, his companions asked him to lead their prayers. Despite his father, it made him think again about the ministry. He returned home to say that after all he had decided he would become a minister. Daddy arranged for him to preach at Ebenezer and an excited congregation flocked to listen. He preached well and both father and son felt that he was called. 'My call to the ministry,' he wrote 'was not a miraculous or supernatural something; on the contrary, it was an inner urge calling me to serve humanity.'[39] He found he could now pray and study more easily. Ordination preceded training and on February 25th, 1948, Martin was ordained and admitted as an assistant pastor at Ebenezer.

He chose to go to *Crozer theological seminary in Pennsylvania*, a small college of some 100 mainly white students. His grades began to improve from C to A by his third year. He read Walter Rauschenbusch on the socially active church in an accepting world, Reinhold Niebuhr on the reluctance of sinful humanity to forgo power and Gandhi on non-violence; he thought Gandhi's ideas impracticable, though fellow-students noted the quietening effect of his own non-violence when a riled student pointed a loaded gun at him.

It is said he hoped to marry a white girl but was advised not to because it would prevent him from working in the South. One confidante claimed the split broke his heart.[40]

He graduated from Crozer with glowing reports and went to *Boston* to read for a PhD under Professor Edgar Brightman. King valued Brightman's emphasis on the ultimate value of persons, because it made arguments for segregation impossible. His difficulty was how to find an effective way of restoring racial justice when it had been lost, especially when neither liberalism nor the social gospel seemed to make any impact.

Martin seems to have learnt early a confident approach to the girls and he was evidently attracted and indeed attractive to them. Certainly his first meeting with Coretta Scott suggests a young man supremely confident of his personhood. He was recommended to meet her by a friend. Coretta's family lived near Marion in Alabama and she was studying music and singing at the Boston Conservatory. He rang her immediately, sweet-talking her into meeting him the next day. On their first date he told her, "'You have everything I have ever wanted in a wife.'" Coretta protested, but he persisted, "'Yes, I can tell,'" he said. "The four things that I look for in a wife are character, intelligence, personality and beauty. And you have them all. I want to see you again. When can I?'" [41]

Daddy King was not pleased. He had plans for Martin to marry a local girl and he hastened to Boston to put a stop to their budding romance. Martin had developed the art of the non-committal grunt to cope with Daddy and simply waited for the propitious moment to put forward his alternative proposal. Coretta herself had reservations about marrying a minister, especially a man who assumed himself, despite what he said, to be superior. She feared also that it would end her musical career. Nonetheless she decided to go ahead.

For Martin's part, marrying Coretta was the true beginning of his adult way. His ordination, when he was still in his teens and before he had been trained, was too early to celebrate all his decisions, though he had decided about his role. His faith had grown simply and naturally from his experience in his family and community, in Church and school and it had now become his own faith. His big problem was his relationship with his powerful and dominant father. He had only been able to recognize his gifts for ordination when he had been away from home and even then, after he was convinced of his decision, his ordination had been by his father. He had decided for a role but it could so very easily have become a subservient one to the dictates of his father. He had overcome his embarrassment about his father's emotional preaching and through his teachers had developed a more social, less fundamental theology, but he was still worried about controlling his own passionate feelings. Finding his own identity, the kind of person and pastor he was himself to be and deciding to marry the person he himself wanted to marry, was something he recognized he had to do and unlike brother AD who never really did break away, he managed it. In fact he lived out his parents' vision to such a depth that later they often became more frightened than he did. These decisions were sealed and celebrated when Martin and Coretta were married on June 18th, 1953 when he was 24.

Angelo Roncalli was born in *Sotto il Monte* on a very cold November 25th in 1881. Sotte il Monte is a scattered village some ten miles from Bergamo in Northern Italy. When we visited one blazingly hot summer's day in the late Sixties, we arrived on Saturday evening and camped. We awoke the following morning to find ourselves in the midst of a melée of happy Milanese enjoying the 'convenience' of our field and preparing for mass by eating a jubilant breakfast. They were a few of the hundreds of pilgrims to Pope John's birthplace making carnival that day.

Angelo was the first son and fourth child (of 12) of Giovanni and Marianna Roncalli. As in any Italian family, he was the apple of his mother's eye. They lived on the first floor, their animals beneath them on the ground. The extended family was already large, some 31 before he was born, a stolid farming people of modest means. Don Rebuzzini, the parish priest, was away in Bergamo on the day of his birth, so his baptism was late. The men folk celebrated with a glass of wine.

As was the custom, Angelo shared the marriage bed until he was displaced by his brother Zaverio some 18 months later. He remembered his mother carrying Zaverio and Maria while shepherding Ancilla, Teresa and himself aged 4 to a nearby shrine for Candlemass. They were late and she lifted him up to a window and said, "Look, Angelino, look how beautiful the Madonna is. I have consecrated you wholly to her."[42]

His father was austere, a man who worked hard and communicated little. When hoisted aloft on the papal chair[43] he remembered being similarly carried as a boy by his father to see a parade in Ponte San Pietro. Angelo was a lively child, and one can imagine him in his mother's kitchen, chattering merrily to her about everything and anything, eating what fruit and food was available and basking in the love. He was a bright boy. An inspector once visited his school and asked the class, "which weighs the most, a quintal of hay or a quintal of iron?" Angelo was the only one to get it right! [44]

In the family hierarchy, great uncle Zaverio led the family prayers in the kitchen each evening and as a reader of John Bosco's paper the *Bolletino Salesiano,* demonstrated also a concern for Christian social action. From the age of 5, Angelo attended mass on weekdays. Don Rebuzzini had once told him that Luigi Palazzola, a priest in a neighbouring parish who had just died, was a saint. Angelo aged 6 told his cousin Camilla that he too would become just such a priest and saint.

He was confirmed unusually early for the time (February 13th, 1889) and made his first communion a fortnight later. After the service, he was enrolled by Father Rebuzzini in an apostleship of prayer which required him to say a morning prayer 'in union with the Sacred Heart.'

Angelo started his education in the village school. He also began learning Latin from an aggressive priest, who beat him for his mistakes, and was then enrolled in the episcopal college at Celana as a weekly boarder. It was not a success. He returned home to be prepared for the Junior Seminary by Don Rebuzzini.

Angelo was almost 11 when he arrived in **Bergamo**. The seminary, now renamed in his honour, is in the upper city looking down upon the expanding conurbation below. He was very young and carefully protected. When 14, as one who was showing promise, he was enrolled in 'The Sodality of the Annunciation of Mary Immaculate' and given rules to guide his spiritual life The *Journal of a Soul*, which he started in 1895 at the behest of his Spiritual Director, begins with these exacting rules[45], adapted and copied out in his tiny writing. He kept to them for the rest of his life. (See chapter 3)

The entries for the Bergamo years are the most extensive, describing his efforts to become perfect like the three Jesuit saints held up to him as models of correctness and sexual propriety. "I must keep myself in the background ... and never mention ... certain topics that are no business of mine ..." he counselled himself, "still less should I scatter my words of wisdom about ... telling (people) how to behave.[46] He refers to "hellish dreams in which I find myself entangled unawares."[47] He was more challenged by his liking for food. 'I am really very greedy about fruit. I must watch myself. Recollection and mortification above all in enjoyment of what the palate desires."[48]

He found the holidays difficult. Some of his extended family resented his absence from the fields and during the 1899 Easter holidays complained to a visiting friar who reported him to the college. "My Superiors received an account," Angelo wrote, "I think exaggerated, of my having behaved arrogantly during the vacation and I have been duly rebuked. So I have had to humble myself against my will. But as a matter of fact, there is a grain of truth in this."[49]

Three days into the summer holidays he felt he could no longer bear his home and cried out, '"Save us, Lord, we are perishing."'[50] During the same holiday, on September 25th, 1898 [51,] while Father Rebuzzini was preparing for Mass, his beloved parish priest suddenly fell and died on the spot in front of a devastated Angelo. Angelo felt as if he had lost his father. Since going to the seminary he had been turning from his natural parents towards Don Rebuzzini as the Christ figure and to Mary as his holy Mother. On the feast of the Immaculate Conception, he wrote, "I consecrate myself to you, my Mother ... bring me to Jesus, the final goal of my affections."[52]

Eighteen months later, rising 18 and feeling himself spiritually mature, he rebuked his mother for some question she had put. "She was deeply offended and said things to me which I would never have expected to hear from my mother, for whom, after God, Mary and the saints, I bear the greatest love of which my heart is capable."[53]

He valued the simple goodness of the seminary and the training which was forming him as a follower of Christ.[54] At the beginning of 1901 he moved to the less restrictive atmosphere of *the Roman Seminary (Rome)*. His joy in life came to an abrupt end in November when he was called up to do his national service. He found the barrack room talk distasteful and described the service to himself as his 'Babylonian Captivity'[55]. He was made a sergeant by the end of the year and some of the soldiers were considerate.

His year away had contributed to his maturity. In January 1903 he reflected: 'I am not St. Aloysius, nor must I seek holiness in his particular way, but according to the requirements of my own nature ... I must not be the dry, bloodless reproduction of a model, however perfect. God desires us to follow the example of the saints by absorbing the vital sap of their virtues and turning it into our own lifeblood ... If St Aloysius had been as I am, he would have become holy in a different way.'[56]

During Passiontide in 1903 he made a ten day retreat in preparation for his first ordination as sub-deacon on Easter Eve in St John Lateran. On a third retreat, preparing for the diaconate, he reflected on the Sacred Heart of Jesus 'throbbing mysteriously behind the Eucharistic veils.'[57]

Despite disappointing exam results and, as he judged, slow progress towards sanctity, ordination to the priesthood and his 'Jordan' day was nearing. His faith had never really been in doubt, nor indeed his early decision to offer himself for the ministry. On the day of his baptism, his first day indeed, Zaverio had dedicated him to the Sacred Heart 'so that I should grow up under its protection, a good

Christian,'[58] and a few years later, his mother had told him she had consecrated him to Mary. Both were significant, both to him and to his family, who had offered their beloved child to God for the ministry as Hannah had offered Samuel to Eli, and from the day he acknowledged the offering as he had done to Camilla, he had in effect begun to leave his natural family.

He had accepted from the beginning of his training that his life was to be celibate, so his sexual way ahead was prescribed and for him not too difficult. He knew whom he was and had come to see that he needed to become a priest in his own way. The day of his ordination itself (August 10th, 1904, St Lawrence's day – he was nearly 23) was so overwhelming that he could not bring himself to describe it in his *Journal of a Soul* until an anniversary some 8 years later. He remembered how he had walked silently across Rome to the church of St Maria in Monte Santo in the Piazza del Popolo. 'When all was over' he wrote, 'and I raised my eyes ... I saw the blessed image of Our Lady... She seemed to smile at me from the altar and her look gave me a feeling of sweet peace in my soul and a generous and confident spirit, as if she were telling me she was pleased, and that she would always watch over me.'[59] The next day he celebrated his first Mass in the crypt of St Peter's and later attended an audience with the Pope. He told Pius X that he wanted to dedicate his life to Jesus and the Church. "Well done, well done, my boy ... this is what I like to hear, and I will ask the good Lord to grant a special blessing on those good intentions of yours, so that you may really be a priest after his own heart."[60.]

*   *   *

The two significant moments of the way so far have been baptism - or some spiritual ceremony - at the beginning and the Jordan day at the end. Baptism begins the spiritual journey and also defines the way; that in losing life it is gained. It reveals the nature of change through the different crises, that every transition to come will be a revisiting and reliving of the original baptism. Each of the four was baptized and where appropriate they were also confirmed. Iulia was baptized and confirmed as an infant according to Russian Orthodox tradition. So too in their different Churches were Angelo and Dag. Angelo was confirmed when he was 7, Dag as a teenager, but too early to confirm his personal decision for faith   Martin as a Baptist was baptized long after he had made his 5 year old offering. All in all, confirmation or its equivalent tends to be done at the time which suits the particular churches and is nowadays more to do with admission to communion and further learning than with marking a transition to adulthood. This is a major reason for fastening on a later spiritual occasion as a Jordan day.

Angelo Roncalli's Jordan day clearly brought together all three of the challenges of his adolescent way, his faith, his role, his relationships and made of it a celebratory day of the Holy Spirit. It was the same for Martin Luther King when he married Coretta Scott. Iulia de Beausobre was not yet clear about her faith and in accordance with her position in society settled for a conventional role at this stage, but she was changed. Dag Hammarskjöld too had not resolved questions about faith and was not really all that certain what he should do, perhaps even about his relationships and the nature of his transition reflects that. The day was marked for the four of them by an ordination, two weddings and a graduation ceremony, each of them a liturgical or a secular occasion with baptismal overtones. None of them had yet fully discovered their vocation, even Roncalli and Luther King. They had found their direction, but their real calling was, as is usually the case, yet to emerge. Two of the four persons celebrated the three decisions on the one day, but many Christians, like the other two, take more than one occasion, as it were evolving slowly into the maturity of young adulthood.

This chapter has been about the long period of childhood and adolescence which all souls negotiate as they travel and are prepared for the way. The whole of childhood is the setting for God's address, many occasions preparing and summoning the young person through John the Baptist intermediaries to the way as the four biographies have shown. But specific events are only a part. God also speaks through the general loving of parents and those others who provided a background of disciplined care and security so that children learn to trust and to grow in love, loving in particular their inner selves, the little boy or girl within, that they may both love others and be inspired to live in hope for the future.

Not everyone of course looks back upon a happy childhood and there are those who can remember nothing about it, such experiences speaking of a frightened and weeping child thoroughly hidden away within. Even those whose childhood has been normally happy, as in the examples given, has much that goes wrong. Part of the wilderness journey (see chapter 4) is about the rescue and healing not only of the lost but of everyone. The healing of the former may be a central task of the whole of a journey.

A main message of each chapter is to illustrate the journey itself and the various 'stations' on the way where each soul pauses. So far and it is a striking fact for the end of this chapter, each of the four had had the good fortune to move little. Iulia remained in St Petersburg, Dag in Uppsala and Stockholm, Martin in Atlanta and Angelo primarily in Sotto il Monte and Bergamo with a foray to Rome. The stability gave their young souls roots and security before they embarked on their adult way.

The dying and rising in Christ which is symbolized by baptism and recalled in the Jordan day is at the heart of the early way. It follows that if a person has been baptized it is worth savouring and meditating on the event. There is a tendency nowadays to denigrate the importance of early baptism, partly because it occurs before a child can understand what is happening and partly because it is imposed before a child can say 'No.' That is true, but then the same can be said of every other nurturing experience of the early years, all of which are equally imposed and beyond recall.

Baptism, when it occurs early, is a gift. Apart from its sacramental significance, it speaks of parents who thought of their child as a gift from God, who wished to share their faith and who regarded the birth as so wonderful that they wanted their friends and relations to gather with them to share their joy. In later years then, visiting the place to celebrate where it happened is – or so I have found - worth a pilgrimage.

Tabley is a small village near to Knutsford in Cheshire. The hall there is now both a residential home for the elderly on the ground floor with a stately part on the first floor, a large Palladian house set in grounds overlooking the A556. For centuries an earlier house had been on an island in a nearby lake until the owners, finding it too damp, decided to rebuild it on higher ground. Two hundred years later, they decided to move the chapel also, brick by brick. It was transferred to its present location again beside the hall. Not the easiest place to get into these days, even more locked than the average church, but worth the effort. My father had been the curate of Great Budworth in the Thirties with responsibility for various big houses on the periphery of the parish and he baptized two children there; one a policeman's son, the other his own. To stand by the font and to pray in the church one day during Easter was to recall that early moment when a soul died with Christ in the waters to rise in him to the beginning of the way.

CHAPTER 3

DISCIPLINE AND TRAINING

Order and Spontaneity

'And the Spirit immediately drove him out into the wilderness. He was in the wilderness for forty days, tempted by Satan.' (Mark 1, 12-13a)

Each year, Methodist Churches hold a Covenant Service, usually on the first available Sunday in January, on or near the Sunday, which celebrates the Baptism of Christ. John Wesley's first formal Covenant Service was in August 1755 [1] and his emphasis then and always was to urge Methodists to 'renew their covenant with God,' to start again on the way. As was being argued in the last chapter young adults covenant themselves at some ceremonial occasion – on what I have called their Jordan day - when they begin their adult Christian way.

The words of the covenant prayer, like the prayer of Ignatius which begins his Spiritual Exercises[2] and the vows a couple make to each other in the marriage service, are 'I am no longer my own, but yours. Put me to what you will, rank we with whom you will; put me to doing, put me to suffering; let me be employed for you or laid aside for you, exalted for you or brought low for you; ... .'[3] This is the spirit in which new Christians begin their response to Christ's total self-giving of himself to them.

In these next two chapters on the challenges of the Galilee/Wilderness Way, this first one is about patterns of living, the rules or habits which people form so that they can live their day to day lives in some sort of order. Some of the examples are from events which occur later, but illustrate the point. How a person lives his or her day and in particular, how and when the person prays are the major emphases. In the next chapter the focus is on the actual way as it leads up to the crisis of 'Caesarea Philippi'.

St Mark begins his gospel with just such an ordinary day[4] which would end at sundown but in fact in the description given goes on to include the early morning of the next day. Significantly the day was the Sabbath and Jesus attended the synagogue during the morning, preached, and then healed a disturbed man in the congregation. He then went with his disciples to lunch at the Barjonah home, where

Peter's mother-in-law was unwell and helped her to recovery. They then shared a meal before resting through the Sabbath afternoon. It was in the evening of what was understood to be the following day that the crowds began to gather at the door with their problems. After bed and sleep Jesus rose early in the morning for prayer. (Mark 1, 21-39)

The day had been full but spaced, Jesus giving his full attention to each of his activities; worship on the Sabbath and time for prayer in the early hours of the following morning, a healing during the service and later in the morning the cure of Peter's mother-in-law. He was with Peter's family for lunch and for a quiet and restful afternoon .so that he was able to give his full attention again to the sick and needy in the evening. There was worship and prayer, time for leisure and in the midst of it the work which flowed naturally from the communion with God and his friends.

This is the fundamental order, first of all prayer, secondly leisure, third work. The word 'leisure' is perhaps difficult. When I was speaking to a diocesan group about this, the whole audience seemed to understand leisure as merely recreation and rest. "Can you think of a better word?" the bishop whispered as I floundered in my explanation. I wish there was a word which does the same, but I do not think there is. 'Schole' is the Greek word for 'leisure', 'school' and 'scholar' being words that come from it; 'aschole' is the word for work, not-leisure, which is in itself an indication of the priority of leisure. St Paul [5] wrote to the Corinthians about having leisure for (scholazete) prayer. Leisure then is more than recreation and rest it refers to the creative things to be done such as study, relationship, creativity, even prayer.

A story which Baron Von Hugel used to tell is relevant here. A politician, the Duc de Chevreuse, who was 'racketed and distracted' by his endless activity and was unable to pray once turned to Archbishop Fénelon for help. Fénelon advised him to take some time each morning to go carefully through his diary and to pare it of all unnecessary detail. Then, he said, he should do what he had to do with as little fuss as possible. 'In this way,' Von Hugel added in his inimitable style, *'he would succeed in placing each action within a circumambient air of leisure – leisure for the spirit of prayer and peace.'*[6]

Christians often have a problem about leisure, the need for which too many seem to understand as some sort of personal weakness which they would be sinful to indulge. It is interesting that religious communities have no such problem. Prayer for them is at the heart of their life, they have firm rules for eating, for fellowship and study and the chores and the work, which has to be done flows naturally out of the life they have in God and in community. When it comes to the community of the Christian couple, thinking seems to change, probably because one party to the relationship is a woman. Leisure is then thought of as a guilty luxury rather than as a fundamental requirement. One of the main reasons for considering what sort of order is helpful is to make certain that persons do put their relationship with God and their intimates first. The spiritual life is not a call to be heroic it is to a life of love shared in 'community'.

When I was first ordained and with four years experience in a second curacy and thinking of myself as both seasoned and senior a young deacon joined our staff. Now retired with a distinguished forty years of significant ministry behind him, he was then wonderfully laid back. "I think I will have a bath, David" he would announce in the middle of a working morning, "and then I will make some lunch". The lunch was excellent I remember but I was a bit shocked. After all this was a working day. Yet his relaxation was such that people would stop him in the street, accompany him to a bar for pastoral conversation, talk with him about important issues which was something they would have found much more difficult with the rest of the staff. He had time and his ministry flourished in a different way from my rather ordered, segmented life style where there were correct times for baths and cooking. I seemed to need a clear routine, while he was able to be much more spontaneous. True, he was at the beginning of his ministry, wondering what to do, but there was a fundamental difference of style.

Underlying the difference between us was the tension between grace and law, between what Kenneth Kirk once called in a sermon, beauty and bands [7], between the creative work of responding to the movement of the Spirit and the more mundane organizing of time to do the necessary tasks – equally of the Spirit as Kirk emphasized but less glamorous. Somehow both beauty and bands have to be accommodated. As Von Hugel was seeing and as the gospel passage about Jesus's day also shows, space for prayer and relationship with others is as necessary as careful thinking about how it is all to be organized. And, whether persons are spontaneous or ordered by disposition, both space and time need to be allotted to the essentials. Life can all too easily dissipate into trivia. As Dag Hammarskjöld observed at the end of his opening poem 'Thus it was', 'how grievous the memory of hours frittered away.'[8]

*   *   *

The first pole of the spiritual life is the provision of 'leisure for the spirit of prayer and peace,' especially how we apportion time for this. Angelo Roncalli started his *Journal of a Soul* with the 'Little Rules'[9] as they were called, which were given at his college to those 'who wished to advance in the way of perfection.' They worked on the principle of little and often, and to the modern reader sound demanding in the extreme, but were probably less difficult once they were being observed. Each day on rising, he would begin with a quarter of an hour's meditation before attending mass. He would then read a chapter from *The Imitation of Christ*. Before dinner and on going to bed, he would examine his conscience, and throughout the day, he would take opportunities to visit the Blessed Sacrament, make acts of devotion and say Our Fathers and Hail Marys. Each week he would make his confession and each month organize a special day of recollection. Annually he made 'the Spiritual Exercises here in the seminary during Carnival time'[10] Towards the end he added proposals for four days of prayer in honour of St Francis de Sales, who was so like him in temperament.

This was before the First World War, an example of post Tridentine Roman Catholicism, which was designed to form him as a late 19th century Catholic priest. Essentially it was advocating a Benedictine and Ignatian form of prayer built round the rhythm of Office and Eucharist together with a scattering of personal devotions to keep him conscious of the Presence.

When he was ordained and back in Bergamo, the early period of his Galilee/Wilderness way, he had modified it a little and had decided to go to bed by 11-30pm. 'I shall have six hours' sleep, which ought to be enough.'[11] he wrote, and then he changed his rule about meditation to allow a greater flexibility, ten minutes to half an hour before Mass, and to continue with his daily visits and devotions. He counselled himself to read the newspapers when he had the least energy for anything else.

Thirty years on he had only changed the rule a little. Now he proposed rising at 6, as a concession to his greater age. He continued to meditate before mass and to say the little hours. At midday he proposed eating less and going for a healthy walk. Before supper he planned to say the rosary with his household, before ending the day with Matins, the news, some music and a final hour's work before bed. Saying Matins on the evening before sounds odd, but he said it after Compline to ease the pressure on the following morning.

Towards the end of his ministry, when he was Patriarch of Venice and in his 70s, he wrote a letter to his dying sister Maria telling her that he had gone to bed the night before at 9. He was now an old man and was feeling much more tired in the evenings but 'six hours of sound sleep' was still enough. 'I got up at precisely three o'clock this morning. After an hour of prayer here I am with my Maria.'[12] He continued to write letters until a quarter to seven before presumably saying mass. The solid discipline, the six hours of sleep, time for prayer and the flexibility arising from years of habitual practice had given him an inner freedom to pray and be and do within a busy schedule, and in this case also write a long and loving letter to his sister. The outward forms had not changed very much as he grew older, but inwardly his response towards God had deepened.

Dag Hammarskjöld's programme was similarly disciplined and he too seemed to be able to manage on comparatively little sleep. He used to start work at 9-30am and continue steadily until the evening when he joined his parents for dinner. He would then go to the theatre before returning to his desk to work far into the night, only interrupting his toil for an 11pm visit to a café. Next morning he would again be at his desk at 9-30 refreshed and alert for another day.

W H Auden was critical of Dag Hammarskjöld for so rarely attending corporate worship, 'because' he said, 'it is precisely the introverted intellectual character who stands most in need of the ecclesiastical routine, both as a discipline and as a refreshment.'[13] He did go to church a little, though as a shy and prominent man who could spare little time, he tried to be inconspicuous. Certainly it could not have counted as a routine. His prayer was a more private, solitary activity, as is clear from *Markings,* a reflective, meditative literary search in the course of which he moved towards a contemplative stance. He quoted from the Book of Common Prayer and was familiar with spiritual writers such as Eckhart, St John of the Cross and Schweitzer whom he regularly quoted.

Martin Luther King had a much more spontaneous style of praying. When he first arrived in Montgomery he had to complete his thesis and like Roncalli used the early mornings, from 6 until 9 together with evenings so that he was free to do his church work during the rest of the day. His prayer probably followed the patterns of his home, morning and evening prayers, grace at meals and spontaneous prayer at important moments. When he was leading the Human Rights campaign in Birmingham Alabama, the authorities had been granted an injunction to prevent the Southern Christian Leaders Conference (SCLC) from marching on Good Friday morning. The campaign at the time was flagging and he was the main person who could raise money, so that if he marched and was arrested, which was bound to happen, there would be an impossible predicament. And if he did not march, what would that say to his supporters? To resolve the dilemma he left the group and went into an inner room to pray about it. Half an hour later he re-emerged knowing clearly that he should march.[14] That was his style and his way of incorporating prayer within his life. He was a part of a community which lived prayer and worship. It is significant how easy it was for a group of young people to invite Martin to lead them in their prayers.

Like Dag Hammarskjöld, Iulia de Beausobre was to become a woman of prayer and contemplation, but this was to emerge later. There is no evidence as to how she organized her life. In her childhood she had experienced the mystery enshrined in the splendour of the Russian Orthodox liturgy and she was to rediscover it when she eventually settled in England. Later she was to develop a style of prayer based on the Jesus prayer - Lord Jesus Christ, Son of God, Have mercy upon me, a sinner.[15] It is the prayer of the publican brought together with the plea of Bartimaeus and is central to Russian spirituality. In a work towards the end of her life, she traced its history from the teaching of St John Chrysostom, who taught a simpler form, 'have mercy on me, O Lord,' and like him she advocated that all Christians should use it like a regularly repeated mantra.[16] There is more about her teaching on prayer in the final chapter.

So whether the person tends to be ordered or more spontaneous the important thing is that the priorities should be right; not "how am I to squeeze prayer into my busy schedule?" but rather "How is my schedule to be altered in order that my prayer is put first?" Having said that, it is a great deal easier, certainly for those who have an orderly disposition, to pray in the quiet of the day, in the early morning or within the naturally quiet spaces, than it is at other times of the day. The danger for the ordered soul is that prayer becomes merely a routine, dull and wooden, while for the spontaneous that it becomes so haphazard it rarely occurs.

Leisure is the second corner stone of the spiritual life of which the most important element is the nurture of the intimate relationships of family and friends. So often, persons run away from these in order, so they argue, that they might do the work of God. Work to avoid a frightening intimacy, is probably a greater reason. As St Vincent de Paul observed, a great trick of the devil is to compel persons to work all of the time so that they are in effect unable to do anything at all.[17]

Relationships are primary and if persons neglect them, not only are their children often seriously damaged and other people made unhappy, they themselves are impoverished and can become depressed. Further discussion of this is postponed until later in the chapter so that sexuality which comes later in the chapter can be discussed in the context of relationship. Each person is a bodiliness, a relating being as much as a sexual one, and it is best to talk of the two together.

A second reason for the importance of leisure is to study or develop some interest which is perhaps in contrast to the main area of work and yet of some vocational importance. Such interests keep the soul fresh and alive. To give examples from the histories, Dag Hammarskjöld was translating Martin Buber's *I and Thou* on the plane in which he died and at earlier times he had been instrumental in having the work of Djuna Barnes translated for the Swedish stage. Not to great enthusiasm, it has to be said, as her writing was difficult but he and Karl Gierow valued the stimulus of working at the text. His membership of the Swedish Academy, which decides the Nobel Prize for literature, was another opportunity.

After some years in Bergamo, Fr Roncalli was delighted to discover the 39 volumes of papers relating to St Charles Borromeo's episcopal visitation of the 16th century. At the time, 1906, the papacy was hoping to impose curial visitations on the dioceses and Peter Hebblethwaite speculated that Cardinal Ferrari might have wanted to know how the Council of Trent had decreed that these should be done. In the end Roncalli's work of editing took him almost his entire life. The final volume was published in 1957.[18] He thought it would be his major contribution to posterity. For Martin Luther King and Iulia de Beausobre, leisure and the work of writing flowed into each other. Apart from his thesis on the different conceptions of God in the thought of Paul Tillich and Henry Wiemann, Martin Luther King had too little time for study, though James Washington's 'A Testament of Hope' is witness to the extent of what he did write. Iulia de Beausobre found her creativity initially in her painting, only beginning her vocational writing once she had found her way to England.

A third component is reflection, spiritual refreshment and rest. Holidays naturally come to mind in terms of rest but as the term 'holy days' suggests, perhaps they should be for prayer in its wider sense of living in the presence, on pilgrimage and in contemplation, discovering a taste of heaven as it were within the joys of family life and friendship, opportunities for stimulus and refreshment of various kinds. The joke, that people often need a rest when they return to work is maybe how it should be. Hammarskjöld and Roncalli had holiday homes to which they could go. Both Roncalli and Luther King took time out for retreats, every year Roncalli made the Spiritual Exercises and much of a 'Journal of a Soul' was written during these annual breaks of eight days. Luther-King's retreats were rather different, more workshops to talk things through but time out nonetheless. More important than holidays for refreshment is living a balanced day and week with rest naturally built into the structure of each day and each week as Hammarskjöld observed by walking in the hills at weekends and as Roncalli did by taking a post-prandial siesta in his armchair. Holidays can be a time of rest but their effects are not long lasting if changes are not built into the rhythm of a person's ordinary day. The effect of a holiday is a bit like dieting to lose weight. Persons may be wonderfully thin at the end of their diet but without a new regime of discipline they will soon be as fat if not fatter than before. Similarly, without a disciplined regime of refreshment, persons are soon as tired as they were.

*   *   *

So to complete these reflections on the priority of prayer and leisure, it remains to look at the three disciplines to do with food, money and sex and how the four handled them. The disciplines refer to the first three stages of life, the oral, the anal and the genital. Abstention from the oral intake of food relates to the growth in trust and obedience to Christ, the right use of money to the learning of self-control with generosity and living as a bodiliness to the task of learning how in intimate relationship with other persons to love both truthfully and appropriately.

Roncalli's Little Rules only specify fasting on Fridays and Saturdays and say nothing about what it involved, though it was probably a formal discipline of the seminary as fasting was for Iulia de Beausobre in her home in St Petersburg. For Fr Roncalli food was difficult. When he left Bergamo for Rome – see the next chapter - the anxiety of his leaving was tempered by having his two sisters Ancilla and Maria move with him and they no doubt began to provide him, perhaps rather generously, with the comforts of home cooking. He began to put on weight, even more so when he left Rome for Bulgaria, and while from an early age he had counselled himself to eat less fruit and take more exercise now he was beginning to expand. It was hard not to ease negative feelings by eating more than he needed, though it has to be said that if he was going to overeat fruit was not a bad thing to choose. Peter Hebblethwaite jokes that he had not yet joined weight-watchers.[19] Neither took it as seriously as they might have done.

Fr Roncalli liked his food and as both he and Martin Luther King were short and broadly made they naturally appeared rather more tubby than their middle sized, even thin body-shaped counterparts. Even if the latter had eaten a lot they would have shown less evidence of it. Anyway it was probably not an issue for them. Iulia de Beausobre associated asceticism[20] with trying to achieve power and control and had found it particularly offensive in the communist system, disliking it for its addictive and masochistic tendencies. Nevertheless the religious traditions have always urged fasting as a discipline, especially in association with petition or intercession, perhaps because oral intake is so related to the learning of trust. There is a place for the person genuinely wishing to live simply in association with the poor and there are the great saints like St Catherine of Siena who put fasting at the heart of her response but in general it is probably wiser to practice abstinence as part of a corporate or Church discipline rather than as a personal one. Much more important nowadays, and indeed probably more difficult, is learning like the religious communities the art of sitting at table and eating sensibly and moderately in company with others.

Almsgiving does not appear anywhere in the Little Rules, probably because the students had so little money. Perhaps it should have done because what is done with money is so very revealing about attitudes of mind. In psychological terms money is a product, as faeces are perceived to be by the infant in the anal phase, the doublet 'filthy lucre' of dishonest gain being suggestive here, which children try to hoard as something of themselves or part with uncontrollably. Persons can either be similarly tempted to hoard money as if to lose it would damage their security or they splash it about in an orgy of spending.

Both Hammarskjöld and Roncalli spent money on houses for their holidays, the one a cottage in the Swedish countryside, the other 'Camaitino' in Sotto il Monte where his Roncalli forebears had lived. Roncalli was thankful he had enough money for his own needs and that he could use the rest for his family and for others. "We are always poor and humble,' he told his family in 1940, 'but never destitute. We live from day to day."[21] When at about the same time he had been given some money he spent most of it on improving the entrance to the Istanbul delegation.[22] He thought people would judge him foolish but he saw it as a matter of obedience and peace.

Martin Luther King found it difficult to spend money on himself or his family, which makes it ironic that the Alabaman authorities should have chosen financial irregularity as the ground for attacking him after the Montgomery boycott. He postponed buying a bigger house for their expanding family until 1965 despite Coretta's pleading because in the spirit of the first beatitude he felt it was distasteful to be providing for himself while others were so poor. But he did buy it.

Iulia de Beausobre experienced both the highs and lows of riches, plenty in her childhood, poverty in mid-life as we will see. When she arrived in England as an asylum seeker she had little more than what she was wearing. When she married

Lewis Namier he wanted her to dress and live in a style appropriate to his feelings about her personal stature and to her alarm decided he would gamble his savings on the stock exchange to bring it about. His stockbroker was successful, which made Lewis happy for Iulia, while she uncomfortably felt she could only justify the excess by planning to relieve the rigours of Lewis's old age. She was cheered when Lewis told her that his fundamental belief was that 'in our dawning day of self-help and do-it-yourself, human dignity could best flourish on the astringent soil of personal frugality.'[23]

There is always a place for the abandoned act of giving of a St Francis of Assisi but for the majority, it is probably better to aim at simplicity, to use the word preferred by the Taizé community, [24] than poverty. Simplicity embraces a self-controlled and prudent living balanced by a concerned and outgoing generosity to others.

Sex and relationships form the third discipline. The capacity for relationship comes to its first maturity in the genital stage of childhood, which is both a time of close relationship and burgeoning sexuality. Persons are creatures of relationship. As souls, each a bodiliness, there is no way in which the physical can be separated from the emotional and spiritual without inflicting severe psychological damage. Persons respond to others physically, sexually in fact as Jo Ind demonstrates so clearly in her writing, [25] to almost everyone, though for the most part unconsciously. It is one of those facts which makes some Christians uncomfortable, as if for some reason to be a sexual being is to be unspiritual. Persons respond to one another physically and emotionally; they are moved in various parts of their bodies, they touch, they shake hands, they embrace, they kiss in order to express the nature of their feelings. There is the beautiful story of Roncalli when as Apostolic Delegate he visited the troops in Greece during the war. A corporal stepped out of line and knelt to kiss his ring. Roncalli asked him what he required. "'*Monsignore*,'" he said, "'may I embrace you in the name of all of us?'"[26]

As an Italian Roncalli was a warm, tactile man, at ease in his bodiliness who had no difficulty in responding appropriately to those he met. He may have been single, but he was not in fact ever alone. He lived with colleagues usually in a priestly household apart from the Rome time (see the next chapter) when he was with his sisters and he maintained throughout his life a steady correspondence[27] dispensing spiritual advice to his many brothers, sisters, nephews and nieces.

As a young boy of 15, his first retreat was on the theme of purity and sex, not that he could have known too much about it at so young an age, any more than the young Iulia Kazarin at the same age, when she was making her confession to the Moscow priest. His rules and his teachers advocated extreme caution about visual and tactile stimuli, to a severe degree, anything which might arouse 'memories of bliss which develop into fantasy'[28] in the head and so to sexual activity. It was the 19th century and his teachers were really trying to point out that sexual desire is always potent, which was possibly a surprise to a 15 year old Roman Catholic ordinand who might have supposed himself protected from such things by God. However, Roncalli acknowledged his sexuality, if with some distaste and he used its energy in the creativity of his work. From time to time he did rather over emphasize the discipline, as if it was more powerful than he liked to admit but when he had offered himself for the priesthood he knew that he was also committing himself to celibacy, not simply because his Church required it, but because he felt it to be right for himself. This knowledge, that he had made his decision, made sexuality much easier for him to handle and allowed him to be at peace with his body and himself and with God and generally in his relationships with men and women.

For all his solitary nature, Dag Hammarskjöld valued his friends, especially those who shared his artistic tastes, like Karl Gierow of the Swedish Academy and Uno Willers of the Swedish Library. He loved the tussle of argument with colleagues and the friends he made throughout his life. Friendship, Digby Anderson has said, quoting Aristotle and then Aelred of Rievaulx gives us someone who can share a similar morality and virtue, a person with whom we can be tender and affectionate, a person with whom we can talk intimately about personal issues[29] Iulia was close to her friend Tamarah and Martin to Ralph Abernathy, whom he met in Montgomery. Martin loved too his meetings with colleagues where humour and banter together helped form them into a band of companions who were together in a common endeavour. Aelred of Rievaulx's 'Spiritual Friendship'[30] is an essential text for today with its emphasis on the warmth and physicality of human affection between people of whatever sex and it sets it all within the context of relationship.

Dag Hammarskjöld decided to remain single for the reasons already discussed. In a different way Roncalli made of his singleness a strength, willingly consecrating his virginity to God so that like Mary he could respond to the seed of the word of God as it penetrated his heart. Freed from desiring the bodies of others he could desire their spiritual blossoming.

When the overt expression of sexuality is a true expression of the relationship as it was for Iulia de Beausobre and Martin Luther King then it has three purposes, to ensure a good genetic mix in propagating the species, to bond couples intimately to ensure that they remain together to nurture their children and to enable a couple to release tension in play. Human beings, in line with their mammalian ancestry, are capable of many kinds of sexual relationship, too many of them sadly to do with dominance and submission, too few with supportive and companionable relationship which is the ideal of the human and Christian way of relating together.

As will become clear in the next chapter, after early difficulties largely to do with the unsettled times, Iulia and Nicolay de Beausobre had to work hard at a relationship before it could develop into the deep union it became. After Nicolay's early death and Iulia's exile from Russia she married again. Some of Iulia de Beausobre's friends, so Irina Prehn told me, could not believe she would, but she considered it the right way forward for her, which she writes about in her biography of her second husband, Sir Lewis Namier. By that time in her life, she had known much about the dark side of sex from her experiences in prison and of her father and she was relaxed in talking about it. Lewis's attitudes to sex, she described as 'European'. He thought of it, she wrote, as 'an inevitable and ever present factor in everybody's life', which he would indulge with any 'amiable amateurs' who would oblige him.[31] Nonetheless he was shocked when Iulia proposed studying the problem of male prostitution after doing some voluntary work in Wormwood Scrubs prison. Lewis's marriage to Clara had gone badly wrong and he had found a way of satisfying his sexual needs by having a woman visit him for sex on a weekly basis. Certainly Iulia could not contemplate an intimate relationship with him while Clara was alive or the relationship with 'Deirdre' was continuing. She had no desire to compromise her bodiliness by entering a tawdry relationship, but in the event Clara died and Lewis gave up 'Deirdre' (Chapter 7).

Martin Luther King lived in a much more puritan country. He had, as is clear from the previous chapter, an easy and authoritative charm with women to which they responded with evident warmth and he was an Afro-American, with a much more human attitude towards sex than the colder more narcissistic European one described by Iulia de Beausobre. The relationship with Coretta when they were together in their first year seems to have been a very happy one but there were to be problems not least because of the massive pressures laid on him by the demands of the Human Rights movement.

David Garrow reports some as saying that sexual intercourse between Southern Baptist pastors and some women in their flock was 'standard ministerial practice in a context where intimate pastor-parishioner relationships had long been winked at'[32]. Well, maybe; certainly a number of Martin Luther King's colleagues took this attitude. Stephen Oates thought he had a need to demonstrate that he was as virile as his father[33] but his preaching suggests that it was not what he wanted to do. Against his moral judgement, he indulged in one-night stands and towards the end of his life two long-term relationships, one of which was to become emotionally important. That of course is always a danger, that a new relationship might oust the original one and some colleagues thought that had Martin lived his marriage would have come to an end[34] but it did not and anyway their comments are speculative. The dyadic structure of the marriage[35] – the experience of being an inviolate couple within the mystery of their own personal life – held and despite the other relationships, continued to hold.

The knowledge about Martin Luther King's extra-marital relations was discovered by the FBI when they started to bug his hotel rooms and apartments. Early in 1965, as will be referred to again in chapter 6, Coretta King received an audiotape and an offensive letter from the FBI telling her of sexual happenings in a hotel. In the event it was Martin who was the more upset by it when she and friends listened to the tape with him. She simply commented: "I just wouldn't have burdened him with anything so trivial ... all that other business just didn't have a place in the very high-level relationship we enjoyed."[36] Whatever Coretta meant by this, she decided not to talk about it then and she has not done so since. She put a high interpretation on their corporate vocation, she knew the political reasons for the attack and for her part she did not wish it to become a reason for destroying her, her family or their vocational task. Nonetheless, for a political and religious figure the sex made him vulnerable and he was terribly aware that this was so.

It is unlikely there was any trouble before the Montgomery boycott described in chapter 6. There were hints during it, after the birth of Yolande, which is not uncommon with some men after their wives turn their attention to a newborn baby, but the main difficulties came much later as the pressures grew and he became more and more isolated. He told a friend that being away for three weeks in four, sleeping with a woman served as 'a form of anxiety reduction'[37] and in one sermon he noted that the fear of what life might bring led among other things to sexual promiscuity which had the power 'to transform the sunrise of love and peace into a sunset of inner depression'[38]

The damage in this is not the sex; it is the injury to fundamental relationships. As a compulsion it seems to have seized him when he was highly aroused, after a major sermon for example, but also when he was bordering on despair, which he was towards the end of his life as he became exhausted and depressed. Sex with the women who gathered around him like pop-star groupies, gave him some immediate relief and seemed to help him to escape the pain and find some comfort in the arms of a mother, as he used to do as a boy when he was running from a beating to the embracing physicality of grandmother and mother.

Sex is an all too common indulgence, but a dangerous one for a prominent religious figure. The media world loves to report such things both to titillate and to have a figure to condemn and thereby relieve so many of their anxiety about sexuality. The problem for Martin Luther King was that he had become vulnerable to his personal needs for female affection. The sexual desire is strong and never really diminishes even if it loses some vigour as the years go by. It is not something which is ever 'conquered.' If it is repressed, it emerges in unpleasant, sometimes dangerous ways, if it is not, persons are sexual beings, each a bodiliness, and all are always open to the temptation to act out. Relationships are not something persons can indulge when they have time, they are the life blood, the heart of their being as persons and servants of God and they cannot function without them.

The paradoxical thing about this attention to prayer and leisure and to these three disciplines is that a good pattern of 'leisured' living is a recipe for hard work and sacrifice. This is important when there is so much pressure to do more and more in less and less time, which quite apart from being so unproductive is such a terrible enemy of the spiritual life. St Paul urged the Philippians to strive for the prize[39], 'strive' meaning here working like an ox at full stretch but not beyond full stretch! Any farmer who overstretched his oxen would soon be out of business. No one can avoid doing too much at times especially under the pressure of a crisis or a deadline, as Martin Luther King was so often facing, but they need to be wary. Recovering from such strain is not easy, as a modern doctor treating heart patients and following the methods of Hippocrates has found.[40] Hippocrates used to require his over-stressed Athenian patients to take total rest for the first half of their treatment and then follow a programme of exercise and physical training in the second.

Sets of rules perhaps work better for men than they do for women. Some, men as well as women, prefer to arrive at their pattern in a more spontaneous and relational way. Whatever the way the order of priorities is first prayer and secondly leisure, in fact the order of the Shema, [41] that persons should put God first and their neighbour second – and the first neighbours are those to whom they have committed themselves in Christ and in love. The disciplines flow from that in order to minimize damage to these relationships and to help souls grow in love and generosity. It is hard enough dealing with sins and shortcomings at any time (see chapter 4) much harder if persons are exhausted. It is perhaps well to remember that while those who have mislaid their vocation tend to become lazy, those who are committed to them are the ones who burn out.

John Townroe tells the story of a parish priest who once asked the Anglican Spiritual Director, Reginald Somerset Ward whether he would be his director.

Somerset Ward gave him the advice argued for in this chapter, to put time for prayer first, to make provision for his leisure second, and only then to consider all the work he had to do. When he heard about the rule of rest, the vicar 'protested that he was far too busy for any of that.' Somerset Ward then, with a stern kindliness softened by humour, which was a mark of his style, responded, '"Well, then, I am sorry I cannot help you, you see I do not direct madmen!"'[42]

CHAPTER 4

CLAMBERING IN THE FOOTHILLS

Acceptance, Healing, Forgiveness

'He was in the wilderness for forty days, tempted by Satan and he was with the wild beasts; and the angels waited on him.' (Mark 1, 13)

In the medieval Church there were two kinds of pilgrimage. One was the pilgrimage 'ambulare pro Dei' (a journey for God) and the other, the penitential journey, an arduous pilgrimage to do penance for serious sin.[1] The overall journey is of both sorts, but this stage, the purgative or Galilee and Wilderness way is more akin to the second. It is not penance for past sin, which to the modern ear sounds both extraordinary and rather glum, though many still do it, but an opportunity to gain a deeper awareness both of the love of God and of the truth about the self.

St Mark sets the first part of the journey in Galilee, Galilee of the Nations as it is so often called in the Old Testament, where Jesus came from and ministered. Martin Luther King spoke in one of his sermons of Jesus walking round the sunny villages of Galilee[2]. The first part of the journey is for many a joyful time, a time of feeling alive, filled with youth and vigour, an adult at last in charge of a promising future. It is how Galilee feels when reading about it, Jesus bringing his message of acceptance and healing and forgiveness to the oppressed and poverty stricken people living there who had been so long neglected by both religion and state.

The Wilderness is a much starker image. St Mark says of Jesus in the wilderness, 'He was with the wild beasts.'[3] He was in danger from predators, which roamed there, as they do in the unconscious and dreams of people. When Angelo Roncalli meditated on psalm 51, he compared the natural human tendencies he found in himself to 'wild beasts, bears, wolves, tigers, lions and leopards' which if allowed to leap the internal barriers might 'rush to sate their appetites!'[4] In *Flame in the Snow* Iulia de Beausobre describes a bear scraping its claws on the window of Serafim's hermitage, greedy for his blood.[5]

All this makes the barren and rock-strewn emptiness of the wilderness, whatever form it takes in different countries, an apt metaphor for the purgative way, both the uphill nature and hardness of the terrain and the interior struggle which has to be faced. Walking through such places is hard enough if we are feeling bright and cheerful, when we are feeling low it is much more difficult. Persons struggle to cope with underlying and unresolved problems, which tend to surface at this stage in life. This is where the hard work of the spiritual life begins

To give an illustration of how severe this can be for some, a psychotherapist once told a story, recounted in *the Tablet*[6] of a young woman who after following her catechumenate through the rite of initiation for adults, was baptized and confirmed on Easter Day, to great rejoicing by the local Church and by those who loved her. Three days later she had a massive breakdown. It does happen, though mercifully not too often as badly as that. Others find that after the thrill of finding a new faith and everything going well they suddenly become inexplicably depressed, overwhelmed by mental turmoil when they thought they had at last found a safe haven and were free from such danger. What had happened in this young woman's case was that finding herself in a place of safety she was at last able to let go, which then, albeit unconsciously, allowed her to release her deeper problems into her consciousness. Persons only engage in the wilderness with their 'demons', all those past behaviours which have puzzled them, wrong decisions made, poor actions done, memories that disturb, attitudes which are sinful, perhaps even serious problems, when they know themselves to be safe. It is a bit like what can happen when people go on holiday and as soon as relaxation sets in, promptly fall ill. The bodiliness lets go and the person becomes vulnerable. The healing in the young woman's case was hard work and took three years of weekly sessions with a psychotherapist before she emerged as a new woman, knowing herself accepted and healed and forgiven in a way that she had known only as a promise before.

The young woman's experience points to two important truths about this stage of the journey. She needed first to know herself loved before she could as a result come to know herself. The old way of pouring through lists of faults to see what souls might discover about their inner state has now given way to the probably more exacting and certainly more useful telling their stories to themselves or to someone else. The value of the second alternative is that it is demanding, it pierces to the marrow of the soul and reveals the roots of the problem. In the end, purgation is not a fierce scouring away of dirt but far more an exploration with a torch into the crooks and crannies of the darker places so that souls can be gently helped to discover what love is and who or what they are hiding in their depths.

Facing this is the interior work of the relationship with God in this first part of the journey, a necessary preliminary before persons can begin to know what needs to be accepted, what of their problems can be healed and what of their past they need to take responsibility for and seek forgiveness. Forgiveness then in drawing the soul from personal disintegration and separation into relationship includes both acceptance and healing as well. Souls are welcomed back from isolation into full relationship. Naturally they yearn for it and pray:

>'Give us today our daily bread.'

And that they may know themselves forgiven:

>'Forgive us our sins, as we forgive those who sin against us.
>Lead us not into temptation,
>But deliver us from evil.'

This wilderness and Galilee way began on the Jordan day which was described in chapter 1. It is a paradox of baptism that what has been declared and enacted and in a deep spiritual sense wholly done has yet to become a present day truth for the person. It is the constant of justification, that as persons are accepted they are still to become what they have been made. They have to grow into the reality of the relationship which has been forged within them. The Galilee/Wilderness way is then a time of formation, very much in the three areas of the 'Jordan' decision, growing faith in God, learning on the job, deepening relationships with intimates and friends, of becoming a person who can love and serve.

*   *   *

These are the concerns of the first two stories of healing which Mark relates; the first (1, 40-end) of the healing of the man cut off from his fellows by his symbolically unclean and separating disease of leprosy and of the paralysed man brought by his four friends (2, 1-12). The one was looking for healing and welcome back into the community, the second for release and healing and both were searching for the three gifts, to know that they were accepted, to be healed of their afflictions and to know that they were forgiven. At the start of the first story Jesus welcomed a soul back into relationship and in the second showed how after penitence he could be accepted and healed and forgiven.

The story is significantly followed by the summons to another outcast, the despised income tax collector Levi (2, 13-17) and after teaching on the disciplines of fasting and rest (2, 18-end) by the healing of the man who came for help on the day reserved for religion and prayer. (3, 1-6) Healing, Mark is arguing, is at the heart of the whole journey, not something that can be postponed to secular occasions. The crowds responded warmly and flocked to hear more (3, 7-12)

Mark then says that Jesus appointed a group of twelve to continue his work. They were to preach and heal and deliver in the power of the Holy Spirit as the Church was doing in St Mark's day. Vital healing work on the one hand, opposition increasing on the other from clergy who thought his cavalier Sabbath behaviour must be provoked by evil. There was hostility even from his family who feared he might be mad. (3, 13-end)

Parables follow about growth and fruitfulness beginning with the parable of the sower. The kingdom of God and the persons within it need to grow despite variations in the terrain, some of which might be lush, others of it rocky, barren or generally unproductive; Some, not necessarily perhaps those on the poor ground, would fail completely, others would be able to produce a variety of healthy crops. The theme is reflected in the parable of the seed growing in the soil and of the tiny mustard seed, which is to grow into such a considerable bush. Souls who are growing within the kingdom are to be like lights in the darkness, persons who are developing their gifts. (4, 1-34)

At the end of the chapter, St Mark introduces a storm. The disciples thought they were in danger of being capsized and were outraged to see Jesus comfortably asleep on a cushion in the stern. A large expanse of water is often a symbol of the unconscious and it has this meaning here as St Mark recognized in his own Church the critical difficulty of their circumstances. No doubt there were complaints that Jesus was largely asleep to their troubles. Mark counsels them to consider that Jesus brought calm to the boat and queried his disciples' lack of trust. (4, 35-end)

The stories following are all sited around the lake of Galilee, a font as I suggested above, to remind readers that as Christians they are to live out their baptism, the disciples crossing and re-crossing the expanse. The stories of healing are now of people with types of mental illness, first of the multiple personality of the man who called himself Legion, and then while going to Jairus's daughter, of the woman who had been searching so long for relief from her bleeding. (5, 1-end) The degree of difficulty seems to increase with each event, which is further enhanced for Jesus by his experience of rejection at Nazareth, and after the disciples' mission, by the political execution of his colleague in faith, John the Baptist. The external circumstances are becoming tougher, only relieved by the promise of the disciples as they returned from their preaching and healing and by the gathering and the sustaining of the 5000. (6, 1-44)

These passages set in the midst of increasing threat prepare the reader for further turbulent times. Again the disciples are crossing the lake, confronting a new crisis as they strain at the oars against a head wind. Jesus had climbed a hill to pray and in the midst of their trouble comes to join them, as it were in intercessory prayer for them, crossing the water and bringing calm both to them and to the sea. (6, 45-end)

The preparatory stories in the last part of the Galilee ministry are of the growing conflict with formal religion in the persons of the Pharisees about the nature of purity which is followed by two healings. In the conflict about purity Jesus asked the disciples to consider whether purity is to do with an outward or inward display of goodness (7, 1-23) like that shown by the sprightly and witty Greek woman whose daughter was sick. (7, 24-30) She trusted Jesus as someone who could free her daughter from her sickness, described by Mark as caused by an impure spirit, and he makes the girl whole and well. Similarly with the man who could not hear or speak. A Gentile and a Jew both cleansed and enabled to hear and speak, purified, because their hearts were now focussed on Christ. Mark has Jesus again in a wilderness feeding the hungry with the bread made from the yeast of God. (7, 31 – 8,13) Even so, the disciples, Mark emphasizes, do not understand what Jesus is asking of them nor indeed why he was so distressed by their inability to grasp where they were heading.

They were at Bethsaida on the North bank of the lake. St Mark's story is of a man who could not see, and even after Jesus's first efforts, still could only see a little. Very like the disciples and every other Christian in their response to God. Only after further ministry was the man finally able to see, Mark emphasizes the conclusion three times. 'He looked intently, and his sight was restored, and he saw everything clearly.' (8, 14-26)

It is a moment of readiness, the soul poised for change. Slowly and after much preparation the disciples have come to know that Christ is someone who brings calm and peace, who sustains and contains[7] their pain, who teaches, accepts, heals and forgives them. On two occasions in the Galilee ministry Jesus has fed the people with bread in the wilderness. There has been teaching about the way, some seven stories of healing and as the way has become harder, stories about disturbance in the unconscious. For some, like the young woman who had the breakdown three days after her Jordan day, the whole of her wilderness way must have felt severe, but for the majority difficulties are more subtle, steadily increasing in perplexity as work or living becomes generally more demanding.

The early years were certainly tough for **Iulia de Beausobre**. Both her parents had died and at the age of 23 she had married Nicolay days before the fall of the Tsar in

February 1917. The new Kerensky government sent them immediately to join the Diplomatic Corps in London. They were in London when Lenin took over the government in October 1917 and friends, as well as Iulia herself, all advised Nicolay to remain in England while he could. He for his part felt that this was not the time to desert his country. A patriot, he felt, should return. He was a man of firm convictions with perhaps less discernment of the risks than Iulia, who feared they would put themselves in great danger, but she set off to return with him in early 1918 travelling home via Norway. When they reached Oslo, Iulia fell ill with the influenza, which was devastating a debilitated Europe after the war, again needing time to adjust to the enormous changes and risks of her circumstances. She was not strong enough to continue their journey until November. Early in April she conceived so that by the time they reached Russia she was 7 months pregnant. Civil war between Lenin's Bolsheviks and the White Russians was raging so they moved to what they imagined would be the greater safety of the Crimea, only to find that the whole countryside was being harassed and in utter misery and hunger.[8] It could hardly have been worse as a place to give birth.

Her son, Dimitri Nicolaiovitch was born on January 6th, 1919, Christmas in the East. She was half starved and as a result did not have enough milk to feed Dimitri herself. They bartered what belongings they had to pay for milk but there was none available. Early in April, at barely three months old, Dimitri died. As they both knelt beside his grave, Iulia thought of the massacre of the innocents. '*Their* massacre is an essential step in *our* (adult) spiritual advancement' she wrote later, 'because mankind is an inseparable wholeness in the divine mind, which can hold together a plurality of singularities.'[9]

Nicolay and Iulia very nearly died too. This time, perhaps because she was so wracked by Dimitri's death, a major and external emotional event so taxing that it overrode her unconscious vulnerability to sickness, Iulia remained well and it was the bereaved Nicolay who fell ill with typhus fever. Clearly the two of them were divided about where they should live, Iulia really preferring to be in exile, Nicolay in Russia. She decided on this occasion that they must leave and she managed to drag Nicolay to an internment island in the Sea of Marmora, eventually to Istanbul; and finally to London.

Their travelling back and forth by different routes was an enactment both of their predicament as aristocrats in revolutionary Russia and their personal struggle to adjust to their married life. Iulia was looking for safety, possibly survival in the West, Nicolay for service in the East, and felt sure that even though there were dangers they were surmountable. Or might it be spiritual death in the West and spiritual life in the East? Their child was conceived in the West and born – and died - in the East, Nicolay's illness understandably following soon afterwards. All their illnesses somehow symbolized their personal dilemmas within the corporate disaster of the Russian revolution, Iulia ill on the way to Russia, Nicolay on the way back from Russia. At this point Nicolay was angry to find himself back in London and after working for a Russian cooperative returned to Russia in 1923, leaving Iulia to await his return. On being refused permission to leave Russia he wrote to tell her that she must stay in London; he now feared hardship and possibly prison for them both. Become an emigré, he advised her, and divorce him. It was a fateful moment. She had to choose between a life of constant danger with her husband or a safe exile alone with friends in England. In the end in a decision, which was to determine the entire direction of her future life, she opted to return to Nicolay. There had been an element of over dependence in her character until this stage, not least because she was so very impractical in her domestic skills. Eva Bruni tells of visiting Nicolay once while he was cooking something for Iulia and asking him why he did it. "Because," he replied, "I have a wife who if she heats water, it starts burning."[10] Much more important was that she was conscious of being spiritually committed to Nicolay. She felt that to be far more binding than any lesser concern. Practically, she could go to Nicolay. He could not come to her.

She returned to a traumatized *Moscow*. They moved into a flat in a house already occupied by several families. Sasha, a countrywoman who had been a servant with them before, chose to join them. Iulia found it hard being in Moscow but felt that she was in the right place. They were regarded by the authorities, she said, as 'amenable intelligentsia' who had 'a regrettable family history, but no future.'[11]

As a child she had spoken French and English more than she had Russian and it was not until these Moscow days that she deepened her love for the music of her native tongue. She also painted, in bold vivid colours. She had met the Brunis, Lev and Eva, mentioned above, who were not afraid to call themselves Christians, and their friendship was to be of great spiritual significance. Meanwhile, Nicolay was full of ideas for relieving the miseries of their life. "We will arrange a fancy dress ball,"[12] he told Eva Bruni once and despite the shortages they did so.

They had survived appalling difficulties, her illness in Norway, Nicolay's in the Crimea, the going to and fro between Russia and England, the tragic loss of their son Dimitri and through it all Iulia had responded to Nicolay's love and they had grown together, their marriage acquiring a depth of love as they shared their hardships. She had made a great act of faith and sacrifice in returning to Russia and at each opportunity before and since she had given her inner 'yes' to the challenges which were set before her. In the encounter with the Brunis she was beginning to see in the Moscow wilderness some new possibilities.

In turning to **Martin Luther King** things could not have been more different. For him and his new wife it was more Galilee than Wilderness. His training at Crozer and Boston was completed and at the age of 24 he was about to begin his ministry. Daddy King had expected him to work at Ebenezer. Coretta hoped to remain in the North but Martin, who had no intention of working with Daddy, planned to start in the South. The Dexter Avenue Church in Montgomery was looking for a pastor and, liking Martin's preaching, offered him the post. Coretta dreaded returning to segregated Alabama but agreed with Martin's discernment; that this was a sacrifice required of them. 'We both felt that God guided our lives in the way that he wanted us to serve, so that we might be the instrument of His creative will.'[13] she wrote.

Dexter Avenue is the Mall of the State of Alabama. Gracing the city at its highest point, the capitol stands with the elegant brick building of the Baptist Church just alongside it as its immediate neighbour, a touch of colour against the white of the capitol. Visitors nowadays are shown a lower room decorated by a wall-length mural about Martin's life depicting his final arrival in the Promised Land.

Martin determined to educate his new Church into social awareness and consciousness of society's needs. The deacons responded warmly. The minister of a nearby church, Ralph Abernathy with his wife Juanita were also looking for a new Christian order; and the two husbands became spiritual brothers, each able to relax with the other in the earthy banter of close friendship. Martin completed his thesis in the June of 1955. He used to spend 15 hours a week writing his sermon, which he memorized before delivery, apparently spontaneously. Some thought these first sermons the finest he gave.

It was a happy if all too short a year for Martin and Coretta and it was crowned by the birth of their first child Yolande Denise on November 17th, 1955. It was a moment of great joy before the conflicts ahead. It is gracious that they had this good year, an obedient living out of the deuteronomic principle[14] that the newly married couple should have at least one year before they are called upon to undertake their community responsibilities.

It is hard to comprehend just how deep the racial hatred and distrust was and is in the Southern States.[15] To have gone to the heart of Alabama was courageous, a deep responding to where the work of the Lord really needed to be done. That alone would have blessed their journeying, but they also experienced great acceptance from the congregation and the Abernathys. Personal problems were not yet in evidence and anyway getting married and moving away from Atlanta were both statements of health. Martin's faith expressed itself in the teaching programme he instituted and in his preaching. Neither of them could have known what was on the horizon, but they had offered themselves and were prepared.

Angelo Roncalli had a much longer Galilee/Wilderness way. After training in Bergamo and three years in Rome – which included his year's national service in the army – at the age of 23 he had been ordained on August 10th, 1904. He began his ministry by moving back to *Bergamo* as secretary to the newly appointed bishop of Bergamo, Giacomo Radini Tedeschi, a former chaplain of an organization called the Opera dei Congressi, which had been suddenly shut down by the Curia. Radini, who was deeply devout and also a pioneer of social action, was removed from Rome by the ancient device of making him the bishop of a remote diocese. Like Don Roncalli, he was strongly attached to Mary and to the adoration of the Eucharistic presence. He loved pilgrimages too and almost immediately after they got there they set out on a pilgrimage to Lourdes.

Bishop Radini preached widely on social matters, urging his people not to ignore Catholic Action. 'If we were to behave with such obstinacy' he taught, 'God would one day ask us to give an account of our buried talent, and would condemn us as faithless servants.'[16] It affected the young Roncalli profoundly, informing a thinking which was to reach its fruition in the two great encyclicals of his pontificate.

From 1906 Roncalli became a professor, lecturing on history at the seminary. His appointment coincided with the disquiet of the Church about modernism, which reached a head with the publication of Pius X's anti-modernist encyclical, 'Pascendi.' The encyclical had an order attached that all scholars and lecturers must take an anti-modernist oath. It was an un-nerving time and the fact that Roncalli kept as calm as he did must have been in large part due to the example of his bishop who had had experience of handling such curial disapproval.

Even with Radini's backing, it took some courage to give an address praising the 17th century historian Cesare Baronias as 'the founder of historical criticism.' The following year, as a prudent sign of loyalty to the Church, he joined the local congregation of the Priests of the Sacred Heart. As things quietened, he thanked the Lord 'for having preserved me safely in the midst of such ... agitation of brains and tongues.'[17]

Bishop Radini was only 57 when he died. Roncalli was a little prepared but found it hard to take his own advice, so often given to his family, and become resigned to it. His gratitude glows, to use his own word, in his hagiographical appreciation of Radini's life. He was 'the guiding star of my service as a young priest' he wrote.[18]

After Bishop Radini's death, Don Roncalli continued his lecturing at the seminary. A year later, in May 1915, Italy declared war on Austria and Roncalli was called up as a sergeant in the Medical Corps, later becoming a chaplain. There is little in the journal about the time and only a few letters to his family, because he was so busy caring. He felt he had been ennobled by the service and imbued 'with a more burning apostolic zeal. I am now of mature years,' he wrote.[19] Photographs bear witness to this; he had become an assured young man, confident in his identity.

Towards the end of the war he was appointed warden of a hostel for a new brand of students and a year later, he became their spiritual director. He felt that inspiring young priests with a 'love and enthusiasm for … ministry' was to be his vocation and he was stirred that God had made it possible for him.[20]

At this time, Pope Benedict XV, who knew Roncalli slightly, thought he would make a good secretary for a new missionary fund the Pope had founded. Roncalli feared that ambition might be his main reason for accepting such preferment and told his director that his intuition was that he should continue his pastoral ministry in Bergamo. Cardinal Ferrari had no such reservations and, speaking as a man of prayer who knew Roncalli well, what his gifts were and the needs of the Church, wrote and told him 'the will of God is as plain as can be … So go ahead. Whenever God calls, one goes, without hesitation, abandoning oneself in everything to his divine and loving Providence.'[21]

He took up his new appointment in January 1921. Benedict XV's encyclical about missions, 'Maximum Illud' advanced three principles; the establishment of indigenous ministries, work for God's kingdom in opposition to nationalism and the involvement of all Christians in prayerful giving for the work. The new domestic prelate, now to be called monsignor, was to address this third purpose.[22]

He moved into a flat in *Via Voltomo in Rome* and was joined there by Ancilla and Maria and the former Rector of his Roman Seminary, now retired, Vincenzo Bugarini. They moved a year later to *a roof top eyrie in the church of Santa Maria in Via Lata.* They were good years. During them Roncalli began to relax his rule, allowing himself more time in bed, noting that 'he who is always in a hurry, even in the business of the Church, never gets very far.'[23] He came to like the work and more than doubled the fund's income.

The power of the Fascists was growing. Mgr Roncalli observed of Mussolini that his 'aims may be good and honest, but the means he employs are wicked and contrary to the laws of the Gospel.'[24] On the 10th anniversary of Bishop Radini's death, he preached in Bergamo Cathedral about the importance of freedom for both Church and people based on the ethics of the Ten Commandments and the Gospels. The Fascists were not pleased and they lodged a complaint.

Shortly after, in February of 1925, Roncalli was told that he was to become the Apostolic Visitor to Bulgaria. There had not been such a person since the 13th century and what he was to do was vague. Mgr Bugarini had died but he was concerned that his two sisters might be left homeless. The problem was solved by them both moving into Camaitino in Sotto il Monte, a house which he rented and subsequently bought. Apart from the war, he spent a month there every year until 1958.

Mgr Roncalli was to be consecrated bishop. 'I have not sought or desired this new ministry,' he wrote, [25] but he felt he should accept it in 'obedience and peace'; words spoken by Cesare Baronius as he daily kissed the apostle's foot in St Peter's, Rome. 'These words are in a way my own history and my life,' he wrote.[26]

His role in *Sofia* was to forge links with the Orthodox, to open diplomatic channels and to discover the needs of the Catholics in the country. He set out immediately on a visitation of his charge and completing it by August had formulated his ideas by October. On October 14th he presented them to the curia in Rome. One proposal was accepted; that a Bulgarian should be consecrated as bishop; Stefan Kurtieff was duly chosen. Roncalli was then left wondering what he should do in a post, which to all intents and purposes had become redundant. It seemed he was to vegetate alone in a Bulgarian wilderness.

He was now in his 40s, at the height of his powers and he could very easily have become embittered. His apprenticeship with Bishop Radini had been invaluable, especially working with a man who combined such a devout spirituality with a concern for justice and righteousness. In the Rome years he basked in the care of his two devoted sisters. He had continued to grow as a man of prayer and concern for his fellows, especially in the war, in his teaching and in his work in Bergamo and subsequently as the head of the missionary fund. Leaving Bergamo and the work with the students was a hard, life-changing decision, though the major transition of his middle years was yet to come. He was now a bishop in a small backwater of the Catholic Church wondering whether there was a worthwhile ministry for him to do. This was the crucial predicament that God was to put before him.

For the very much more detached, introverted **Dag Hammarskjöld**, the Galilee and Wilderness way was inevitably going to be much harder. After tertiary education at Uppsala University he was now 25 and about to move into the Civil Service at a fairly high level. Inwardly there was much that dissatisfied him as he continued to struggle with problems of identity, relationship and purpose. He was preparing for what was to be a massive personal crisis, which would take him back to his as yet unresolved adolescent searching and would become part of the inner battle of his transition to the way of the cross. (See chapter 5)

Hammarskjöld had moved back to *Stockholm* and to begin with continued to live with his parents. After a short time as Assistant Professor in Political Economy, he had been appointed Secretary to the National Bank of Sweden. In his spare time, he had been studying for his doctorate, which culminated in the debate, which was described in the first chapter. Then, in 1936, still only 31, he was made Permanent Under-Secretary of the Ministry of Finance. There he remained until 1945.

He did not consider marriage.[27] His main relationship seems to have been with his mother and as he told enquirers, he felt he could not ask a woman to undergo what his mother had suffered from his father's absences. His mother died on January 21st in 1940 when he was 34. There is no reference to it in any marking of the time and none indeed until much later, but writing 17 years later on the anniversary of her death, he suggests that the loss had been cruel: 'Destruction! What fury in your attack, how cruel your victory over this poor old. body! You razed everything, you plunged a mind into abysses of anguish – and released this smile of joy.[28]

The smile of joy was perhaps his discovery that he was beginning to find a surer faith. He had not been writing *Markings* at the time of his mother's death, but he had started again in 1941 in a section headed 'The Middle Years'. He described himself as like a top, only kept upright by the lash of the whip.[29] What is it, he asked, to be an authentic, selfless person? His mother had had a lively faith? Was such a faith possible for him? He did trust to a point but his faith lacked objective spiritual confirmation. True self-knowledge, he reflected, could only come when he was prepared to follow the fleeting light into the depth of his being and grasp what faith really was.[30]

He and his father were now living together and though Hammarskjöld admired his father greatly, he felt himself distant from him. The difficulty was that he saw in his father what he detected in himself, a need to depend on a mother. In the same marking, he comments, of both his father and himself, that they both felt a similar cold and loneliness. There are two sections of *Markings* covering this period, the first written in the year following his mother's death between 1941 and 1942, the second after the war when he was working in France between 1945 and 1949 entitled *Towards New Shores*.

In his penetrating analysis he identified a void within, which he found himself trying to fill by endeavouring to attract praise and attention. It drove him to ask as deeply as he could just how his life might acquire real value? Only, he concluded if he could listen to the voice within and follow a path which led in some way to the right kind of death: 'Is this the starting point of the road towards the union of your two dreams – to be allowed, in clarity of mind to mirror life, and in purity of heart to mould it? [31]

Outwardly everything continued as before. He rose rapidly within the higher echelons of the Civil Service to a position in the Cabinet as the Adviser on financial and economic problems and after the war, increasingly into foreign affairs. In 1946 he negotiated a trade agreement with the States and a year later was appointed head of the Swedish delegation to the Organization for European Economic Cooperation set up in **Paris – he lived mainly in Paris and had a flat in Stockholm -** to implement the Marshall Plan after the war. When he had time, he toured France, on one occasion visiting the St Mary Magdalene Basilica on the crest of Vézelay; such an evocative memory later.

Inwardly he continued to struggle. Hammarskjöld's dating of *Markings* in these pre-UN sections is of the most general kind, so that it is impossible to relate inward reflections to any outward event. In the *Towards New Shores -?-* section which introduces the least abstract part of the book he begins by asking how he might choose 'his' true self. What is the precise, the only way for him, given the thousand possibilities he might choose between what he would personally prefer and finding the one true path where there is a 'congruence of the elector and the elected'? [32] He will never find it, he tells himself, unless he can cast anchor 'in the experience of the mystery of life' and consciously embrace the talent entrusted to him as his personal identity.

As he searches for his particular way forward he gives a series of vivid vignettes of people and places, [33] which describe individuals who have in some way diced with death, in most cases, he thought, in foolish ways. They are explorations of the meaning of death and sacrifice, allowing him to ask whether suicide is ever a meaningful act of sacrifice. He was partly asking this for himself because he was lonely and unfulfilled but he was also struggling to understand the meaning of sacrifice. What, he asked of himself, was involved if he were to live a sacrificial life and how could he avoid doing something ridiculous? The sad marking of the mother knitting and praying that her son might achieve the freedom he longed for when he was in fact 'as free as anybody can be in the economic mazes of a modern society'[34] was one example of such foolishness. He was striving to see and to hear and to find his own way but was mortified that he was still so obsessed with himself. 'Behind his talk of freedom lay hidden a child's wish to conquer death, a lack of interest in any piece of work the result of which would not be *his*, even long after he was dead.' Or, as he put it starkly, early in his 1941-1942 reflections, summarizing his self-discovery 'you are your own god.'[35]

This was the fundamental insight of the many he had received in his search to understand himself. He had discerned the narcissistic attitude within himself, that like everyone else deep down he considered himself to be a god to whom others, if he would allow them any existence at all, were necessarily of lesser importance. They were merely mirrors, on whom he could cast his reflection, like Narcissus gazing into the pond and falling in love with his own beauty until his metamorphosis into a flower. Like Adam and Eve, who on taking the fruit and thinking they had become independent found that instead they had become existentially alone. Hammarskjöld identified this ultimate truth not just in himself but as a truth of the human condition, that human beings are in a state of separation from both God and others.

*   *   *

One of the great psychological findings of the first half of the 20th century was that a person who is cut off from relationship eventually despairs. A spilt occurs, the heart as it were breaks and, to use Michael Balint's [36] analogy, a basic fault-line occurs splitting one part of the heart holding on to some semblance of relationship from the other which withdraws into what Hammarskjöld described as a "ring of cold,"[37] This is where the pain of the human condition lies, and the wilderness is the beginning of the struggle to move from this spiritual state of centredness in the self to a new and lasting encounter with the Other.

How is it to be done? In a letter to her spiritual companion Monna Alessa dei Saracini, Catherine of Siena advised her to create a spiritual dwelling place within her soul, 'namely the cell of true self-knowledge, wherein you will find knowledge of God's goodness (at work) in you. ... Self-knowledge alone would result in confusion of mind, whereas to abide solely in knowledge of God would lead you to presumption. Each needs to be seasoned with the other ...'[38] This in summary form is the essence of the purgative way as a penitential pilgrimage, a learning about the love of God however mediated in order to have the courage to learn more about the self. To meditate just on the love of God as Catherine says without any inner exploration would not only be presumptuous but also a discourteous avoidance of unpleasant truths about the self. To discover self without knowing love would bring about breakdown, its severity depending on how serious and disturbing early experience had been.

Hammarskjöld and de Beausobre certainly had personal difficulties which it was going to take them a long time to work through and in a different way, so had Roncalli and King, but all four had been brought up within a Christian tradition from the beginning of their lives. They had their sins and weaknesses: obsession with self and pride, aristocratic distance, greed, a tendency to gossip, lust, infidelity and problems which would emerge later, but they were ordinary human difficulties. None of them had suffered severe abuse. But like everyone else they still needed to know that they were accepted, healed and forgiven. The way to it is a five-fold process: first an ever expanding experience of love, secondly an encounter with the self, thirdly acknowledgement of who the person is and of the need for healing, fourthly cooperation with the healing process and only then and finally the joy of knowing acceptance, healing and forgiveness.

The learning of the way begins with the experience of love. Each of the four had come to know themselves loved by Christ through their prayer, King and Roncalli through the worship of the Church, possibly de Beausobre also, and all four, Hammarskjöld included, through their personal searching in prayer and reflection. As they prayed, so their apprehension of God deepened and changed.

Dag Hammarskjöld yearned to know God and sought to reach out to him, finding it impossibly difficult to feel that God might be reaching out to him. It had not happened, he thought, and he did not know how it could. He, like everyone else, was projecting his perceptions onto the face of God, unconsciously positioning his image so that, like mixed pixels hiding an identity on a television screen, he could not make out the Countenance. In all relationships when one person loves another and hopes to become intimate, the true person of the other is equally obscured. It is just as long a process of maturing before the one can accurately see the other. The difficulty is well illustrated in the relationship of Iulia and Nicolay. They took a long time to see and know each other as they were. Each saw the other in the light of their expectations and past perceptions so that what they in fact saw was in terms of their imagination rather than the other as he or she really was. Projections cloud the mystery of the other person. When persons come to realize this, through experience of love in the relationship, they begin to see beyond their distortions. They begin to be more present to the other; in personal relations as much as in the relationship with God. They begin to see beyond what they had assumed that God was like to discern the reality revealed in the face of Jesus Christ.

They were also coming to know the love of Christ through others. Martin experienced the love of Coretta. They had too the friendship of the Abernathys. Learning about love was at the heart of the De Beausobres' struggle and they were also cared for by Sasha and their friends the Brunis in particular. Angelo Roncalli valued and was cared for by his sisters and his mentors, Bishop Radini and Cardinal Ferrari. Dag Hammarskjöld knew the love of his parents and his friends. It is a truism but one which needs constantly to be restated: that persons do not begin to seek healing unless they are first of all aware in some part of their being that they are loved. The whole process is like the person being slowly healed in St Mark. (Mark 8, 14-26, see above) They begin to see better, their eyes open, their vision is enhanced.

It is only in the light of God's love which is exhibited both directly and through the love of others that persons are able to move on to the second step of healing, to learn more about the self and begin to identify and discern any underlying fears and problems; for example Iulia de Beausobre, that she would fall ill when difficulties became too much, Dag Hammarskjöld that he was lonely to a narcissistic degree. Neither were things easily healed though they were both of them able to find later that as they matured they could discover resources actually within the severity of the problems.

In one of his early sermons, Martin Luther King identified his underlying problem as to do first of all with fear, and in his case a fear of death. As he put it, 'I have been tortured without and tormented within by the raging fires of tribulation.'[39] He noted that at times he had asked God, to 'solve this problem for me' and added, 'I can't do anything about it.'[40] He recognized he was powerless to solve it himself but equally that God was not going to solve it for him. He had first to recognize that he had a problem, secondly to acknowledge that it made him afraid and only then discover that he might be able to bring it out into the open. It was either that or become depressed and bitter. Learning the truth about the self is the task of a lifetime and it deepens the further on the way persons are. In fact a conviction of sin is usually a later development on the journey and not something which is very much there in the beginning.

The third step of healing is the need to acknowledge this truth about the self. It is as if the soul has to say, 'this is the truth about myself, I am the person who has had these thoughts and have spoken and done these things. Maybe it was not possible for me to do any other, but nonetheless it is I who did them.' One of Roncalli's tutors used to say of the temptation to shift or project the blame onto someone else or even onto forces outside, "Devils? What devils? ... We are the devils, we are the ones responsible."[41] Indeed as all souls do find as they journey into a deeper communion with God, they are able to identify more and more clearly what the truth is about themselves. Taking responsibility for the self is a necessary preliminary to recovery and healing.

Then comes the fourth step, the arduous task of rebuilding disciplines, finding things that help; practical ways of prayer, going on a pilgrimage, therapeutic especially cognitive-behavioural tools which encourage healthy living. Roncalli often felt guilty about his temptation to gossip but he learnt from Mgr Radini the value of Augustine of Hippo's[42] rule that conversation at the table should always be governed by generosity and charity. 'Never' he commented as his bishop was dying, 'was there a single reference to a Vatican official, from the Holy Father downward, that was lacking in ... respect.' [43]

He also kept a journal, encouraged by one of his earliest spiritual directors, Luigi Isacchi, to do so since he was a boy. A diary draws out what is inside and places it outside the self, and in the writing renders events less alarming. It puts a stop to the constant whirl of repeating thoughts and helps identify causes of behaviour. *Markings* served a similar purpose for Hammarskjöld and painting for de Beausobre. Once thoughts and ideas are on paper they are already half-healed.

Forgiveness, the fifth step does not mean, Martin Luther King once told a congregation 'ignoring what has been done or putting a false label on an evil act. It means, rather that the evil act no longer remains as a barrier to the relationship.'[44] Souls are welcomed back within a relationship in which they are changed and can once more engage with the demands of life.

'Forgiveness' Hammarskjöld wrote in *Markings* 'is the answer to the child's dream of a miracle by which what is broken is made whole again, what is soiled is again made clean ... In the presence of God, nothing stands between Him and us – we *are* forgiven.'[45]   Roncalli when he made confession would hear his confessor say, "... of his great mercy, forgive you your sins; and by his authority committed to me, I absolve you from all your sins, in the name of the Father and of the Son and of the Holy Spirit."   Not at this stage of her story, but certainly in later years, Iulia de Beausobre would have heard similar words when she and her confessor stood together before an icon.[46]

Martin Luther King once told a story of how God spoke to him of acceptance and forgiveness. It was through a priestly woman who was known among the Afro-American community as Mother Pollard. One day she had accosted him after a service. '"Something is wrong with you," she said.' He tried to deny it but she persisted. '"Now you can't fool me,"' she said; '"I knows something is wrong"' and she speculated what it might be. Then, before he could say more, she said, '"I don told you we is with you all the way." Then,' rummaging in her faith, 'her face became radiant and she said in words of quiet certainty, "But even if we ain't with you, God's gonna take care of you."' As he heard these words he felt something coming alive in him, so much so that he shook, quivered is the word he uses, with a new and powerful energy within him.[47]   To be forgiven, Roncalli once said, is like the dawn of a new day; the darkness fades 'as the rays of the sun increase as it rises.[48]

Forgiveness is one of the gifts of Baptism, the sacrament associated with this part of the journey by Pseudo-Dionysius.[49]   Part of baptism's definition of the way, referred to at the end of chapter 2, is this demonstration that there is a way back when souls have fallen from the path. Reconciliation is an extension of baptism, in that souls metaphorically speaking return to the waters to be cleansed and purged and made new again for the journey. Forgiveness begins in the experience of being loved - Jesus said plainly, 'I have come to call not the righteous but sinners.'[50] - so that they may be strong enough to take the necessary steps towards reconciliation. The traditional terms for the four steps beyond the experience of being loved are self-examination, confession, penance and absolution.

As the Galilee and wilderness journey draws towards its close, it is interesting to reflect how dramatic the beginning of it was for three of them. Martin and Coretta King moved together to their first home in Montgomery, Iulia and Nicolay de Beausobre moved fairly immediately to London and Angelo Roncalli from Rome to Bergamo.   Only Dag Hammarskjöld stayed where he was. Then there was a considerable contrast between the surprisingly peaceful, even joyful, journey of the Kings in Montgomery and the de Beausobre journeying back and forth between

Russia and England before they eventually settled in Moscow. Angelo Roncalli remained in Bergamo apart from his chaplaincy years before moving to Rome and then finally to Sofia. Dag Hammarskjöld remained primarily in Stockholm with a number of years in France helping implement the Marshall Plan.

The beginning of the way is often accompanied by a move to a new home to start what for some is an adventure while for others it is a hard struggle. It is often during this young adult period of life that any serious problems, hidden through the childhood years, begin to emerge. Any age is appropriate for help of course but if therapy is to be done, then this is a good time to look for it. As the gospels suggest, the young adult way is a time of cleansing and purification, of becoming open, untrammelled by disturbance and learning to discern the ways of God because they have found themselves accepted and healed and forgiven and they now want their gifts and talents to be made available for use in God's service.

Sometimes people find it hard to believe that they can be forgiven. Others may be forgiven, they think, but they doubt they can be included among them. This is particularly troubling to persons who think that what they have done is especially repellent – and it may indeed be so, though it is often small things that cause the most worry – not only to others but to themselves. It is worth re-iterating that God knows what persons are capable of and that every penitent soul can be forgiven.

Harry Guntrip once told me that over his years as a therapist, he had never heard of a thought or feeling, a capacity for sin, which he had not at some time been able to identify within himself. He knew both the dark places and the light within his own soul, his envy and jealousy as much as his gifts, his capacity for hatred as much as his capacity for love, the grandiosity within him as much as his humility. He discovered this about himself because after a long journey he had come to know that he was deeply loved.[51]

The Meeting of the Waters above Hexham. The trees in the background stand behind and in front of the village of Warden and its church.

CHAPTER 5

CAIRN ENCOUNTERS

Caesarea Philippi

'Jesus went on with his disciples to the villages of Caesarea Philippi; and on the way he asked his disciples, "Who do people say that I am?"'
(Mark 8, 27)

In the figure of the spiritual dynamic (page 12) in chapter 1 there is a gate. As persons journey through their Galilee and wilderness and begin to discern more of the love of God for them and more about themselves, they reach a frontier, a barrier of some sort, which in effect generates a kind of personal crisis. It is a crucial moment, the transition from the Galilee/Wilderness way to the Way of the Cross - traditionally the purgative to the illuminative way - which includes in terms of the spiritual dynamic a new call from Christ to take up the cross. It is followed by a fresh celebration before the disciple engages once again on a new way.

It is a crisis insofar as it is a change of direction, not in the sense that a person has an active choice in the matter. In the histories in the last chapter, Angelo Roncalli made an important decision to move to Rome and Iulia de Beausobre to join her husband in Moscow and both were hard choices over which they spent much time considering how to decide. They weighed up the pros and cons, took what advice they could, prayed for wisdom to discern the best path and eventually made their choice. In the transition here the situation is more passive. There are elements which are similar, the need to respond with a decision, but primarily it was something, which happened to them. Events around them were having an effect, making them ask large questions about their life and about God, to which they had to make a response, which in its turn brought about a major internal shift of consciousness within them.

Erikson identifies a crisis in the middle years as coming somewhere between the ages of 35 and 55, sometimes earlier, sometimes later and in terms of his epigenetic cycle at the time when the children of the young adults are about to leave home and the mature couple to become grandparents. Not that that is the case with any of the four, but the middle age upheaval is one that is easily recognizable. Many people feel that their youthful enthusiasm has started to evaporate into a middle-aged ennui when they wonder if life has anything more for them. Erikson puts the conflict as one of generativity versus stagnation.[1]

In Fowler's [2] thinking his stage of maturity of faith can be earlier or later, but not usually before 30. Ken Wilber[3] does not really give his equivalent level an age. He says that it could be as early as 21 and St Catherine of Siena is an example of this, but for the majority even 30 is early. Most reach it in their middle years having traversed the Galilee and Wilderness way and come to realize that the neat package of faith that has served them well enough until this moment has become frayed. Fowler observes that the symbols, myths and stories, which they had rejected as juvenile in the early 20s, are now beginning to return in order to help them handle the paradoxical nature of the many religious and philosophical questions they find themselves facing. They can no longer ignore persons of other faiths and understandings. In effect they are maturing as Christians, their eyes are being opened to discover new ways of responding to the complexities of life before them.

Wilber[4] identifies a change in consciousness from ego levels of adolescence and early adulthood to what he calls the Centaur or existential level. He has used mythological creatures to illustrate two of his earlier childhood stages not referred to here and in this one the half human half animal nature of the centaur (presumably derived from the horsemen of the Central Asian steppes who appeared to be sealed to their mounts) symbolizes for him the coming together of body and mind in a maturity of bodiliness. The change in consciousness is from thinking verbally to an ability to comprehend visually through image, symbol and myth. It is interesting in connection with this how much the language of the gospels at this point is to do with receiving sight and acquiring vision. The person is now centred and autonomous, able to intend or will the direction in which he or she is going.

The transition to this new stage is the Caesarea Philippi crisis of which the Galilee/Wilderness of the last chapter has been the preparation and address. It is a creative crisis in contrast to the crises that dominate the news which often are disasters of one sort or another. Creative crises are different in that they lead to some significant change for the better. To give an example, my son-in law was for a time Vicar of a deprived parish in Newcastle when he and his congregation were planning a reordering of their church. It was an ambitious scheme which was to cost about £500,000. Half the money had been raised but there was still an enormous shortfall which needed to be found from somewhere. It so happened that at the same time one of the Newcastle Building Societies, Northern Rock, was making £200,000 available for another unrelated scheme to provide a Nursery school in the area. The idea suddenly struck him; why not site the new nursery school within the church? A creative idea, an instance of lateral thinking, a bringing together of two different streams of thought and making of them one! I can remember his excitement as he shared the vision. Once the idea had come, of course, it seemed obvious, but it had been anything but obvious before. Seeing the magnificent new interior when the project was finally brought to completion brought joy to both Building Society and Church community alike.

Wondering where £200,000 was going to come from when there was no idea where it could be found had the making of a crisis. The struggle, casting around for a way forward until the surprising idea became actual might be called the preparation and having the idea was the critical event which changed the whole situation. Once the agreement was made, then the crisis was resolved. The actual process of change in the resolution of a crisis is similar whether it is a crisis leading to an improvement in affairs or a destructive event which leads to a catastrophe. They are much the same too if the moment of change happens after a long period of agonizing or very speedily. Once the critical event or creative moment has occurred, there is a further predictable dynamic; amazement and wonder, sometimes an inability to believe at first that it could have happened in this way which leads in its turn to an emotional response and adjustment until things can be fully accepted as part of a new reality. In sum there are three main parts in any resolution of a crisis, the long or short period of preparation, the critical event itself and all that follows afterwards.

Wilber[5] speaks of such a change as a transformation or metamorphosis and he too identifies three stages in the process. When an existing level of consciousness ceases to be enough, some symbol from the one to come draws the person onto a new level of consciousness. There is the *existing* level, the 'call' as it were urging the person to *identify* with a new level, *differentiation* from the past one and *operation* in the new one. It is not so much a series of steps upwards, more an expansion into a deeper consciousness which includes what has gone before.

Similarly, Nancy Burkin[6] writing in *The Way* about conversion identified the same process. She described her threefold way as time of preparation, critical point of decision and resultant life. The preparation, she said, was all that preceded and prepared the person for conversion, the critical point was the actual experience that required a change, an opening up to a new way of seeing both God and the self and the third was the result, all that followed in new life.

The similarity here between these various analyses and the spiritual dynamic described in the first chapter will be apparent. The engagement of the previous stage serves as the preparation, which leads to an address from God of some sort which demands a response, which then leads to some 'liturgical' celebration of the call and response to be finally followed by an engagement to the new way. What happens at the address is the spiritually creative moment and usually it is a fairly brief 'critical event.' It is usually a surprise or at least has a surprising element. It may be dramatic but it does not have to be. What can be said is that at this critical moment, two or more previously opposed ways of thinking - frames of reference, patterns of thinking – have been brought together into a new unity. To bring things together into a harmony is a work of the life-giving Holy Spirit moving gently within the heart to bring about a creative outcome.

Arthur Koestler[7] in his study of creativity explores how such different matrices of thought come together. He noted that the creative event seems to occur most readily when the rational mind is at rest, the person gently ruminating through a dilemma in the netherlands of sleep. The brain waves in such a state are in the theta mode, in which they as it were roam about so that the synapses make sudden and often bizarre and surprising connections. For many this also occurs in sleep itself. A recent survey by Ulrich Wagner of the University of Lubeck in Germany showed convincingly how persons go to bed with a problem and wake up with new and fresh insights to resolve it.[8] Dreams can do the same thing. At such moments the soul becomes open to the creative surprise, to the life-giving movement of the Holy Spirit within, making new and previously unknown possibilities out of an impasse. It is what Ian Ramsey[9] used to speak of as a disclosure of God, the moment of sudden clarity when the penny drops and a person comes to a new understanding.

Near my home, the river Tyne runs through the city of Newcastle, the river flowing from the higher central regions of the North of England all the way to the coast. It begins as two rivers, prosaically called the North Tyne and the South Tyne, the first rising in the borders of Scotland, the second in the East Cumbrian hills the two of them eventually coming to meet just above Hexham. I have stood there at this meeting of the waters on several occasions, struck by the mystery of these two rivers gently coming together to form a new river, which must be twice as large as the two separate rivers but looks not all that much bigger. Presumably it has to be. The new river is both wider and deeper, like a creative change in the spiritual life. Much the same in surface appearance, massive change interiorly! The Saxons honoured the spot with churches at the three angles: Hexham Abbey to the South, where Aelred of 'Spiritual Friendship' was the son of the parish priest, St John Lee to the East where St John of Beverley once made his Lenten retreat and healed a deaf and dumb boy, and Warden to the West where a recent Vicar cared for wayfarers and others. Three Saxon houses of prayer at a place of spiritual significance![10]

*　　　*　　　*

The spiritual transition being considered in this chapter is a similarly creative moment. In St Mark's gospel it is what occurs at Caesarea Philippi. Shortly after the healing of the blind man, the disciples were walking behind Jesus as he set out for the town of Caesarea Philippi. Apart from the visit to Tyre and Sidon, this town is the most northerly place Mark records Jesus as visiting. He turns to the disciples and asks them, "Who do people say that I am?" His address was phrased as so often in spiritual communication as a question. They responded by giving him the opinions which were circulating round Galilee. Jesus then asked them "but what about you? 'Who do you say that I am?'" (Mark 8, 27-29)

Peter as the man who represents all the disciples is the one who gives the reply. As a first century Jew sharing the common expectation that a Messiah would be sent to deliver his country from Rome, he also knew, though neither he nor the rest of the disciples had a conscious knowledge of it, that the Jesus they had come to know and the Messianic ideas that they had inherited were not really congruent. Power and glory, yes, suffering and service, no! The Old Testament had both, of course, but suffering was not part of the popular view. When Peter acknowledged the truth which he felt was in Jesus, even if he had not grasped its full significance, he brought the two matrices of thought together, the fact of his changed life on the one hand with Jesus's work of teaching and healing and living on the other and made of the two a creative act of faith; "You are the Messiah," he said. (Mark 8, 29-30)

Immediately Peter had given his response, Jesus spoke openly about what this entailed for him and for them. He was to suffer and he would undergo rejection. Despite his words, Peter could not grasp this. He was unable to make the further leap of understanding and comprehend what Jesus was saying. Could the person he had recognized as Messiah possibly let this happen to him? Urgently he challenges Jesus to acknowledge his new status so that Jesus, in concern for their souls, had to respond with angry vigour to defuse Peter's dangerous misunderstanding. He explained to them the nature of his vocation and the vocation of all Christians. (Mark 8, 31-33) Following me, he said, is to walk the way which leads to the cross. You cannot allow anything, least of all the self, to distract you from the true way of holiness and righteousness. "If any want to become my followers, let them deny themselves and take up their cross and follow me," Jesus said, "For those who want to save their life will lose it, and those who lose their life for my sake, and for the sake of the gospel, will save it. (8,34 – 9,1)

Jesus then leaves Caesarea Philippi for the celebration and commissioning on the high hill of Tabor which lies to the South East of Nazareth in the middle of Galilee. St Mark's account refers back to the ascent of Mount Sinai by Moses and of Mount Carmel by Elijah and describes Jesus with Peter, James and John ascending the mountain and in the mystery of the stillness of his prayer becoming radiant and transfigured by the light of God's Holy Spirit. In the company of his Old Testament precursors he is disclosed, as he will be at the fulfilment of his journey. As the cloud of the presence of God descends upon them they hear again the words spoken at Jesus's baptism, "This is my Son, the Beloved; listen to him."(9, 2-13)

So the threefold dynamic is repeated. There is the address of Christ, the questions he put to the disciples, the response he received and then the clear and direct call to walk after him on the way of the cross. His close friends, the three apostles, Peter, James and John then accompany him as he is transfigured before them in his baptismal glory.

Each Christian follower at some point or another on his or her pilgrimage comes to such a Caesarea Philippi moment. It began famously for **Martin Luther King** and in a thoroughly ordinary way with Rosa Parks[11] refusing to give up her seat on a late Thursday afternoon Montgomery bus. Martin Luther King had now been the Minister of the Dexter Avenue Church in Montgomery for a little over a year and his and Coretta's first child had just been born. Rosa Parks was tired after a busy day at work and when a white traveller got onto the full bus, the bus driver, with whom she had had a bad encounter some years before, insisted that Mrs Parks should stand. She refused and after a confrontation was forced off the bus, arrested and taken into custody. Rosa Parks was a prominent person in the black community, the local secretary of the NAACP, and someone with a reputation for probity and concern for justice. Her arrest was the catalyst the community were waiting for. One or two earlier cases had been considered, but this one gave them their ideal opportunity to act. They planned their boycott of the buses to start on the Monday following, on December 5th.

After the first meeting, the organizers realized they were going to need a new chairman. Dr King had attended meetings of the NAACP before and indeed Rosa Parks had invited him to join the executive but both he and Coretta had decided that it would be wiser at this stage for him to concentrate on his Church work. At the planning meetings, the one to elect a new chair, there were two candidates being considered, neither of whom was Martin Luther King. It was not until one of those who might be elected spoke up to say, "'Mr Chairman, I would like to nominate

Reverend M.L. King for president,"' that he realized he was a candidate. There were no other nominations. A little nervously, wondering what Coretta was likely to say, Martin said, "'Well, if you think I can render some service, I will'"[12] The call had come totally unexpectedly and he could hardly have had any conception of the enormity of his 'yes', nor much sense at the time that he was responding to an address of Christ, but it was a spontaneous response for which Coretta and he had been well prepared by their earlier offering to work in Montgomery.

That night he found a telling phrase to sum up the mood of the community. 'There comes a time,' he said, 'that people get tired. We are here this evening to say to those who have mistreated us so long that we are tired – tired of being segregated and humiliated. ...'[13]

Their demands were modest enough; for courtesy from bus-drivers, white seats in the front going back, black at the rear coming forward, which passengers could take on a first come first served basis, and black drivers. They expected the company to accept them all as they had done elsewhere, but the whites were confident that they could break the boycott. Police harassed the cars transporting the workers and on January 26th they arrested King, at first refusing bail until growing crowds began to mass outside the jail and were becoming aggressive.

Martin and Coretta had been elated to be involved in such an historic moment, but the hatred and menacing phone calls frightened them both. Martin wondered whether it was right for him to continue. Some few weeks later, when the boycott was beginning to bite someone rang with yet another threat to kill him and he began to feel that he had had enough. He was tired and desperately worried about the safety of Coretta and their infant daughter Yolande. Had he accepted this dangerous task without proper consultation and even if Coretta had accepted his decision, was it right to put them into such intolerable danger? "I got to the point," he said " that I couldn't take it any longer. I was weak." He could not call on his parents for help when he had worked so hard to find his own identity and anyway they were far away. He began to doubt that he could go on. It was in the stillness of this moment, as his mind was exploring these unassailable reasons why he should give up, confessing to God the extent of his fears, that his arguments suddenly clashed with the strength of his faith and the reality of his vocation. At that moment he heard within himself the voice of Christ saying, "Martin Luther; stand up for righteousness. Stand up for justice. Stand up for truth. And lo, I will be with you, even until the end of the world." Over the years, as he came to preach about it he would add his conviction that the Lord would be with him in his fight. "He promised never to leave me, never to leave me alone. No never alone."[14]

Martin's faith had grown into an implicit trust in God. His father Michael had taken the names Martin Luther and given them to his son because they represented to him, and he prayed to his son also, someone who had been prepared to stand up against evil for righteousness sake. This came to Martin in the kitchen, as his mind was idling round the terrible things happening to him and his people, and he was able to draw upon this concern for righteousness and bring it together with his awareness of the presence of God within him and make of them a synthesis of strength. God was going to be with him whatever happened.

The images and language in which the experience was couched came clearly from his background in the Church. They spoke to him of God's presence in such a way that he would tell the story in his inimitable way again and again. It was a spiritually creative moment, an immense sense of encounter with the mystery of God, his early experience of being addressed massively confirmed by the words welling up within him that Christ was beside him and would stay with him.

Both he and Coretta had needed to know that God was with them. "In the midst of lonely days and dreary nights," as he described this in a sermon, "I have heard an inner voice saying, "Lo, I will be with you." When the chains of fear ... have all but stymied my efforts, I have felt the power of God transforming the fatigue of despair into the buoyancy of hope. I am convinced that the universe is under the control of a loving purpose, and that in the struggle for righteousness man has cosmic companionship'[15]

In terms of the dynamic, the order is different from St Mark. This is probably because he and Coretta had responded to their vocation already by moving to Alabama. Martin was still very young and perhaps it was easier to understand that he had a vocation than it was to know that Christ was with him and would give him the spiritual strengthening he needed for the hard task ahead. His vocation was confirmed when he was elected as chair but it was not until his kitchen encounter that Jesus asked Martin who he thought he was. There in the kitchen he was assured of his presence. There was nothing about removing the difficulty. It was the assurance of presence which he needed and was given. Neither he nor Coretta were to turn back.

Shortly after the kitchen event, a bomb was thrown at his house. Fortunately Coretta and Yolande were in the back but the crowds gathering at the scene were angry. Martin was in church at the time but it was his quiet authoritative presence on his return home and his wise words that persuaded the crowd to leave. He had been able to accept what had happened in peace. '"My religious experience a few nights before had given me the strength to face it,"' he said[16].

There are similarities in the experience of **Iulia de Beausobre**, though her vocation and her understanding of it was to grow more slowly and her main vocation was to come much later. She had returned to the hardships of Russia after a time in England towards the end of 1923 or early 1924 and now aged 30 was living with Nicolay in a small flat in Moscow. It was at the behest of her friends the Brunis, that she and Nicolay took their 1925 summer holiday in the then dissolved monastery of Optino. At the time Nicolay was in and out of prison and Iulia was frequently ill, and they were in serious need of a break. In her edition of Macarius of Optino's letters[17] the importance of this visit is emphasized by her detailed description. She said, they reached the nearest station, Kozelsk and hired a peasant's cart to make the journey through the fertile countryside and forest to the monastery which was some four miles away. The onion-domed monastery or skete (meaning 'wilderness' in Russian) was a low-lying white building reflected in the lake which lay opposite. They crossed a wooden bridge, entered the forest and stopped when they reached a high wall, whitewashed and topped by a colourful tiled roof. Through the door was the orchard where Macarius had lived, the garden which had also inspired Dostoievski to place his staretz Zosima with his spiritual disciple Aliosha in the same place. For Iulia the experience in a place of stillness and prayer brought her love of literature and her yearning for the contemplative life together and awoke within her a new sense of the reality and presence of God. This was the beginning of a deepening encounter with the mystery.

She could not remember exactly when it was, but when she was back in Moscow and Nicolay was once again in prison, she had another profound experience. She and Sasha had been making weekly visits to deliver food and fresh clothes and both were wilting under the strain. Iulia suddenly felt overwhelmed by the futile cruelty of it all; and in a frenzy of inner anger cried out against the sadistic idiocy of the torment. "To what end?" she demanded. As she said the words, she suddenly felt a blow at the back of her neck as if she had been severely cuffed, and she was knocked reeling forward. As she recovered her balance, she heard the unspoken words of "Another" within her, "Of course it's no earthly use to any of you. But I will share in every last one of your burdens as they cripple and twist you. I will know the weight of your load through carrying it alongside of you but with an understanding greater than yours can be. I want to carry it; I need to know it. Because of my Incarnation and your baptism there is no other way – *if you agree.*"[18]

What had happened? Partly she was feeling a weight of anguish both upon herself and her husband as well as upon Sasha, but perhaps also she was acknowledging her guilt for being so resentful and angry when things were so much worse for Nicolay. It may be that a cuff or a slap around the head was the punishment in the Kazarin household, so that the blow was a way of punishing herself for what she felt she deserved, getting it literally in the neck, as the saying goes. Interestingly, the Tibetan Buddhist, Chögyam Trungpa[19] writing about the great Tibetan gurus Marpa and Milarepa says that a moment of enlightenment is sometimes brought to consciousness, as it was for one aspirant by his spiritual guide, by a firm slap about the face. Iulia found herself challenged to wake up to the reality that the Lord was with her and wanted her to be more consciously aware of his being. Then there were the final words of encouragement, "I want to carry your load. 'Because of my Incarnation and your baptism there is no other way – *if you agree?*'" [20]

Again the language comes from the riches of her strong liturgical background and her understanding of the real significance of her baptism. There is also the telling end, that even in the extremity of her predicament, she was not to be compelled. She must make her own free response. The address required her to make the choice herself and she felt as she did so that the "simultaneous question and answer had made of that fleeting moment a first day."[21] She was now called to a new perilous way of the cross, aware now that as she journeyed "Another" would be with her using her suffering, in Christ as a result of her baptism, as part of his redemptive work for the world.

In both these accounts there has been a clear sense that God had clearly spoken to each of them with questions similar to the ones in the gospel. The order in Iulia de Beausobre's experience was a question, more perhaps a statement from Christ as to the nature of his identity, carrying with it a clear baptismal, celebratory reference. The direction of her work, living in the fearful days of the Russian terror, would be with Christ because she was in him through her baptism, on the way of the cross.

In the two accounts which follow, both of which are closer to the gospel order of events, except that the celebration which marks Roncalli's response is embedded in his sacramental living, his daily mass and worship rather than in some extra liturgical occasion and Hammarskjöld's takes a long time from the inception of the crisis to its resolution three years later.

Dag Hammarskjöld's work in Paris, part of his work as a senior civil servant had come to an end in 1950. He was now 45 and he returned to Stockholm to become

First Secretary-General of Foreign Affairs and then Vice-Minister and he also joined the Swedish Cabinet as a non-party Minister without Portfolio. Despite the importance of these appointments he told Gunnar Myrdal that he found the return to Sweden limiting.[22] Myrdal advised him to write, but he was reluctant. He felt called to a life of public service and he wondered whether he was doing enough and where his life might now be going. He ended his *Towards New Shore* section of *Markings* by remonstrating with himself because he was reluctant to carry burdens, yet acknowledging that he could choose the path ahead: 'O Caesarea Philippi', he wrote, 'to accept condemnation of the Way as its fulfilment and presupposition, to accept this both when it is chosen and when it is realized.'[23]

Each New Year when the Hammarskjöld family gathered together for prayer, they used to read the Bishop Franzen hymn about preparing for death, *Den korta stund jag vandrar ha*. The final verse reads:

> How vain the worldling's pomp and show,
> How brief his joys and pleasures,
> The night approaches now, and lo!
> We leave all earthly treasures

WH Auden translated the third line, 'Night is drawing nigh,' familiar from Baring-Gould's gentler hymn, 'Now the day is over,' but the Swedish is more demanding.[24] Hammarskjöld prefaced each new year for the next four years which follow immediately after the 'Caesarea Philippi' quotation above with these words and he discerned that he was entering a dark night in St John of the Cross's sense. He felt that he was encountering a spiritual darkness of soul within, an aridity within his person as he yearned for God whom he felt was not responding. He found himself moving deeply into his unconscious, knowing that if he was to become his own person, 'a bridge for others, a stone in the temple of righteousness he must somehow penetrate his deepest recesses in order to find himself,'[25] not only himself, but God also:

> The longest journey
> Is the journey inwards.
> Of him who has chosen his destiny,
> Who has started upon his quest
> For the source of his being.[26]

Is there a source, he wondered? Yes, he thought, there must be but he knew he was not in relationship with what or whoever it was. In the years of the night, mainly from 1951-1953 he describes his spiritual experience. In his enigmatic way he teases the reader to try to find psychological explanations for his sufferings so that he can deplore their findings as a diminishment of his spiritual reality. 'How easy Psychology has made it for us to dismiss the perplexing mystery with a label which assigns it a place in the list of common aberrations.[27] What he is really exploring is his relationship with God and his coming through his Caesarea encounter to a new understanding of his vocation. He found himself yearning for death, not for his actual death, although he had a fascination with the possibility, but for the ability to abandon himself in an act of sacrificial self-giving. He castigated himself as foolish for wanting to find meaning in his life, of weakness for finding loneliness so utterly debilitating, and despicable, because he was so obsessed with himself and longing so much for public acclamation. Was loneliness to be his lot for ever? Was there a meaning in life for him?

It was in part the adolescent struggle he had still not completed, Hammarskjöld acknowledging that he suffered from a lingering immaturity. His had been a 'long spring'[28] he said. The markings in 1950 are a statement of where he found himself in his relationships; with his father for example, who seemed to attach such importance to position and was now resting on his laurels having provided for his sons. If only instead he had given them the simplicity of his love and appreciation, how warming that would have been. He knew in the marrow of his bones that he worked for him. The 'him' might be his father; it might equally be the Father beyond his father.[29]

The trouble was that he was alone. He felt that he was slowly dying within, his life made pointless by his inability to commit himself to anyone, let alone to God, afraid that he might bore or intrude on another if he did. He loathed the triviality of social occasions, feeling as he observed himself that he became like a blown egg, an empty shell floating well enough as a good mixer circling around a gathering but making no contact.[30] He found intimate friendship just as difficult. Why, he asks, do we glide past each other, in vain reaching to each other and he answered, 'because we have never dared to give ourselves.'[31] He felt he had 'a ring of cold around the Ego', which was slowly percolating into his being.[32] If only he could be like a sea-bird above the waters and be able to plunge into the depths.[33]

In so ruthlessly exploring the nakedness of his aridity in the wilderness, he reflected that Jesus had been similarly alone in the wilderness with stones for a pillow and only a star as a brother. 'But' he reflected, 'loneliness can be a communion.'[34]

'Perhaps', he wrote a page or two later, 'a great love is never returned.' Again there is an enigma. Is he talking of human or divine love? He may be speaking of both, because they are so connected, but the main meaning here seems to be his love for God and his perception that if he had always been aware of the presence of God perhaps he would have rested in it and remained immature. St John of the Cross considers the barrenness of the understanding, the blankness of the memory and the feebleness of the will at this point as necessary disciplines if the soul is to abandon the comforts of sensual awareness and make the leap of faith into closer communion. The Other ''gives' us nothing', he wrote, 'But in its world of loneliness it leads us up to summits with wide vistas – of insight.'[35]

It was during 1951 that he was asked to negotiate with the Russians about a Swedish plane they had by mistake attacked and destroyed. In general he listened well, could discern the essential nub of a problem and when things became especially complex, could present the issues in a masterly summary. He was a natural conciliator. The Russians were impressed and although they found him tough they also thought him reasonable.

He was now nearing the climax of his struggle. On the one hand he felt himself like Narcissus enchanted by his ugliness[36] congratulating himself that he had enough courage to admit it and loathing himself for doing so. On the other he had a hunger for righteousness, a desire to be a real person called to serve others. The conundrum was how could these and the other conflicting currents in his unconscious be guided into 'the channel of prayer'? [37]

As another year of night – 1951 – began he felt himself at a crossroads. 'Before an important decision, someone clutches your hand,'[38] he noted, as he realized he was nearing a 'point of no return.'[39] It was tempting to 'remain at the cross-roads'[40] and avoid the dilemma of choosing one path or the other. As Passiontide approached, his mind was drawn to meditate on Christ, ' a young man, adamant in his committed life' washing the feet of the disciples. Here, he knew, was a man who was his own person, someone who had assented 'to a possibility in his being', who was prepared to walk the road without self-pity or demand for sympathy to an end which might be 'a death without significance.' To die for his own sake would be monstrous, to realize himself for the sake of others would be a way of love.[41]

Easter was early in 1951 (March 25th), and Hammarskjöld follows the drama of his Maundy meditation with two peaceful Easter scenes, the beautiful singing of a blackbird and the sight of a young girl in a second hand frock enjoying the sun with her father, two telling consolations to express his joy in his new discovery. He had seen the morning star and knew that in the light touch of Christ and in his company he could escape from the chains of his personality into a world of freedom and reality.[42] He then describes three dreams. The first is of birds on a cliff edge above the sea looking towards the coming night. The second is of a road behind him leading to a house which with the people inside it is hidden in the dark. A solitary bird calls and he goes to the house. In the third dream it is dawn and there are flowers and in the gentle breeze of the morning he walks out of the ravine onto a wide open slope.[43] Now, having traversed all this, he knows himself to be at what he describes as 'the frontier of the unheard-of.'

The whole process, he says, had been training for taking 'the plunge into the deep'. Expecting no response, he had found that in giving the other was able to respond, Love dissolving his self into light and becoming radiant and liberating within.[44] He had come to see that his intellect could not give him an answer and that only faith could take him further. At the end of 1951 he thought of himself as like Conrad's Lord Jim, who after his great failure, stood untroubled and happy before his fellows, at the frontier of the unheard-of. 'Now when I have overcome my fears – of others, of myself, of the underlying darkness:

at the frontier of the unheard-of.

Here ends the known. But, from a source beyond it, something fills my being with its possibilities.'[45]

There was still to be another year of searching. At the beginning of 1952, he reflected that he had needed every second of his life to learn about the road. He is still puzzled by his destiny and wondering how he might die rightly but he had seen the frontier. He wavers, as persons like Hammarskjöld tend to do, not quite being able to believe fully that he has had the experience, yet knowing that he has, trying to accept it in the face of his inveterate desire to analyse his every motive even if it leads to his own destruction. As he puts it, he does not know how to put his head under water yet somehow he has learnt how to plunge into the sea.[46] 'Thy will be done' – he prays twice.[47] He has an awareness now of being supported by ' ... a sustaining element, like air to the glider or water to the swimmer,'[48]

Finding a meaning for his life as a relief for his loneliness is the subject of several of the final 1952 markings. He prays that his loneliness might spur him to find something to live and to die for, and in an almost final despairing shout, 'I do not see how I shall ever be able to believe that I am not alone.'[49] That was the reality of his night. The loneliness was never to leave him and at times as at this one, without some degree of restraint could easily have spiralled into unbearable despair. But then he had come to know that there was an alternative. Despair in desolation was one way. The other was 'to stake ... on the 'possibility' that one acquires the right to life in a transcendental co-inherence. But doesn't choosing the second call for the kind of faith which moves mountains?'[50]

Precisely. He faced a stark alternative: either he must have faith or he must die in despair. This challenge was the essence of God's address in Christ to the intellectual Hammarskjöld to which he had been able to reply, 'Yes'.

He prefaces the New Year in 1953 with the same words; Night is approaching, but then:

> For all that has been – Thanks!
> To all that shall be – Yes! [51]

He was never precisely clear when it was that he found himself able to say 'Yes'. 'I don't know Who – or what – put the question, I don't know when it was put. I don't even remember answering' he was to write a few weeks before he died. It seems to have been a growing conviction within him, first realized in 1951 but still needing the struggle and confirmation of 1952 to convince him of what he needed to do. From that moment he was certain that his life had meaning 'and that, therefore, my life, in self-surrender, had a goal.' [52]

If there were any lingering doubts they were dispelled by his totally unexpected election as Secretary-General of the United Nations. Trygve Lie, the Secretary-General from the UN's inception finally resigned on November 10th. In looking for a successor, the Security Council wanted 'a careful and colourless official' who would concentrate on administrative matters[53] and thought they had found such a one in Hammarskjöld. 'When in decisive moments,' he wrote, '- as now – God acts, it is with a stern purposefulness, a Sophoclean irony. When the hour strikes, He takes what is His. What have *you* to say? - Your prayer has been answered, as you know. God has a use for you, even though what He asks doesn't happen to suit you at the moment. God who 'abases him whom He raises up' '[54]

Word came late on March 31st, at the beginning of Holy Week of 1953. He responded: 'With a strong feeling of personal insufficiency, I hesitate to accept the candidature, but I do not feel that I could refuse the task imposed upon me.' [55] The General Assembly elected him on Easter Tuesday, his first dated entry in *Markings*[56], and the ceremony surrounding his inauguration a week or so later gave him the public celebration of his spiritual vocation that had been so much less clear on his Jordan day.

Angelo Roncalli's young adulthood had been normal enough. He had been ordained 21 years before, had served in Bergamo, been in the army during the war and then he had moved to Rome. He had been consecrated bishop when he was 43 in 1925 and had since been the Vatican's Apostolic Visitor to Bulgaria. After his initial six months his life had become an endless retreat from the work he had been expecting to do. He faced a struggle to cope with the disappointment he felt and the sheer puzzle of his appointment. He was ambitious in a quiet way, but he was not the kind of person to plan things to advance his career, if anything he was inclined to the opposite. Now in his 40s and at the height of his powers he felt he had been put out to grass. Had he failed in some way? Had the Church come to regard him as ill equipped to take on a more responsible position? Was it he that was at fault? If it was, could he discern in what way he had failed? And the Church's behaviour? It was certainly very mystifying, even destructive he sometimes felt. As a secretary of Bishop Radini, he was not one to deny that 'one must learn how to bear suffering without letting anyone even know it is there,'[57] but there were surely limits.

His interior crisis came to its climax in 1930 when he was 48. He wrote to Ancilla and Maria to tell them that he was going into retreat at Rustchuk [58] which he described in his journal: 'All around me in this great house is ... magnificent solitude, amid the profusions of nature in flower; before my eyes the Danube; beyond the great river the rich Rumanian plain, which sometimes at night glows red with burning waste gas. The whole day long the silence is unbroken.[59]

He was 'absorbed all day in prayer and reflection.' He opened his notes with the words, 'Make me love thy cross ...', then listing the discontents of his work, his uncertainty about the nature of his mission, his frustration that he could do so little, being forced to live like a hermit, he seemed to be about to pour out his soul in a great wail of bitterness and misery, when instead and very simply he gathered all his thoughts into an act of faith: 'All this,' he said, 'makes it easier for me to enjoy this sense of trust and abandonment, which contains also the longing for a more perfect imitation of my divine model.'[60] It was in effect the beginning of a simple response to a possible question, 'if you are a follower of me, what is the nature of the Christian way?'

Each day of the retreat he prayed and read and meditated in the silence. He had taken a book by Fr Plus, *The Folly of the Cross* and delving deeply into his own spiritual resources, his time with Bishop Radini, his knowledge of Ignatius's *Spiritual Exercises*, his episcopal motto 'oboedientia et pax', his love for Francis de Sales and the example of St John Eudes, he found words to respond to Christ's question, "Who do you say that I am?"

Using a prayer of St Ignatius, he prayed "that I may become more like (Christ) in all I do, I desire and choose poverty with Christ who was poor ...; scorn with Christ who was scorned ...; and I prefer to be counted worthless and foolish for the sake of Christ ... rather than wise and prudent in this world."[61]

Then, turning to the words of St John Eudes, he prayed that he might "embrace the spirit of your Cross, and in this spirit ... I welcome with all my heart, for love of you, all the afflictions of body and soul which you may send me."[62] Quoting St Francis de Sales he prayed that he might become 'like a bird singing in a thicket of thorns.'[63] He concluded, 'When I leave this holy retreat I will take up my cross once more with joy. Ever forward! ... "always crucified, under obedience."'[64]

It was a singular spiritually creative moment, which well illustrates the distinction Erikson drew between stagnation and generativity. In the midst of the desert, when his life appeared to be drifting into the sand, he heard the address of Christ urging him simply to embrace the way of the cross. In welcoming such a future, which he knew now was to be one of little consequence he set the tone for the rest of his ministry. His vocation was to become a person of love. It was not now what he was proposing to do with his life, rather it was what God was going to do with him. He was to follow, obediently and peacefully. His life in the 'desert' of Bulgaria, which was to continue for a further five years, was to blossom like a rose.

*   *   *

In each of these accounts from the histories, the central point of the Caesarea Philippi experience has been the change in the quality of the relationship with Christ. Each from assuming that they were leading the relationship with God had come to realize that in fact it was they who were being led, that he was with them and inevitably drawing them into a greater closeness of prayer. However they had prayed to this point, and it is probable that their actual style of praying did not change very much, they were now more responsive, less active in striving to know God, more passive in listening to what the Lord was saying to them. The relationship had become properly adult, a supportive and companionable togetherness within a respect and reverence proper to a relationship with the Creator of all things.

Much of the psychological critique of the relationship between soul and God is that the soul is required to be submissive to a dominant God. The criticism rests on the principle of projection raised in the last chapter, that in the early stages of the journey persons thrust their personal longings onto an ideal figure largely created by their imagination and fit this onto the face of God. This simply asserts accurately enough that much of early relating is compromised by projections. Spiritual adulthood, the transition which Caesarea Philippi is about, means that souls who have been coming to see beyond these projections, acquire a more adult view of God. As baptized persons in Christ they now relate to the Father, not as subordinate children in Arian submission to a dominant Patriarch, but as adults sons and daughters who have become friends with Christ, minors no more.

Souls who have become mature – and it can only happen when they have – then hear the paradoxical call to deny the self and follow him. It will be the process of a life-time, a call to deny all that is false in the make-up of the identity and ego and to move from centredness in the self to an identity in Love. They are to become persons of heart as they willingly abandon themselves to divine providence. As mature sons and daughters they will essentially engage with Christ in the spiritual work of God, not as slaves, but as persons invited to cooperate freely with the Lord. Taking up the cross, a metaphor for the hard task ahead, will require them to focus totally on the Lord so that they carry out his purpose regardless of what will happen, whether they die on the journey because of it or not. They are enthused by their vocation, prepared to allow nothing to deflect them from their purpose, things peripheral, other people's vocations, alternative concerns, they are ready for the way of the cross because their will is aligned with his.

Only spiritually mature adults can be called to live out their vocations on the way of the cross. There is the general vocation to all Christians to follow, which is the essence of the early Christian way and there is the corporate vocation which all have as members of the Church, but there is also the personal vocation of each disciple to use the gifts and charisms each has been given in the service of God and the kingdom. There are of course those who know what their vocation is from an early age, especially those with spectacular gifts. There are those who wrongly suppose they have no gifts. There are many who in originally choosing a role had a strong sense that what they were choosing would be their vocation for life, while only really becoming fully aware of it as a vocation at this Caesarea Philippi moment. The founder of the hospice movement, Cicely Saunders once received a letter from Brother Roger of Taizé in which he advised her to take the part of the gospel she understood and simply to live it. [65] Writing about vocation, Francis Dewar has taught that persons need not only to develop their awareness of God's general call to follow, they should also listen for their personal call which will draw on their gifts and enthusiasm and engage them for action. [66]

The gifts of the four were considerable: Martin Luther King was a great speaker, one of a remarkable tradition of black preachers. That he was to be one of the great orators of the 20th century with a gift for elegant construction, a stunning ability to coin a summary phrase and a musical baritone to deliver his speeches could scarcely have been known when he was elected to lead the boycott. It soon became clear that he had a majestic gift which, as he honed his speeches by constant delivery, was to empower a people. Add to that his power to inspire, his ability to chair meetings and his wise leadership he was formidably gifted.

Iulia de Beausobre's greatest gift, in addition to her personal courage, fidelity and artistic talents, was a profound sensitivity which was eventually through her experience to give her a deep spiritual insight into others. She had what St Paul describes as the gift to discern spirits.[67] Similarly, Dag Hammarskjöld who had a brilliant and penetrating intellect and a legendary capacity for work, was able to use a similar gift of insight in the political arena to distill the issues in an argument, as much in his reading as in his diplomacy. He learnt early how to steer a discussion on a complex issue towards a sound conclusion. Angelo Roncalli too had a considerable intellect and like Hammarskjöld an immense capacity for work. His spiritual creativity and his clear vision and warm disposition of love towards others equipped him magnificently for the work he was to do.

These were personal gifts given to each of them by the Holy Spirit, a bit like the three or more gifts given to heroes about to set out on a quest in great myths. Gifts are never merely personal; they are charisms and talents from God, which are primarily for the common good of humanity in his service. Each of the four persons of the histories used their gifts to the full as they lived out their vocations.

Interestingly in terms of their journeys there was virtually no movement either during or after the transition. Martin Luther King remained in Montgomery, Iulia de Beausobre in Moscow and Angelo Roncalli in Sofia and they were to stay there for some time to come. Even during Dag Hammarskjöld's longer crisis he did not move about during the actual crisis. Compared to the earlier Jordan crisis when three moved and Hammarskjöld stayed put, in this one it is the other way about, they stayed in one place and Dag Hammarskjöld made the dramatic move to New York. It may be that that is just how it happened, that it was to do with the rhythm of his particular life, but it may also be because there was also something of the Jordan moment within his Caesarea Philippi upheaval.

The essential element of this Caesarea Philippi critical change is that it is interior. The young adult soul is invited to recognize Christ after journeying through Galilee and the Wilderness and passing through the gate. The address in this transition seems usually to be in the form of a question, different in each case, inviting the soul to a deeper communion of prayer and companionship with Christ on a new and demanding way of the cross. As each responds, God gives to the beloved disciple in whom he delights an appropriate and transfiguring assurance of his presence

Perhaps one of the reasons why there is so little said about a vital transition like the Caesarea Philippi one is that people do not know how to talk about it. In the Sixties and early Seventies when the group movement was in full sway, it was generally found that participants would willingly talk about their faults but found it much harder to speak about their gifts and strengths. Persons need to discover how to do so.

Not long ago, a group was involved in some remarkable work and they met on one occasion to talk about why they were doing it. Embarrassment was intense. Everybody was afraid of appearing pretentious or in some way immodest. Much easier, they felt, to say that they were mad to be doing what they were doing than to articulate a vision of intimate and spiritual things and possibly be judged to be pious. Sadly, though, it meant that the Christians in the group could not share their undeniable conviction that Christ had called them to follow. Perhaps the group was too large a setting to explore their motivation and perhaps anyway they felt that talking of spiritual things might be damaging - and sometimes it is. But the modern world needs a language to share these important intuitions and understandings if persons are to find their vocations and engage on the way. After all a call from God to serve is the most 'natural' thing in the world

CHAPTER 6

THE PATH IS STEEPER

The Way of the Cross

'He called the crowd with his disciples, and said to them, "If any want to become my followers, let them deny themselves and take up their cross and follow me." (Mark 8, 34)

Both St John's Lee and Hexham Abbey, the churches mentioned in the allegory of the meeting of the waters in the previous chapter, stand on high points on either side of the Tyne valley. The church of St John Lee, rebuilt in the 19th century on a 7th century foundation, has a spire, which is just visible above the surrounding trees while Hexham Abbey, substantial within its market town, its blue clock face on the tower catching the light, commands the dale. The churches stand out, as does the hill of transfiguration above the Galilee plain, a significant marking on the road to Jerusalem. At the end of every Eucharistic celebration of the Church the worshipping community is dismissed to engage with the world; 'Ite missa est' in the Latin Mass, Go out and love and serve the Lord. Set out on the road through the valley and live out your vocation in holiness and righteousness in the world where you are set until you reach the goal of Jerusalem.

Martin Buber has described religion as being about the way to a goal and politics as the means to an end. It is a fundamental distinction: one of the tasks of religion being to reveal the underlying vision of where our society is going, while politics is about finding the practical means for getting there or at least achieving some small contribution to whatever the goal might be deemed to be.[1]

The Biblical writers were circumspect in articulating their vision of what they thought the goal was. They identified it as 'shalem' (Hebrew for peace, wholeness, fulfilment), Jeru-'salem', the city of peace, essentially a spiritual vision, a statement of hope that eventually, as Martin Luther King put it, the beloved community might come into being.

The goal is defined in the New Testament as the kingdom of God, the parables never saying specifically what this might be. The evangelists speak of it by analogy, as like seed sown in a field and growing into a crop, like a small seed becoming a large garden plant, or like a net holding all kinds of species of fish, something of small beginnings which of itself grows and expands. They speak of it as near, that it is within, and give enigmatic sayings about a final rule of God, which will spread to include everybody and be a time of righteous love and justice of which at this stage we only have tentative intimations. It is both a present reality and something far in the future, possibly only to be realized in heaven. Ultimately it is a gift of God and yet something for which the world strives. "I have a dream ... " Martin Luther King proclaimed in his speech at the Lincoln Memorial in August 1963, "(of) that day when all of God's children – black men and white men, Jews and Gentiles, Catholics and Protestants – will be able to join hands and to sing in the words of the old Negro spiritual, "Free at last, free at last, thank God Almighty, we are free at last."[2] The goal is inevitably couched in such visionary terms. The problem is converting this spiritual goal into practical politics.

There is further tension in that the work of the moral person acting personally is very different from the political activist striving for a better society. The spiritual goal can easily get lost in the intrigues of politicians trying to govern a community. The problem is well stated in the title of Reinhold Niebuhr's book *Moral Man and Immoral Society*[3]. The soul who acts in a personal capacity is capable of behaving morally, the group acting politically even when wanting to do some good for the community often finds itself drawn into immorality. The personal agent sets out to help single persons make their own changes while the politician gathers people together to make changes in society on their behalf, whether they agree with the proposed changes or not. The personal worker supports the one in a companionable way, the politician seeks to dominate in order to effect a policy. The personal agent values the unique potential of each person, the politician convenes a group with its ideals for a fairer society and struggles with them to overcome any opposition. And so on. There is always a tension between serving the needs of the one and the demanding and conflicting needs of the many, between personal holiness as the aspiration of the one and political righteousness as the end of the many, between the two aspects of the goal, personal salvation and the kingdom of God. If persons are to attend to them both it is often perplexing how it is to be done.

People have tried to resolve the tension in various ways. One option has been to drop out of politics altogether and care for persons alone in the hope that by improving individuals it might be possible to change enough people to make a decent society. It cannot be done and totally underestimates the degree and complexity of corporate power and indeed the power of evil. Another has been to concentrate on political activity alone. Marxism-Leninism was an experiment of this kind and inflicted misery on millions. Other theorists have tried to deny that there is a problem, that in fact persons can act both personally and politically at the same time, the result there being that one or the other dominates, the political becoming personalized or the personal becoming politicized. Paul Halmos[4] from whom these ideas are largely drawn, argued that there was only one possible way forward and that was to equilibrate between the two under the spiritual rule of God, to balance both concerns and act politically when that was the better way and to act personally when that was the more appropriate. How in fact persons act will depend on three things. First their discernment of what God is already doing in the world and working together with him, secondly on the particular vocation they have been called to follow and thirdly on their ability to equilibrate between the personal and the political.

Discernment grows as persons pray. 'Your kingdom come, your will be done on earth as in heaven.' God is already active in the world and has a purpose for it and for those called within that purpose and their task is prayerfully to work in harmony with him. 'Who stands fast?' Bonhoeffer asked in one of his letters from prison. 'Only the man whose final standard is not his reason, his principles, his conscience, his freedom, or his virtue, but who is ready to sacrifice all this when he is called to obedient and responsible action in faith in exclusive allegiance to God.'[5].

Secondly, they are to go forward in obedience to their vocation. Who knows whether what they have to offer will be valuable or not? Niebuhr[6] insisted that if a person truly believed that something could be done and was prepared to act on that assumption and indeed to believe in it against all the odds, then he or she would achieve something significant.

Thirdly, they need to equilibrate between acting personally or politically. Equilibration is to balance the two in such a way that equal weight is given to each, the personal vision on the one hand, the practical politics on the other. Martin Luther King was particularly adept at this. He had a clear vision of his ultimate purpose but as a politician he insisted that the SCLC should aim to achieve clearly defined objectives which they could express in simple and summary form so that the whole organization knew what was intended and could work with single-minded determination to achieve it. It was then important that they should be satisfied with whatever small victory they could win. They knew their goal, but the practicalities of getting there was another matter. That remained hidden and ultimately a mystery within the purposes of God.

*   *   *

When Jesus and his three companions walked down Mount Tabor and before they met the other disciples, Jesus once again warned them about the suffering of the way ahead, that he would be ill-treated, that he would die and that he would rise again, the same threefold dynamic of crisis which occurs at every stage of the way. When they reached the other disciples, they were faced immediately with the first impossible situation, the group not knowing what to do about a father who wished his son who was suffering from epilepsy to be healed. "All things can be done for the one who believes," Jesus tells both the father and the disciples, adding that such situations, as indeed the way of the cross itself, can only be undertaken by persons who give themselves to prayer (9,14-29)

Jesus then repeats to the rest of the disciples his stern warning about a coming betrayal and death and resurrection, which are to be the marks of his way and contrasts it, as he will in the two chapters following, with the way of the world. The disciples, Mark judges, are not persons of great faith, discernment or even prayer, their discussion about which of them might be the greatest and his record of John's jealousy of those outside the company doing good work in Christ's name, making his point. They needed rather to become persons of prayer, persons who were seasoned with salt, fired by the Holy Spirit, trusting like a married couple or like a child with his or her parents, that they might genuinely become agents of the kingdom and act in his name. (9,30 – 10,16)

In the rich young man's question about inheriting eternal life which follows, Jesus teaches that disciples are to give all they have and are to God. He gives another warning, that while those who follow and live out their vocation to the full will receive a reward, they must first walk with him along a path of betrayal, poor treatment and eventually death (10, 17-34)

The warnings seem to make little impression. Even James and John were concerned more about the reward they were going to receive than any dangers there might be on the way to it. Jesus did not deny them their hopes but wanted them to think through the deeper implications of their following, that they would share his baptism of death and resurrection but that the rest would be a matter of faith. In the conversation later with their indignant peers Jesus emphasized again that the essence of the Christian way is not glory; it is service of the kingdom, service of the goal (10, 35-45)

When Jesus and his disciples reach Jericho, Mark tells a story very like the one he had told before Caesarea Philippi, of a blind man wishing to receive his sight. Bartimaeus pleads with Jesus that he might be able to see. The disciples had discerned something of Christ's nature at Caesarea Philippi when Peter had made his declaration of faith but now after the journey towards Jerusalem this blind man symbolizes that they needed to see still more if they were to discern the full nature of Christ. On the one hand Jesus is welcomed into Jerusalem, the people spreading their cloaks on the road and waving palm branches and proclaiming, "Hosanna! Blessed is the one who comes in the name of the Lord!" On the other he was entering Jerusalem in readiness for his passion (10,46-11,10)

So begins the final ascent. After a night in Bethany, Jesus and his disciples leave for the temple and walk past an un-fruiting fig tree, a metaphor perhaps for the altar at the heart of the temple, which should have been the spiritual centre of the nation but had instead become a shopping arcade. To the disciples, after the high moments of Caesarea Philippi, Mount Tabor, the long walk from Galilee to Jerusalem and the gift of sight before the final ascent to the holy city, it must have been crushing to reach the temple and find it corrupt. The end of their journey was not the goal they had dreamed about, life did not resound there. Jesus entered Jerusalem and had to lay about him to insist that the heart of the nation should be reconstructed into a place of prayer. (11, 12-19)

The next day, when they passed the fig tree again, it had died. When the temple, or the soul, is no longer attached to the God who gives it purpose it loses its in season and out of season fruitfulness and dies. On entering the temple itself, Jesus was waylaid by the leaders who wanted to know his authority for his action on the day before. They needed to silence this person who was acting so 'foolishly' in such a dangerous political environment. (11, 12-end)

Jesus simply proceeds along his way, concerned to live the kingdom in his being by serving love and justice, holiness and righteousness heading towards a goal which Mark highlights in a final cumulative prediction of the passion. Between the parable of the tenants who seized and killed the owner's son and the Sadducees question about the resurrection, in the place of the usual warning of death Mark places the question put to Jesus about whether he should pay taxes to Caesar or not   It is another trick question, designed to incriminate him however he answers, but its position in the narrative at the critical point of the warning pattern, highlights the harsh reality of the conflicting dialectic between the rule of God on the one hand and the authority of government on the other. Without anxiety, Jesus sidesteps the trap and advises giving what is due to each pole of power. The sovereign rule of God is in the long term the arbiter of power but equally the political force has in the short term the strength to demand that people have to follow its demands on pain in the final instance of death. When the two are in conflict, death is the only means of resolving the inherent tension between the two. (12. 1-27)

Four times Jesus had warned his disciples that the way of the cross would mean suffering and death and that resurrection would only follow after that had happened. He had instructed them to become persons of prayer and to trust as they journeyed with him to the political and spiritual heart of the nation in Jerusalem. In the four histories each follow their vocations on the way of the cross, journeying prayerfully in faith towards the goal.

Martin Luther King was still in Montgomery – aged only 27 – and in the second year of his pastorate at the Dexter Road Church and a few weeks into the bus boycott, which was by no means resolved. Shortly after the bombing of his home, he was visiting his parents in Atlanta and Daddy did everything he could to persuade him to pull out before either he or his family were killed. How could he desert? "I would rather go back," Martin told them, "and spend ten years in jail than not go back."[7] Soon after his return, the Montgomery Council indicted the boycott leaders and King in particular was fined $500 with costs. The Council had miscalculated. The media were alerted and the boycott started to become national news. Had the South, civil rights workers in the North wondered, Bayard Rustin among them, at last produced a Gandhi?

By May the bus company needed to settle but the local authority was adamant until the Supreme Court made its 'Brown judgement' declaring that segregation on buses was illegal, and the Council was compelled to capitulate. On December 21st, Dr King and a white companion waited for the first bus of the day, and at 5-45am, paid their fares and travelled together in the front seats.

Dr King had been leading the boycott for more than a year. He was by now inexorably involved in the wider campaign for black civil rights and wide open to revenge attacks. On January 14th he was leading prayers in the Bethel Baptist Church and in the pain of the situation pleaded with the Lord, "if anyone should be killed, let it be me."[8] He was so stirred he had to be helped to a bench. Next day he could not admit that he had been so emotionally overwrought. It was too like Daddy for comfort. When a little later unexploded dynamite was found on the parsonage path, he told his congregation, "If I had to die tomorrow morning I would die happy because I've been to the mountain top and I've seen the Promised Land and it's going to be here in Montgomery."[9]

He was facing danger without and criticisms within the movement. Colleagues were jealous of his fame, there were accusations of financial irregularities, questions about improprieties with women, all were combining to increase his stress. Nonetheless, progress was made. The Southern Christian Leaders Conference was formed on February 10th, 1957 in New Orleans and King was elected President. Its main purpose was to organize the registration of Negro voters, the campaign for which they planned to launch at Washington with a pilgrimage of prayer. On the actual day, the crowd was not enormous, but undaunted, Dr King urged the government to "give us the ballot!"[10]

On the personal level, for Martin and Coretta the high point of their year was the birth on October 23rd 1957 of their second child, Martin Luther King III.

Dr King spent much of the autumn writing the story of the Montgomery boycott. *Stride Towards Freedom* was well received, though critics noticed that chapter 6 plagiarized Paul Ramsey and Anders Nygren. Later that year, on September 20th, 1958, he was signing copies of the book in a Harlem store when one of the purchasers suddenly stabbed him in the chest. He remained absolutely still, as people rushed for help, waiting calmly for the ambulance. Apparently, the knife had been so very near his aorta that a sneeze would have killed him. When he had recovered he used regularly to refer to a letter he had received from a young white girl who wrote to say to him, "I'm so happy that you didn't sneeze."[11]

Earlier in the March of 1957 Martin and Coretta, together with Ralph Bunche, had represented Black America at the Ghana Independence celebrations. Pandit Nehru had also invited Martin and in February two years later he and Coretta went to India for a month. In the *Ebony* article he wrote about it, [12] he allowed that Gandhi as well as Jesus had been his guiding light in the technique of non-violence the boycott had employed in Montgomery. In a sermon on his return, he spoke about Gandhi's capacity for self-criticism, his avoidance of material possessions and his absolute self-discipline. He longed to cultivate these virtues within himself but wondered how he could do it when he had a family. Ought he, he wondered, to be celibate? A greater challenge was in fact to balance the responsibilities of a family within the demands of his vocation.

SCLC was not making as much progress in registering voters or indeed in training people in the practice of non-violence as it had hoped. It needed above all a full-time president. Both SCLC and the Dexter Avenue congregation were suffering so in November 1959 Dr King announced his departure. At his farewell on January 31st 1960 – he was just 31 - he said, 'What I have been doing is giving, giving,

giving and not stopping to retreat and meditate like I should ... If the situation is not changed, I will be a physical and psychological wreck. I have to reorganize my personality and reorient my life ... '[13]

He and his family moved back to *Atlanta, to 563 Johnson Avenue*, where Martin joined his father as a part-time pastor. "'He's not little M.L. anymore, now,'" a proud Daddy said on his first Sunday back, "'He is Dr. King now.'"[14] Pastor Joe Roberts told me that even in 1988 older members of the congregation still thought of him as 'Little Martin', the child they had dandled on their knees when he was young.

Shortly after his return two lawmen arrived with powers to extradite him to Alabama for tax evasion. He feared it would be the end of his involvement in the crusade, as he could not see how a Southern Court could possibly find him not guilty. By American standards he was not rich; he dressed well but did not drive an expensive car nor was his home large. Money was not in fact much of a temptation to him. His defence was able to demonstrate that the additional monies recorded by the Alabama State authorities had actually been for his necessarily large travelling expenses. To his immense surprise he was acquitted. The next day he preached at Ebenezer about the pain both of the anticipation and the trial.

Meanwhile students of another human rights group, the Student Non-Violent Coordinating Committee (SNCC) managed to persuade King to join them in a sit-in at a local Atlanta store. He did not really judge it wise for him but could not but agree that he should practise what he preached. He was arrested soon after he had joined them. A month or so earlier he had been fined $25 for driving a borrowed car with out of date number plates and unknown to him, he had also been bound over to keep the peace. On this conviction this was taken into account and he was sentenced to four months in prison. On his first night in prison he was woken at half past three, put into leg irons and handcuffs and driven away into the night, he feared to his death. Eventually as dawn was breaking they arrived at Reidsville. He never found aloneness easy and isolated in a solitary cell in the new prison he was filled with foreboding. He wrote to Coretta encouraging her 'to let their common faith ... carry them through,'[15] and then he began plans for a book of his sermons. It was not to be necessary. Large efforts were being made to organize his release and three days later he was freed.

Back in Atlanta, the SNCC felt that their sit-in settlement had been inadequate and said so at a stormy meeting in the Ebenezer chapel. King gave what some regarded as one of his greatest speeches, urging SNCC to accept what they had won and to be satisfied that they had won something.

In early May another Civil Rights group, the Congress of Racial Equality proposed sending thirteen people by bus to New Orleans. SCLC warned the riders to expect a rough reception in Birmingham and a worse one in Montgomery and King went himself to preach for them in Birmingham, He encouraged the congregation to offer their bodies 'as instruments to defeat the unjust system'[16] while a white mob gathered outside and laid siege to the building, holding them there in the building for all of the night. King decided not to join the continuing riders, partly because he feared it would violate his Georgia probation but more because he thought that their purpose had been achieved. A week or so later the attorney general announced that bus stations were to be desegregated.

People meeting Dr King at this time commented on his increasing gravity. On London television he appeared tired, almost withdrawn behind his public persona, speaking quietly in his attractive Southern American drawl. '"It is never easy for one to accept the role of symbol,"' he said, '"without going through constant moments of self-examination ... I must confess that there are moments when I begin to wonder whether I am adequate ... to face all of the challenges. ..."'[17]

In the following month, November of 1961, the civil rights stage moved its campaign to Albany where they were opposed by the wily police chief Laurie Pritchett. Dr King was once more arrested, jailed, released on bail and later sentenced, an experience wherever SCLC was campaigning. However short the time in jail he was always traumatized. In 1964, in Jacksonville he told a cleaner he felt he had been 'treated (there) like a hog.'[18]

Coretta was now pregnant with their third child, who was born at the end of January 1962. They called him Dexter after their Montgomery church.

Albany had been a harsh lesson, because it showed that direct non-violence was useless if the town's rulers used similar tactics, refused to be riled and paid fines secretly, acting in effect in the same way as the campaigners. To be effective SCLC realised they had to have a clear objective, use the law wisely, organize an effective campaign and above all seek out a stupid authority.

Such a one they found in Birmingham. Dr King saw Birmingham as 'the most difficult big city in the United States in race relations.'[19] During a previous visit he had been punched about the head by a white man gate-crashing the SCLC's annual assembly. This time they knew their strategy had to be effective. They planned to boycott three stores and hoped that a hostile reaction would alert the country to the indignities the black community were suffering. They knew it was dangerous and Dr King feared that one of their number might be killed. While SCLC was waiting for the right moment to begin, Martin and Coretta's fourth child, Bernice Albertine, was born on March 28th, 1963.

The campaign started badly with only 65 turning out to sit in. A march planned for Good Friday, which the authorities wanted to stop by injunction, looked more promising but SCLC was in a predicament. The story has been told in chapter 3 [20] the problem being that they had no more money, that only King was able to raise it by his speeches and that if he marched he would be jailed. On Maundy Thursday (April 11, 1963) he told a rally, "we're going to march."[21] By Good Friday he was less sure, but after agonizing with his colleagues, and further prayer, he emerged to say; "the path is clear to me," he said. "I've got to march."[22]

"I'm going to jail," he told the gathered marchers as "a good servant of my Lord and Master, who was crucified on Good Friday."[23] They had hardly taken a step before they were arrested. King was taken into solitary confinement and he described the night as "the longest, most frustrating and bewildering hours I have lived ... I was besieged with worry."[24] News came at last on Easter Day and it felt indeed like a sign of the resurrection; that Harry Belafonte had managed to raise the $50,000 they needed to continue. Further on Monday President Kennedy rang Coretta to express his concern, which Martin urged her to use to the full in the campaign. By Tuesday he was able to begin his shaming letter written on scraps of paper to convict the Church ministers of Birmingham who had judged his campaign to be untimely. 'Frankly I have yet to engage in a direct action movement that was "well-timed," in the view of those who have not suffered unduly from the disease of segregation.'[25]

On Friday King was sentenced to five days in prison, fined $50 and released pending appeal. After the Easter drama the campaign had begun to lose impetus and few apart from High School children were prepared to march. The Press began to leave. A desperate SCLC decided it must use the students. The Public Safety Commissioner, Bull Connor, true to form and to world amazement, set dogs onto them and blasted them with fire hoses. Hundreds were arrested and the campaign was saved.

The Kennedy administration was shaken by Birmingham. Soon after the Government announced a new Civil Rights bill to prevent such a disaster happening again. Philip Randolph had been dreaming of a march on Washington and organizers hoped they could now use his idea to encourage Congress to pass the bill. At one of the meetings Dr King had with President Kennedy at this time, the president had had a private word. For some time the FBI had been monitoring King's friendship with Stanley Levison, considered by the FBI to be a communist agent, and the president, to King's distress advised him that he should drop Levison. He felt he could not. With his need for friendship, the strain of his endless travelling and the amount he had to do he judged that he needed all the help he could get. He decided to keep in touch through another friend.

The Washington pilgrimage followed shortly after, on August 28th 1963. 250,000 assembled, almost double the number expected. Dr King began to speak as people were drifting away. After a quiet start he left his prepared text and moved naturally into one of his oratorical flights of imagery built around a central theme. He had made the speech before but never to such effect. Even hearing it endlessly repeated in the Atlanta King Museum it is moving as he shares his dream of a world made one, 'when all of God's children ... will be able to join hands and sing in the words of the old Negro spiritual, "Free at last, free at last, thank God Almighty, we are free at last."'[26] The final visionary words are on the sarcophagus in the middle of the water enclosure outside Ebenezer church. Since Montgomery he had hoped someone else might emerge as leader. Now it was not to be,

He still kept in touch with Levison, because he needed his help in writing up the Birmingham campaign and on the strength of a photograph of the two of them leaving an hotel room, the FBI persuaded the Justice department to authorize a tap on King's phone. From that day the FBI began to build up a detailed dossier of King's personal life.

King was now away from home for almost 90% of his time and his relationship with Coretta was necessarily under strain. It is not clear when he started sleeping with other women[27] but though he was penitent he found his yearning impossible to control. The FBI recorded a high spirited and bawdy party in the Willard hotel and another of a fierce row between Coretta and Martin about his absences from home. His failure to ring when the boys were to have their tonsils out was an especially sore point.

Dr King visited St Augustine on the Florida coast in May 1964 to march to the old slave market and he returned again in June. He was arrested for taking lunch at a segregated counter. Meanwhile the FBI was beginning to spread rumours about him especially among other religious leaders and from now on he worked continually with this sort of hostility surrounding him. Despite the support and laughter of colleagues he felt increasingly worn down by it all. Andrew Young has said that they were all on the verge of cracking up. Martin himself was so utterly exhausted that in the autumn of 1964 an anxious Coretta arranged for him to be admitted to hospital for a complete rest. When a few days later she rang with news of his Nobel Peace Prize he was asleep. He told friends that it was a 'victory of moral recognition for the cause of justice.'[28]

Dr King left with his family to receive the Peace Prize in Oslo with a heavy heart' knowing that other religious leaders wanted to know if the rumours about him were true. On the plane he talked it through with Harry Wachtel. The ceremony itself was on December 10th, 1964 and he gave his lecture on the importance of non-violent action for peace on the 11th. Back in New York he told a Harlem church that he 'must go back to the valley.... I must go back because my brothers and sisters down in Mississippi and Alabama can't register and vote.'[29]

He was depressed further by the President telling him that a voting rights bill was now unlikely. In Atlanta his mother had once become so concerned that she had rung a policeman friend to see what had happened to him because he had gone out. The policeman found him standing outside a factory, alone and in the dark, waiting to encourage a group of struggling black workers.

SCLC had been planning that the next campaign for black vote registration should be in Selma, because it had backward racial policies and a recalcitrant sheriff. The campaign began as planned on January 2nd, 1965. It was at this time that Coretta received the FBI letter and tape referred to above.[30]

Dr King returned to Selma to take part in the first march on January 19th. It passed peaceably enough, the Sheriff Jim Clark keeping his temper but no one was able to register. The next day 226 were arrested and jailed, King returning to Atlanta on the 26th for a special dinner to mark his Nobel Peace Prize. Daddy King told him that the Atlanta police chief had spoken to him about the Director of the FBI, Edgar Hoover's hatred of Martin. Back in Selma, the next march ended in King's arrest. On release, he was more deeply depressed than before but he fulfilled speaking engagements in Washington and Los Angeles before returning once again to hear that a protester had been killed. Then a minister was killed. Malcolm X had recently been killed. He felt his own life was becoming equally precarious.

The planned marches to Montgomery began shakily, the first being attacked by States' troopers and the second, ignoring an injunction, reaching only the far side of the Pettys bridge. King, to the dismay of many critics, had agreed to a halt before they reached the standing troops. The media was now in full attendance. When a judge lifted the injunction before the next march, the world watched for what might happen.

The pilgrimage began on March 21st, the walkers knowing that the President had decided that a Voting Rights Bill was now essential. King walked with them through the wooded countryside for three days, his fellow marchers noticing that he seemed to be living in his own world. He left to speak elsewhere on each of the days and returned with Coretta to join the thousands who had been bussed and flown in, to be part of the final march into Montgomery. Together they ascended the rising Dexter Avenue, past their old church and onto the steps of the white capitol. "I come to say to you this afternoon," Dr King proclaimed, "however difficult the moment, however frustrating the hour; it will not be long, ... How long? Not long!"[31]

Coretta had for some time felt they needed a larger home. Their new place in **Sunset Avenue in Atlanta** was a very modest little house, Stanley Levison thought, but Martin was afraid that it was too pretentious. The FBI decided they were not going to bug it.

After Selma, SCLC felt it must turn its attention to the North: to the problems of segregation there in education, unemployment and housing. When King visited Watts in Los Angeles after the riots there he had come to the conclusion that the abject poverty he saw was an even more important cause of the troubles than race. Poverty from that time became the focus of his campaigning; that and the war in Vietnam, which he spoke about, as he put it, as a personal concern in creative dissent.[32]

To help Al Raby in Chicago might, Dr King thought, be an effective beginning of a campaign against poverty. He visited the city in July 1965, giving upwards of twenty addresses in one day and as his temperature rose to 102 degrees, staggering from there to engagements in Cleveland and Philadelphia. "'I cannot begin to explain the great burden of my schedule,'" he told Randolph Blackwell, "'the impossible day-to-day demands that confront my life, and the endless travel that keeps me wondering whether I am going or coming.'"[33] He found it hard to understand colleagues who were less prepared to give as much.

Finding a clear focus for the Chicago campaign was difficult. On one occasion when King said he must ask the Lord about it, Bayard Rustin expostulated, 'Seeking refuge in prayer – "this business of King talking to God and God talking to King" –

would not resolve serious strategic questions.[34] They eventually opted for a too complicated assault on estate agents who were refusing to serve black clients.

At this point, events in the South forced a postponement to the start of the Chicago campaign. On June 5th, 1966, James Meredith who was on a 'Freedom from fear' march from Memphis to Jackson was shot. Civil rights leaders rushed to his bedside, King among them, to pledge themselves to continue the march on his behalf. The march marked the advent of more violent tactics in the movement as a whole. SCLC continued to urge "Freedom now!" the new chairman of the SNCC, Stokeley Carmichael, was shouting in contrast, "We want black power." Dr King deplored the phrase, not least because he though it unrealistic. Leading a memorial service in Philadelphia a day or two later for three workers who had been murdered two years before, the worshippers were surrounded by white hecklers. "I believe in my heart that the murderers are somewhere around me at this moment," he said in his prayer, "You're damn right," the Chief Deputy Sheriff said from a position not very far from him, "they're behind you right now."[35] He did not see, he said in his final speech in Jackson how black power could possibly contribute to the creation of the beloved community.

Back in Chicago, SCLC began its campaign on Sunday July 10th, 1966. Only 30,000 of the 100,000 hoped for came. Dr King spoke of ending the poverty of the slums and then, like his namesake Martin Luther, pinned his demands onto the city hall door. Next day he confronted an angry Mayor Daley who claimed that Chicago was already doing all it reasonably could. Two days later the riots began. Martin had rented a flat in a run down part of Chicago, intending to live there for half the year and the other half in Atlanta. His family had joined him for the summer and he and Coretta were on their way to a dinner when they heard the first disturbance. After three nights of rioting, King persuaded the gang leaders to meet in his flat and throughout the night argued with them about the values of non-violence. "'Somewhere,'" he told an interviewer "'there has to be a synthesis. I have to be militant enough to satisfy the militant yet I have to keep enough discipline in the movement to satisfy white supporters and moderate Negroes.'"[36]

The marches and the worldwide publicity forced the Chicago authorities to call a meeting, [37] which did at least agree that they would try to improve the lot of black home seekers but in the end not much more than that. King described it as a first round victory in a fifteen round bout, but inwardly he was disheartened. "America's greatest problem and contradiction" he told one meeting "is that it harbours 35 million poor at a time when resources are so vast that the existence of poverty is an anachronism."[38]

His awareness of a high calling remained fundamental to him. He told a San Francisco congregation, 'To be a Christian one must take up his cross, with all its difficulties and agonizing and tension-packed content, and carry it until that very cross leaves its mark upon us and redeems us.'[39] It did leave its mark but the commitment to which God had called him never wavered.

After Christmas (1966) he left for a month's break in Jamaica to write *Where do we go from here?* He bought a magazine called *Ramparts* to read on the plane and read there about the affliction of the children of Vietnam and was so appalled he felt he could no longer prevaricate about Vietnam. He was preparing for another transition. Coretta joined him for a week. Their relationship was by this time in more distress, under strain because of his other relationships but chiefly because they were so often apart. There was little time to work at things even if they had wanted to.

At this point there needs to be a pause in the story, which has been an all too brief summary of a remarkable period of 20th century history. The tension between the political struggle for human rights for Afro-Americans, against poverty and the war in Vietnam, together with the need sometimes to act against the law, or to use adolescents (even if willing) in Birmingham, illustrates the anguish of his political way. His personal way was even more difficult. He worked of course too hard and at the expense of his family and relationships and indeed his mental health but he was conscious of being called to lead a campaign at a particular moment when a vital change was possible. Such windows of opportunity do not remain open long and if they were to win their human rights he and SCLC had to act, as he explained to the Birmingham Clergy. But the price was huge.

Reinhold Niebuhr[40] writing in the Thirties had suggested that it might be possible for the Black communities of the Southern States to free themselves from oppression if they could produce a Gandhi like figure who could then adopt Gandhi's satyagraha methods. Afro-American people had the spirituality, he thought. It is clear that the community felt they had found such a person in Martin Luther King.

The development of satyagraha (from 'sat' meaning truth and 'agraha' firmness in Gujerati), is one of the most valuable modern attempts to marry a spiritual goal to a political end and was used by Gandhi to expose the underlying untruths of British colonial rule by highlighting and symbolizing the injustices in India by imaginative marches and protests. Gandhi hoped the measures would convict the Raj of wrongdoing and shame it into amendment of life. In King's development, which he did by bringing together Gandhi's ideas with Jesus's sermon on the mount, [41] he and

SCLC, once they had agreed a simple and clear focus for a campaign, usually had a threefold aim: first to expose injustice. As he told a group of young people at Berkeley, California in 1957, 'I think every person who believes in non-violent resistance believes somehow that the universe in some form is on the side of justice.'[42] Secondly, to love those they opposed in order to restore community. 'His soul is greatly scarred,' he observed of the whites, 'he needs the love of the Negro … to remove his tensions, insecurities and fears,'[43] and thirdly to eschew violence because he felt it damaged the spirit of those who used it. 'The aftermath of violence,' King said 'is bitterness.'[44] After fulfilling all three aims, he was then ready to accept even limited victories as small gains on the march towards freedom.

Ralph Bunche, one of **Dag Hammarskjöld's** black American colleagues, who accompanied the Kings to Ghana, invited Dr King early in 1960 to meet the Secretary-General. Coretta King says that Martin was 'deeply moved,' and Hammarskjöld 'most cordial.'[45] Martin Luther King Jr was 31 at the time, Dag Hammarskjöld, 54.

Early in April 1953 Hammarskjöld had arrived in *New York and moved into an apartment in East 73rd Street.* His three-year crisis referred to in the last chapter was over and he was about to begin his major work. He seemed a diffident figure, in some contrast to his irascible predecessor. He told the Press that the UN required the qualities of a mountaineer: 'perseverance and patience, a firm grip on realities, careful but imaginative planning, a clear awareness of the dangers but also of the fact that fate is what we make it and that the safest climber is he who never questions his ability to overcome all difficulties'[46]

1953 was a comparatively quiet year, so he spent the time addressing the low morale of the UN itself. In September, invited to speak at a dinner in his honour, he compared the UN to the *Santa Maria,* [47] sailing on a voyage of discovery in search of peace and necessary change, an analogy which perhaps inspired the *Santa Maria* like shape of the Place des Nations building in Geneva. He reflected quoting Tao Tse Tung (*sic*) that the world cannot be moulded into shape but has to be influenced from within, as something spiritual, towards justice and political and economic equality between nations and within nations. The task of the United Nations, he thought, was to be like a secular Church, a truly international agency free from national pressure pledged to work for this righteousness by moderating conflict and building systems for reconciliation between sovereign states.

A second talk for Edward R Murrow's *This I believe* radio series[48] was more personal, in effect a summary of his discoveries during his three year dark night. He had found, he said, that it was not intellectually dishonest to accept the truth of his basic spiritual experiences, however inaccessible they may be to the normal laws of logic. He acknowledged his debts to his parents, to Albert Schweitzer whose gospel ethics made sense of his ideals and to the mystics when they spoke of love overflowing in self-surrender.

Hammarskjöld's first major test came in 1954. China still held captive eleven American airmen from the Korean War and on November 24th had sentenced them to long terms of imprisonment. The United States, despite threats, had failed to obtain their release and early in December they decided to refer the matter to the UN. Hammarskjöld saw it as a singular opportunity. He felt the way forward was to ask for a personal meeting with Chou En Lai, the Chinese Prime Minister. Nothing like it had been tried before and a failure would have been serious, but his advisers agreed. On December 10th he sent a cable to China, writing in *Markings* 'God spake once, and twice I have also heard the same; that power belongeth unto God, and that thou, Lord art merciful ...'[49] A week later the reply came, 'In the interest of peace and relaxation of international tension, I am prepared to receive you in our capital, Peking, to discuss with you pertinent questions.'[50]

On the same day on which the telegram arrived Hammarskjöld left for Sweden. His father had died the previous year and he was about to take his place in the Swedish Academy. A new member addresses the academy on the life and work of his predecessor and uniquely he also spoke as a son. While he was in Sweden he was also to meet the Chinese ambassador to Sweden at his friend Uno Willers's home to determine whether the question of the eleven airmen would in fact be regarded as 'pertinent.'

On Christmas day, he wrote: 'to have faith – not to hesitate!' and then, on leaving New York on the 30th: 'If I take the wings of the morning, and remain in the uttermost parts of the sea; Even there also shall thy hand lead me.'[51]

There was no immediate outcome. Reward was to come some six months later on his 50th birthday, July 29th, 1955. Hammarskjöld was on his way to Geneva at the time to address an international conference on the peaceful use of atomic energy when the release was presented to him as a personal gift. Hammarskjöld was embarrassed and diplomatically tried to explain that while he and the Secretary-General were indeed the same person, the release was first of all a response to the UN and not to him personally. But he was delighted and typically distressed to note how much he basked in the international acclaim.[52] Had the Chinese discerned the self-centredness he so yearned to overcome and teased him with their 'gift'? He delved deeper to trace the fault observing God's ironic smile at his capering on the international stage.

Hammarskjöld spoke of God, first of all as something or someone but he was now beginning to address him as 'Thou'. He reflected that he was not simply under God but could only be under God. Quoting Eckhart, he said, '"You must love him as if He were a Non-God, a Non-Spirit, a Non-Person, a Non-Substance: love Him simply as the One, the pure and absolute Unity in which is no trace of Duality."'[53] He was now prepared to say 'yes' to whatever life offered.

While in the depths of his unconscious he still felt himself to be a beast without human shape, longing as always for human companionship, he was coming to see that what he sought in human relationship he could only find in the divine. On Christmas Eve he was struck by the paradox that losing himself in a human being might mean slavery, while falling into the hands of God would bring him freedom.[54] He closed 1955 with the words, 'In our era, the road to holiness' – Aulén preferred 'sanctification' in his translation – 'necessarily passes through the world of action,'[55] and in the new year opened his notes with a personal prayer to the Trinity.

In Holy Week that same New Year, 1956, as trouble brewed in the Middle East[56] he was instructed to see what could be done to prevent any further deterioration, and three days later set off to meet the various leaders. He sought to listen to them, he wrote, in the stillness of the Holy Spirit, because 'for the eye to perceive colour, it must divest itself of all colours'. [57] He became close to Ben Gurion, though he strongly disagreed with him, and more particularly to Mahmoud Fawzi, the Egyptian Foreign Minister with whom he kept up a lively if infrequent correspondence.

During October (1956), in collusion with Israel, which was to attack Egypt on the 29th, Britain and France had given an ultimatum to both countries to withdraw within 24 hours or be invaded; they had planned the whole debacle to happen as it did. On October 31st, an appalled Hammarskjöld reminded the Security Council of the Charter and in *Markings* [58] urged himself again to be still. His immediate task was to arrange a cease-fire and help the European nations to extricate themselves. It was Lester Pearson, the UN representative for Canada who suggested the idea of a United Nations Emergency Force. At the time it helped to keep the border between Egypt and Israel secure, but as the UN was aware, it could be no more than a symbol of the world's wishes and hope. It had limited actual power but used in the right way was an effective instrument. Whenever he could Hammarskjöld used to visit the UN troops at Christmas.

Internally 1956 was a time of deepening faith. He reflected that whatever righteousness and humility he had acquired had come from the Father, that faith and courage depended on the companionship of the Brother and that stillness was the gift of the Spirit. Outwardly he was less sanguine. He told Per Lind, 'that no one in my job can run this properly, short of a miracle, without breaking his neck politically. So far it has not happened, but that is, by God, no guarantee for the future.'[59] Yet his underlying attitude, the password of his life as Aulén described it, remained as he wrote at the end of the year, gratitude and readiness to give everything without hesitation.[60]

When the UN had moved into its New York headquarters in 1952, a room had been set aside for personal meditation. During 1957, Hammarskjöld planned to reshape it and asked Bo Beskow to paint a fresco for the back wall. To symbolize creation he had a block of iron ore placed in the middle with light to play upon it. The room is now locked, like so many modern churches after a latter day Guy Fawkes proposed blowing up the UN building from there, but a key is available. The Chagall window outside is a memorial to Hammarskjöld, as the room itself is a meditation on his spiritual vision of a world made one in the silence of God. 'A living relation to God,' he wrote, 'is the necessary precondition for the self-knowledge which enables us to follow a straight path.'[61] During Holy Week he meditated on Christ being taken as a sacrificial victim to his death and prayed that his own self-surrender might be as selfless, that he might be 'merely the lens in the beam.'[62]

This year of tightening resolve culminated on September 26th (1957) on his unanimous re-election as Secretary-General. He attached words from the Lord's Prayer to his acceptance speech.

> *'Hallowed be Thy name,*
> *Thy Kingdom come*
> *Thy will be done,*
> *26 September 57*
> *5:40*[63]

In *Markings* he quoted from Eckhart, 'the best and most wonderful thing that can happen to you in this life, is that you should be silent and let God work and speak.'[64] His inward spiritual progress was matched by similar growth in his political thought, again largely triggered by the shocks of 1956. The UN needed effective tools for preventing violent conflict and in the spirit of article 99 he decided he must alert the UN to potential crises in the world before they actually degenerated into war. He began his second term officially in the following year, on April 10th, 1958. Brian Urquhart, looking back on it, did not feel it was to be as blessed as his first.

Within a month crisis afflicted comparatively peaceful Lebanon and the UN sent 'observers' to find out what was actually happening there, suspected infiltration of arms by lorries moving at night, for example, turning out to be shipments of fruit rather than arms. In Egypt, he tried to use his 'good offices' and his friendship with Fawzi with only limited success to persuade the Egyptians to re-open the Suez Canal to Israeli shipping. He installed Piero Spinello in Jordan as a 'presence', whose role was to keep his eyes open, to advise when asked, to intervene delicately, and to keep the UN and the Secretary-General informed. It was effective in Jordan and was tried in Laos and elsewhere. A German correspondent once asked Hammarskjöld to define the concept. 'I may quote to you as a German: *'Name ist Schall und Rauch'* ("A name is noise and smoke") [65]

After a visit in the Spring (1959) to Vientiane he called in at Nepal for discussions with King Mahenrdra. In the late evening he walked to the Buddhist monastery of Swayambhunath, which stands above Kathmandu and was reminded of the Magdalene Church of Vézelay. He was moved by the silence, the monks' search for the mystery of life and the invisible presence of the Himalayas. The next day he flew to see the mountains:

> Himalayan ice-cliffs
> Beyond the hills
> Of Vézelay at Easter[66]

His photographs later appeared with an article in the *National Geographic* of January 1961.

He took up the theme of truth and humility over his birthday. To be simple-hearted, he said is to be at 'the point of rest in ourselves.' Then he wrote, 'we encounter a world where all things are at rest in the same way. Then a tree becomes a mystery, a cloud, a revelation, each man a cosmos of whose riches we can only catch glimpses.'[67]That summer (1959) he began to write in poetry about his childhood. Greater inward ease was not reflected in the situation of the world outside. He made an extensive tour of Africa in January 1960, beginning with the independence celebrations in Cameroon and ending with a UN conference in Morocco. Africa, its economic weakness and the threat posed by the cold war dominated his speaking and writing. 'Presences' were installed in Togoland and Somalia and Hammarskjöld hoped that the 'presence' of Ralph Bunche might help to avert trouble in the shortly to be independent Congo. It was to be the cause and means of his final crisis.

Early in 1959 a reporter asked Hammarskjöld whether the United Nations should not condemn the wrongdoings of the world. "I am perhaps not a moralist," he had replied[68] The crisis of the 11 airmen held by China, the first major crisis he faced as Secretary-General, is a good illustration of his political acumen and of his prayer and personal reflection at the time. The outcome, their release as a 50th birthday gift gave a personal twist to a political event, which required a careful political interpretation, while he struggled personally to understand the meaning for himself.

Per Lind told me that he regretted that so much attention had been paid to Hammarskjöld's religious ideas and nothing like as much to his political peace-making innovations, which had been so creative. He wrote about the art of negotiation in a skilful blend of the spiritual and the practical in a 1955 passage in *Markings*. Addressing the negotiator, he wrote, you first need to acknowledge the grounds of your own behaviour so that you are able to understand the motives of the other. It is the face of the other which is the important one, 'more important than your own' because you are not there to seek something for yourself but to plead the cause of the other. Indeed, you will only find a lasting solution to a problem if you can see the other objectively, while experiencing 'his difficulties subjectively.' 'The man who 'likes people' he observed, 'disposes once and for all of the man who despises them' Then, with a word about the value of first hand experience and openness of mind, he advised the negotiator to approach persons with the 'youthful ambition to learn a new language and so gain access to someone else's perspective on life.' Lies have no place, 'only an uncompromising 'honesty' can reach the bedrock of decency which you should always expect to find, even under deep layers of evil.'[69]

The two remaining histories are in the personal domain yet both were profoundly affected by difficult political situations, much of which they could do little to change if they could do a little to alleviate. **Angelo Roncalli** was five years into his work as Apostolic Visitor in Bulgaria with a further five years still remaining. Soon after his retreat at Rustchuk the Pope required him, as his diplomatic representative in Sofia, to convey his displeasure to the King, Boris of Bulgaria because after marrying an Italian princess in a Catholic ceremony in Assisi he had repeated the ceremony in the Orthodox Church in Sofia. Roncalli was banned from court for his pains but his chief concern was for the Queen. He gave Giovanna a missal and invited her to attend mass at the delegation. The Pope and the curia thought he had been too soft; but they also noted that he would make a good replacement in Turkey for the severe Nuncio who had preceded him. What had he been doing these 'monotonous years

... ' he asked himself as he prepared to depart from Sofia? 'Trying to make himself holy and with simplicity ... a source of blessings ... for all Bulgaria.'[70]

Bishop Roncalli moved to the Apostolic Delegation in *87 Olçek Sokak Street in Istanbul*. He had come to a Muslim country under the secularising government of Mustafa Kemal Ataturk, who was nearing the end of his life. People of any faith were tolerated little but Roncalli charmed the governor when he called and they ended their meeting by drinking raki together. As with every country he served he started to learn the language.

He had pastoral charge of many varieties of Catholic Christian who lived in Turkey and Greece. His first sermon on St Paul's day was appropriately on unity, which he sought to promote within and beyond the Church especially with the Orthodox; even though he thought of the latter as 'souls to be won for Christ.'[71] 'I try to pull out a brick here and there' he told the Anglican, Austin Oakley. It was 'his ant's work, carrying away tiny pieces of the barriers between men, his bee's work, filling the cells of mankind with small doses of honey.'[72]

On a visit to Greece he fell ill with nephritis, which made him reflect that he must begin to prepare for his death. Both his parents died around this time, his father in July 1935 and his mother four years later on February 20th, 1939. He felt unable to visit them before they died and did not attend either funeral, given the demands, as he explained, of his new family the Church. His mother especially felt his absence. He still continued his care for an ever-extending network of relatives and sent a steady flow of letters often with money and always with guidance.

On Good Friday 1939 Mussolini invaded Albania. Roncalli was in Rome at the time and could not return to Istanbul until late September. He returned to a neutral Turkey at a strategic crossroads of the international community. He became friendly with the affable German ambassador, Franz von Papen, the former Chancellor of Germany, and also took polite tea with the British ambassador. His diplomatic analyses were judged naïve by Rome but he saw his purpose as one who should listen cheerfully and judge mildly and above all remain a bishop of God.[73]

His major work was to help the victims of the war. He began with refugees from Poland and tried hard to relieve hunger in Greece, following the German invasion of the country in 1942, by liaising between the Greek Orthodox Patriarch and the Vatican. He interceded with the Germans to spare the lives of some Greek partisans and with the Russians about the fate of Italian and German prisoners of war but in each case to little avail. His work on behalf of the Jews was a little more successful.

He wrote to Mother Marie Casilda about a ship, which had left Constanza (in Romania, on the Black Sea) in December 1941 with 769 Jews on board only to be blown up by the Turks. "We are dealing with one of the great mysteries in the history of humanity," he wrote. "Poor children of Israel. Daily I hear their groans around me. They are relatives and fellow-countrymen of Jesus. May the Divine Saviour come to their aid and enlighten them."[74] He saw anyone at this stage who was not a Catholic as in need of enlightenment. Through his friendships with King Boris and Von Papen he was able to sign transit visas for Slovakian, Transnistrian and Hungarian Jews, all in all managing to save the lives of some 24,000.

Early in December 1944, Mgr Roncalli received a telegram from Cardinal Tardini. He was to be the new Apostolic Nuncio to France, one of the most senior posts in the Vatican diplomatic service. De Gaulle had entered Paris, the Vichy government had fallen and De Gaulle required a new Nuncio before the end of the year. The Vatican had been looking for someone who could speak French and was above all conciliatory. 'It was all the Pope's doing,'[75] Cardinal Tardini explained when a puzzled Roncalli presented himself and enquired how he had come to be chosen. "In Paris there will be for me no pastoral ministry..." Roncalli told his family. "I shall be almost entirely taken up with religious questions in which politics are frequently involved, and this is always unpleasant."[76]

He arrived on Saturday December 30th, 1944 and moved into *the Paris Nunciature on 10 Avenue Wilson.* He met Cardinal Suhard of Paris on the Sunday, presented his credentials on the following day so that as Dean of the diplomatic corps, by protocol always a Vatican privilege in France, he could grant formal recognition in his New Year greeting on its behalf to De Gaulle's new government.

As had happened in Turkey, his first sermon was during the week of prayer for Church Unity. He dwelt especially on obedience, the virtue that had so informed his own life and work. He spent his first Holy Week at the Benedictine abbey of Solesmes, counselling himself to be wary about speaking his own thoughts. Roncalli's skill as a diplomat was that warmth surrounded his person and while his merry chatter set people at their ease, he could at the same time listen carefully to what people were saying to him.

War came to an end with the allies' victory in Europe on May 8th 1945. Shortly after, Mgr Roncalli visited Lyons to preach for the 7th centenary of the First Council of Lyons. He believed that the Church '... *knows how to find in the past the certainty of mastering the future.*'[77] He used Innocent's condemnation of the Emperor at the Lyons Council as a veiled example of the Church's duty to condemn the Nazi evil. Freedom for the Church, he maintained, was the guarantee of freedom for the people.

His endeavour was to find a style of diplomacy that was commensurate with being a minister of the Gospel. Shortly before he arrived, the Abbés Godin and Daniel had published their study of urban Paris. *France – pays de mission.* In response Cardinal Suhard had inaugurated the Mission de Paris and given his full backing to the Worker Priests who were the front line of the mission. The Vatican was uneasy, fearing for the spiritual lives of the priests who were living among the communist workers. Roncalli feared the same, but disapproved of the harsh messages he was required to convey from the curia. He believed 'kind words full of mercy and forbearance will do more than statements even if made ... for a good purpose.'[78] When a Vatican condemnation of the Worker Priest movement arrived on his desk, he left for a pilgrimage, allowing the French cardinals to interpret the document as best they could.

Archbishop Bruno Heim, who was Roncalli's secretary at this time, told me of one such pilgrimage. Roncalli had wanted to see the tomb of Eligius, the patron saint of goldsmiths, whose tomb he had heard was in a nearby cathedral. They searched it thoroughly, pausing before each chapel for Roncalli to pay his respects – "Ah, St Joseph, Hail Mary ... " The visit became more and more protracted until finally they reached the cross. "Our Lord!" he said and went out. Eligius had eluded them.[79]

Another happy task was studying the history of the nunciature and he was delighted to find that he had a 16th century Bergamesque predecessor, Gerolamo Ragazzoni. As in Istanbul, he set about improving the building, changing pictures and obtaining tapestries. He was aware that the Church in its national and international dress needed to look well and be courteous in its appreciation of the self-esteem of the governments it served.

By 1950, he was 68 and had been a bishop for 25 years, twenty five years of masses offered 'with the splendour of good intentions, and all the dust of the road,' he wrote. In contemplating death, he reflected, 'I am poor, thank God, and I mean to die poor.'[80] As he prepared for the Easter Vigil that year he felt there was no need either for hurry or delay, he just wanted to be open to the future; '"the will of God is our peace,"' he reflected.[81]

Carlo Agostini, the Patriarch of Venice, was dying and Roncalli was asked if he would be ready to succeed him. His joy was tempered by news at the same time that his sister Ancilla was also dying. 'A thorn pierced the most sensitive part of my heart,' he told Mgr Valeri.[82] He made a hasty journey to Sotto il Monte to visit her, thankful to God that he could see which of the two events was the more important. 'I was so pleased to find you full of the desire to live, as we all wish you to do, but at the same time perfectly prepared to obey the holy will of God who sends us both health and sickness.'[83]

At an ambassadorial valedictory meal, there were those who joyfully remembered the time he had had laryngitis and had mimed the words while one of his staff solemnly read out his speech. General Vanier remembered his warm heart, his vivacious spirit and firm strength tempered by grace. Cardinal Feltin thought of him as a far-sighted and subtle person who knew himself and could slip 'through the grasp of those who sought to exploit him.'[84]   Shortly before leaving, on January 12th, 1953 he was made a Cardinal.

Appointed Patriarch of Venice, on March 15th, 1953 he arrived in the city by festive gondola to a tumultuous reception. He reflected in his journal, 'I am beginning my direct ministry at an age – seventy two years - when others end theirs.'[85]   His new staff included Don Loris Capovilla who as his secretary was to edit his journals and writings. He moved *into the second floor flat of the large house near St Mark's* and set out like his exemplar St Charles Borromeo to learn about his diocese.

He wrote his last letter to Ancilla from Rome when he was taking his title as cardinal from the church of St Prisca. 'My heart is still aching from this wound, the thought of my dear sister. I say to the Lord: *Thy will be done,* but it is hard to say this; if it is hard for me, how much harder it must be for you, in your pain and suffering.'[86] She died on the 11th of November. His sister Maria also died two years later.

It was still not long since the ending of the Mussolini era. Preaching at the service held to celebrate the silver anniversary of the Lateran pacts in St Mark's (February 11th, 1954) he observed that such an agreement had had to be made with 'the man whom Providence put in the path of Pius XI.' But Mussolini had also been 'a cause of great sorrow to the Italian people.' Sometimes divine mercy requires 'vessels of clay for the realization of its plans, and then breaks them, as though they had been made for this purpose alone. My brothers and sisters, I know that you can read my heart.'[87]

The clergy and people rejoiced in their new patriarch. Capovilla tells of a visit Cardinal Roncalli made to an alcoholic priest to whom on parting he had given £150; "Padre Giovanni, this is for you. It will help you cover some of your expenses." A delighted Giovanni had sent out for wine to celebrate and was soon drunk. When told the patriarch replied, "Do you really think that I believed one visit would be enough to change that man's life? It wasn't to change his life that I went to see him, but to begin to take away the bitterness."[88]

Over the door of his patriarchate were the words 'pastor et pater'; he understood them to refer to the spiritual father's task of bringing Christ to birth within the people by listening to and leading them to become a mature people of God. By 1957 he had concluded his visitation with a synod to 'adapt, correct, improve and be filled with fervour.'[89]

His brother Giovanni died in 1956. 'I want to hold myself ready,' he told himself, 'to reply *adsum* at any, even the most unexpected moment.' He was nearing the time which was to change his life so completely. He wrote, 'I think the Lord Jesus has in store for me, before I die, for my complete mortification ... some great suffering and affliction of body and spirit.'[90]

Angelo Roncalli was essentially a man of God who did not find political life easy, though he developed through his knowledge of history an enviable ability to find relevant references in the past to illuminate his contemporary comments; his Lyon address is one example, his Venice one about Mussolini another. Ironically his first task after Rustchuk had been to convey the Pope's disgust at the King's second marriage, a distress Roncalli no doubt shared, but he felt that his approach should be a firm and gentle one, appropriate to a bishop not a heavy handed diplomatic rebuke. His careful handling meant that when he did have real need of King Boris's aid in helping the Jews during the war, he was able to call upon him.

Towards the end of his time in Turkey he had noted in his journal some reflections about the kind of person a bishop should be. He had been reading the ideas of the 6th century bishop Fulgentius. Fulgentius said that a bishop should be holy, above reproach, able to speak personally and appropriately to all who looked to him for counsel. He should be a man of personal devotion and peace, someone who always obtained proof before he issued a condemnation, a humble man who worked hard, who was authoritative without being harsh; a person of love and purity to whom exercising the works of mercy were paramount, a person who cared and was hospitable. The unsentimental gentleness of the advice in line with the simplicity of the gospel appealed to Roncalli. 'All the wiseacres of this world, and all the cunning minds, including those in Vatican diplomacy, cut such a poor figure in the light of the simplicity and grace shed by this great and fundamental doctrine of Jesus and his saints!'[91]

Over in Russia, **Iulia de Beausobre** had now been married some 8 or 9 years and was back in Moscow with her husband Nicolay. Aged 33, she was feeling stronger after the experience described in the previous chapter, able to cope better with Nicolay's continuing periods of imprisonment. Shortly after yet another imprisonment, he and Iulia were exiled to **Samarkand**, the city of Tamerlane's blue domed mausoleum. It was 1929 and they were to be there for some two years of happiness. In 1931 they returned to their **Moscow flat.** On January 31st, 1932, Nicolay went to work as usual but failed to return. Iulia and Sasha searched the hospitals, the morgues, everywhere; he had simply disappeared. On February 4th – she was 38 - the secret police came to collect her too. She was taken to *the prison in Moscow's Lubyanka Square*, 'a pocket of hell'[92] she called it, a place of fear and silence, its single purpose to degrade whoever was put into it.

She described what happened some years later in her book *The Woman who could not die*[93] one of the earliest accounts of suffering during the Stalinist terror. She thought people would not believe her so she understated the horror of what happened. Her publishers, Chatto and Windus thought it a profoundly spiritual work.

She was subjected to both physical and mental torture, though she did not mention the former.[94] The mental torment was worse especially the total absence of information. Lying in an almost empty cell, a bucket in the corner, a high window, an observation hole with a naked yellow bulb everlastingly on, she felt she must lose her sanity. She calmed herself by consulting her inner mentor based on Leonardo da Vinci, a wily and detached inner voice counselling her to remain invulnerable. In fantasy she would travel in her mind back to her time with Nicolay amid the fresh beauty of Samarkand and thought of the family they might have had. She was terribly afraid she might betray someone, especially under hypnosis. In the midst of one interrogation, she started to pray and promptly fainted so that she had to be returned to her cell. On another, when they had brought the wrong de Beausobre, the interrogator said, "'Dammit, it's the man we want! the man, the Man, *the Man!*'"[95] As the ordeal continued, she began to move beyond her inner Leonardo and the fantasies of her former life to become increasingly aware of the presence of another; "*Peace, says the other. Let peace stream out before you. Let peace stream out to the left of you. Let peace stream to the right of you. Let peace remain awhile wherever you may tread. May it spread even to the furthest boundaries of the universe ... Peace.*"[96]

She was entirely alone apart from her jailors. She gave them nicknames as she did her interrogators: Snake and Bison to symbolize their cunningly contrived intrusions into the patterns and mosaics of her life. They stripped her comprehensively aiming to leave her as an empty shell, a bodiliness without content. Yet she felt her jailors were victims too, without experience of care or kindness 'flowing towards them from without.'[97] If she could overcome her own pain, she felt, she might be able to make their criminal record less villainous.

Three months after her arrest, on April 24th, her cell door opened to admit another prisoner. Zoia came first, Emma second, Caterina, who told her about St Serafim, third, until the small cell was crammed with six people. She found their presence at first an intrusion but soon became grateful for their company.

In October, without warning, she was moved to *the Boutyrki prison*. She was admitted this time to a huge, dark and smelly cell. 'My soul has partaken unstintingly and richly of all the delights that blood and flesh could give it,' she reflected as she lay half asleep, 'Unstinting and thick indeed should the sordid horrors now be to give me a balanced feeling for true values.'[98] Among her fellow prisoners were Sofia, known as the Cocaine Fiend and Galeena who was a prostitute. One day her name was called and accompanied by a single warder she was taken out to the middle of the Promenade. The two of them stood there alone. "'I shall now read your sentence to you,'" he said. The legal preamble concluded with the statement, "'... sentenced to five years hard labour in the G.P.U Penal Camps, according to Article 58,8 of the Soviet Code.'"[99] There had been no trial, no explanation, no indication of her wrongdoing, just her sentence.

Not long afterwards, she and her criminal companions were loaded onto cattle trucks and slowly conveyed towards Sarov in the East. They were being taken to a penal camp in the Temniki woods where the 18th century St Serafim had lived. She had no idea what article 58,8 was until she reached the camp. There, standing with a roaring temperature before the medical orderly, she learnt she had been convicted as a terrorist who must prepare herself for punitive treatment. She prayed, 'I have presumed to pray for (Nicolay's) life all through the nightmare of the past months, not realizing that our dehumanised existence is not worthy of the name of life. I pray for nothing more. Thy will be done, only veil not Thy face from us, be we living, dying, or dead.'[100]

After a week, she was placed in a hut largely inhabited by nuns, from whom she learnt how to pray the Jesus Prayer. She was feeling steadily worse and eventually was so ill that she was sent to the hospital some four miles away to which she had to walk. She tramped there slowly, struggling to move but valuing the silent solitude of the surrounding forest. There she was put to bed, the full extent of the illness which she had been trying to control taking over and by the evening she had a temperature of 105°. By the morning it was back below normal and each day it fluctuated between the two, she herself existing in a state just short of delirium. She seemed to be dying.

As a person, Iulia de Beausobre was the victim of terrible political injustice, treated as a terrorist simply because of her unacceptable background. Her journey as a Christian had become more than the way of the cross, in fact an early passion in which she struggled to maintain her identity as a person. Some years later when she came to reflect on her experience as a prisoner she gave a paper [101] to Lincoln theological college on the need for redemption as a political victim of an ascetical regime determined to subject its people to the sadistic tyranny of a single idea Suffering, she argued, is more than coping with physical pain or social unease, which are ordinary problems of life. Suffering to her Russian understanding was more to do with confronting the mystery of evil. Evil had to be participated in, she thought, and could only be understood and finally transfigured if the soul was able to become like a holy fool (yurovidny in the Russian), someone whose vocation it was to participate in and live among the dregs of life. She felt she had been made such a holy fool by 'doing time'[102], a phrase she used to identify herself with her fellow prisoners. She recalled being 'examined,' and that in the humiliation she had been presented with two clear choices; either to dissociate herself and mentally withdraw from what was happening to her and in effect psychologically damage herself by doing that or engage with her accusers by what she called 'distilled' sympathy. She counselled herself to be emotionally detached, to avoid any sentimental self-pity either by excusing her torturers of their responsibility, or by giving way to despair but instead, by trying to penetrate their minds, empathise with their emptiness and so come to a state of redemption. She discovered by this that she brought serenity to her heart, to the core of her personality which she described as being built on rock.[103] She discerned that such a way would not be possible for anyone outside the mystical body of the Church, not because she or others in the Church might be peculiarly brave but because they were able to draw on strength from their participation in the redemptive being of the mystical body of Christ.

*   *   *

To Pseudo-Dionysius, the Eucharist is the sacrament he associates with the way of the cross, making the pilgrim one with the body of Christ both on earth and in heaven. In the sacrament, souls are received, given thanks over and when broken are made incorporate within the communion of Christ (Mark 14,22) 'Give us today our daily bread', we pray in the Lord's Prayer.

Returning to St Mark's gospel (12, 28) one of the scribes had asked Jesus about the great commandment. He had replied that it is to love God, to love our neighbour and to love ourselves. (12, 28-34) It is to have a clearer discernment of the person of Christ himself, of the reality of God's love displayed within the ordinary humanity of Jesus who is both son of David and at the same time the one whom the Father wishes to set at his right hand. (12, 35-37) It is to dwell in love and humility. (12, 38-40)

In the prayerful encounter of souls with Christ they are becoming more the person they are meant to be in him, loved into personhood by the Person of God. The final story in this section of St Mark is of Jesus watching a poor widow put her small contribution into the temple box. She gave her whole self in her gift so that it symbolized her achievements, her vocation, all that was valuable to her and Jesus declared of her gift, "Truly, I tell you, this poor widow has ... out of her poverty ... put in everything she had, all she had to live on.' (12, 41-end)

*   *   *

Each of the four gave much. King had fought hard for racial justice, Hammarskjöld for peace in the world, de Beausobre had engaged with political cruelty and Roncalli exercised his ministry as a papal representative with dignity and love. There was more to come, but probably none of them thought as they came to think about what they had achieved that it amounted to very much. Artists who create works of art or engineers who build can at least see what they have done and to that extent, each in the end could have claimed that they had written a number of books, but in the political and personal and religious world it is difficult to measure achievement. When Dr King was asked about the success of the Human Rights campaign in a television interview in June 1966 he said that he thought that conditions might in fact have become worse. Modern commentators assessing his contribution – without wishing to take away from the significance of what he did achieve - agree that advances were not very great and that the treatment of Afro-Americans remains abysmal, but James Washington comments on the profound spiritual effect Dr King had; he was always 'a Christian leader trying to be righteous in an unrighteous world, (who) skilfully maintained a Christian position throughout his public ministry.'[104] The calling is to trust in God, to grow in faith and love, and to give all in service of the kingdom.

In the course of all this endeavour, the four made their particular journeys with Christ on the way of the cross. It was a long and tightly scheduled journey for

Martin Luther King from its beginnings in the middle of the Montgomery boycott, his family's return to Atlanta to his wanderings all round America and visits to India, Ghana, Sweden and many other places. There is a picture of him sitting in a bus station waiting for yet another journey to begin, which symbolizes this all too well. Atlanta was his base but he was rarely there.

Dag Hammarskjöld moved to New York shortly after the experiences described in the last chapter, but his stability too was constantly and necessarily interrupted by journeys all over the globe. Angelo Roncalli's journey, after a further five years in Bulgaria, took him to Turkey, France and eventually to his delight, to Venice, again relieved by holidays back at his home base of Camaitino with his sisters at Sotto il Monte. Iulia de Beausobre, after two sunny years in Samarkand travelled the shortest distance of all from Nicolay's and her flat in Moscow to imprisonment in different parts of the city and in the Gulag. All four had their homes to live in, their 'stations', but to a remarkable extent each of them, for much of the time like Christ who had nowhere to call his home, was without a regular or stable place to lay her or his head.

At the heart of this chapter has been the inherent difference between the spiritual way to a goal and the political means to an end, the inner tensions between the two and the sheer difficulty of articulating a vision at the same time as trying to do something practical about it. Roncalli shared with a great many people a dislike of politics because of the grubbiness that is so much a part of it. That in itself makes it a high calling on what can be a very painful path. Iulia de Beausobre and Angelo Roncalli (Dag Hammarskjöld and Martin Luther King as well in a less sacramental way) understood that they could only manage to travel the way they did because they were both part of the mystical body of Christ, that theirs was a Eucharistic way, that in their responding to the mystery they were broken and yet in that breaking almost immediately brought into a oneness in Christ at a deep level of his communion with the Father in the Holy Spirit.

Once persons have reached their Caesarea Philippi experience, they are called to the way of the cross. Dag Hammarskjöld once said, 'in the Kingdom of God -;- all works are equal there, my smallest is as my greatest, my greatest is as my smallest.'[105] There is a strong temptation when faced by the problems of the world to think that there is not very much that any of us can do about it. But the point is that, however unimportant persons think they are, when they do something with and for God, however small, it is significant. It is not the grandeur of vocation which is the most important, but that whatever souls are called to do, that they are faithful in doing it. Who knows how their work will be used, or valued? At the end of Sarah

Dunnant's novel *The Birth of Venus*, the self-critical and realistic heroine describes her joy in finding that her 'single voice lost inside a great chorus of others' was contributing something to the common task. 'Such is the sound that the chorus made together … to have been a part of it all was enough for me.'[106]

CHAPTER 7

FIRE WIND PLAYING THE STRINGS

Anointing, Thanksgiving, Affliction.

'While Jesus was at Bethany in the house of Simon the leper, as he sat at the table, a woman came with an alabaster jar of very costly ointment of nard and she broke open the jar and poured the ointment on his head.' (Mark 14,3)

In Dag Hammarskjöld's opening poem 'Thus it was,'[1] he speaks of a wind stirring the strings of his expectation and calling from an unknown beyond. His image is reminiscent of the sound the wind makes when it blows through taut overhead wires stretched between pylons high on the hills, the Holy Spirit singing of an unknown mystery towards which the soul journeys.

In chapter 5 the Caesarea Philippi transition was compared to the two Tyne rivers converging at the meeting of the waters, the two rivers symbolizing two different frames of reference becoming one at a significant point on the person's journey towards the mystery. The transition there, like the pattern in all crises, after the long preparation of the way of the cross explored in the last chapter culminates in a new threefold cycle of address, another celebratory occasion and an adjustment to and fresh engagement with a calling, a pattern which Mark has been emphasizing by constantly repeating Jesus's prediction that he would be cruelly used, put to death and then after three days, rise again.

In Erikson's cycle he has an eighth stage to mark the beckoning of old age when the soul faces the choice of either becoming ego-integrated or collapsing in despair. Erikson means by the former someone whose heart has become true, whose life has become harmonious and meaningful, who has come to accept the self and no longer has any need to hide behind a false personage. The soul has become spiritually alert, no longer afraid of a death which is nearing. He gives as his spiritual virtue of this age, wisdom. Erikson writing in the 1960s put this crisis at the point of retirement, at about 60 plus, which is probably now a little early.

It is also Fowler's final stage. For each of his five previous stages Fowler and his team did extensive research but when they came to this one, because of the difficulty in finding people they could interview, they turned to literary sources. Michael Jacobs is not convinced that this was successful and sees Fowler's account as more 'a description of the true direction in which stage 5 people are moving ...'[2] than a new one. In general and in terms of his discussion perhaps this is right but there does nonetheless seem to be some later transition, which is worth examining. .

What Fowler observes of his final stage is that persons have developed a sense of unity with all being, of unity not only with themselves but with all life. They have clarity in their thinking, a more lucid grasp of things and while remaining comparatively free from anxiety, a much greater involvement in life. They have become simpler, more open   It is an ideal, Michael Jacobs thinks, that he is describing.

Nonetheless these traits are visible in the four lives and there are many others who have such intimations of personal anointing – to use the term which seems suitable for this stage – and desire for unity. Certainly a thinker like Ken Wilber[3] would confirm this. He presents a forthright analysis of the later stages of consciousness. After his centaur level he identifies three more - in some of his writing he distinguishes these further – which are the subtle, the causal and the final atman or oneness. He takes his levels from the writings of the mystics and especially the Sanskrit pundits and gurus of the East. Of the subtle level, he says, persons' psychic and intuitive gifts are enhanced, they become more detached and contemplative. This is akin to the interior side of the person discussed in the previous chapter. The causal is the level on which persons begin to become one with the source of all – the subject of this chapter - and the final level is a state of completion, of utter simplicity of heart.

Thomas Merton commented in a paper he gave in Calcutta on East and West dialogue, days before he died, 'that even where there are irreconcilable differences in doctrine and formulated belief there may still be great similarities and analogies in the realm of religious experience.'[4] So here. Wilber in talking about the causal level seems to be referring to the experience of a Serafim breaking his silence to speak with Prioress Xenia (see chapter 1) or St Antony of Egypt[5] emerging from the tomb where he had been praying for the previous 20 years and appearing to his onlookers as someone who had become serene and open and at peace. In the Christian tradition of the desert fathers such an attitude of mind is described by the term 'apatheia':[6] indifference to the cares of the world while at the same time being fully engaged in life, open and attentive to others while undisturbed by the anxieties and troubles around them. As Wilber says such persons have received spiritual gifts of intuition and discernment, they have become full of gratitude and love, longing for a oneness and unity with the God who reaches out to them, souls in their response, as the anonymous English mystic[7] teaches, penetrating the cloud of unknowing by contemplative darts of love. What Wilber is at particular pains to point out is that what he calls transpersonal experience, experiences of union with the Divine which are the result of such prayer, is not a return to oceanic feelings of oneness in the womb, as analysts with their concern for roots tend to assert, but a fresh and mystical union with all that exists. An infant is only at one with the physical and sensorimotor levels, mature persons on the unitive or anointed way experience what in Christian terms are intimations of the fulfilment of their relationship in the Vision of God.

The full revelation of the Vision of God is beyond this life, so whatever is experienced here is an earnest of a later reality, a more complete living of the baptismal gift of resurrection life. For those who come to it, this penultimate transition to the unitive or anointed way is almost a preview of the final one, which precedes death. It has the same threefold pattern as previous crises of long preparation, this time on the way of the cross. It usually begins with a period of desolation before there is again a new address until it finally ends in anointing. The celebratory thanksgiving is then followed by a fairly short – though not always short – living more fully in the resurrection.

Turning once again to the river Tyne allegory, a remarkable feature of the river to a lay observer is the distance the tide reaches from the coast. One winter some years ago the cold was so intense that the river froze over. As the train passed Wylam on the way to Newcastle, huge blocks of ice could be seen strewn about, like slabs of concrete after an earthquake. It was puzzling why there should be such an upheaval just there and not anywhere else. The reason was the meeting with the sea. The tidal limit today is just below Wylam Bridge, some 25 miles upstream from the river mouth. In the allegory the flooding represents the love of God greeting the pilgrim as he or she draws towards the end of their journey.

The effect of the tide on the river is dramatic. Gone are the falls and rapids and sudden changes of course and in their place there is a tranquil and gentle flow. Not long ago I went on a walk from Wylam past the tide post to Newburn and it was snowing. The snow blanketed the sounds and there was a dark and brooding silence, a stillness only occasionally disturbed by a shag diving or a duck suddenly taking to flight. The water seemed scarcely to move. Even with the ebbing tide the river is considerable, but in flood it is even wider. It seemed to speak of a twofold mystery both of darkness in the failing light of a winter afternoon, of death at the end looming large and also of an interior change wrought silently by the infusion of the love of God. At the beginning of this transition, the soul encounters a growing darkness, hostility increasing and making bold to destroy, a desolation of loneliness together with a premonition that this is the end.

It is not desolation for everyone. It depends very much on the sort of person the soul is, his or her personal strength and circumstances. For Angelo Roncalli the transition was comparatively peaceful, for the others much less so. Even when it is peaceful, it does not happen without something visible occurring, just as in the allegory. In the river there is a weir just above where river and sea meet. Otherwise the transition is unremarkable to the casual observer. It is the same with the spiritual transition. In some people it is difficult to notice anything very unusual happening, in others it can be cataclysmic, especially if feelings of desolation are all consuming. In the earlier Caesarea Philippi crisis the struggle was to recognize Christ through the fog of projections, in this the issue is whether souls have any being at all.

Isolation is anyway one of the problems of increasing age. So many loved ones die as the bodiliness becomes weaker. It seems hard, when the faculties are so much less strong, that at such a time so many unresolved problems from the past should rise into consciousness but they do; things done in the past, sins and weakness, unacknowledged fears, all of them come to mind. With it can also come a dwindling awareness of the presence of God, sometimes only of total absence. Souls feel themselves bereft and profoundly alone, in touch with the ultimate human nightmare that perhaps the dread fear is true and they are indeed existentially alone. Could it be that they have simply manufactured themselves a person and illusorily come to suppose that they are alive? Might it be that their consciousness is nothing more than a fabrication?

There is only one way through this and it is to trust. It is not a question of fault or failure, which requires some action on the part of the soul. It requires nothing; they are simply to continue in faith and trust even when what evidence there is suggests that they are in fact existentially alone. They can depend only on the deeper evidence of faith, that they are held. And in the containment of this love by God, as they pass through the experience of desolation, they discover that as persons they are addressed and are becoming infused ʽwith the love of God. These are intimations of resurrection and the promise of a new way marked by a deeper anointing by the Holy Spirit.

The prayer of this new way is contemplation, with incorporation into Christ through the celebratory thanksgiving of Eucharist, that they might be strengthened to join him in the prayer of Gethsemane as they are made one with God. Pseudo-Dionysius[8] spoke of this as the unitive way, which he associated with the sacrament of anointing, an anointed unity with God the Holy Spirit making souls Christ-like (Christ' in Greek, 'Messiah' in Hebrew meaning 'anointed one'), in their anointed status as sons or daughters of God.

Anointing with olive oil is the symbol of this generous outpouring of God's love and Spirit onto his people, described in Psalm 133 as like the dew of Mount Hermon falling on the hill of Zion.[9] Olive oil was used in the consecration of priests, at the coronation of kings and is associated in the New Testament and today with healing. Anointing then symbolizes a maturity of spirit in the relationship with God, souls being now at rest as beloved disciples, healed and commissioned, they are empowered to contemplate the Lord, as they are themselves beheld by God:

Our Father in heaven

Hallowed be your name

is the heart of the prayer, an intimate form of address in which souls contemplate the glory of the Lord. .

Writing about contemplative prayer in notes for a last book Iulia de Beausobre said that she prepared herself for it by a 'steady and persistent stilling of the emotions, for years on end,' to cleanse her 'mind of its inveterate image-making habit.' Everything, she said, needed to be 'gathered into the region of the physical heart', so that the soul might concentrate and learn 'to keep on the alert while perfectly relaxed.' The soul was 'to keep out the flutter of thoughts (those darting, alluring, kingfisher wings) and the creepy-crawlies of the all-too-human emotions' to keep her awake to hear the words, "Know that I am God!" After a lifetime she found the best of herself had come to dwell within the uppermost part of her heart, 'like a tightly coiled spring ever ready for action yet at peace.'[10] St Teresa says the same; that God and the soul become one.[11] and St John of the Cross [12] that after years of contemplative prayer souls began to glow like logs heated in a fire.

With the growing union in the inward relationship with God there is a parallel desire to bring the whole of society into an equal and harmonious conversation. Thought moves at this stage towards goals of peace between peoples and within peoples, of justice and righteousness everywhere. Sights are less on means of achieving these ends, more on a spiritual vision of how peoples might reach out towards such a goal.

*   *   *

In St Mark's gospel the transition to the anointed way is described in the Little Apocalypse of chapter 13. The chapter is first of all a reflection on the corporate end of all things before the coming of Christ, but its placing here suggests that it also has a personal reference within the corporate approach to the end. Jesus's four intimate companions, Peter, James, John and Andrew are with him on the Mount of Olives observing the Temple, the spiritual heart of the people on the hill of Zion opposite. As Jesus said before they sat down, this splendid edifice, this great religious and material adornment of the heavenly city, would shortly be destroyed. (13, 1-2)

Jesus begins with the warning signs; the upheavals, which like the labour pains of a woman about to give birth, precede an actual crisis. The process of birth, of which every crisis is a reworking, is also an image of baptism, the pain and hardship of souls labouring as they die in the waters before they emerge from the depths into a new and risen life. In this crisis souls face a twofold encounter with the deepening darkness of evil in actual afflicting events around them together with an awareness of a growing personal attack on their integrity. This is when unresolved experiences and personal failures flow into consciousness and exacerbate the feelings of desolation. Souls feel their very identity as persons, slipping away. When Iulia de Beausobre stood before the guard on the parade ground (see the last chapter), her crime was that she was not thought worthy to be considered a person. She had been beaten and abused and virtually condemned to death because she was deemed not to have a right to exist. This is the pain of this transition, the identification with nothingness, being out of touch with others, of being out of relationship with God. This reader understands the abomination of desolation described in the text here as something more than Antiochus Epiphanes' altar to Zeus[13], which he put up in the temple at the heart of the nation in 168 BC to desecrate the nation at its heart, it represents also an inner and equivalent desolation of the personal heart. In the midst of this souls need to be on their guard and to watch and to pray and trust as they wait for the Christ to come. (13, 3-end)

Mark at this point tells the story of Jesus being anointed in the house of Simon the Leper by an un-named woman. During the meal she anointed Jesus with an expensive perfume. In the midst of constant misunderstanding from the authorities, from his disciples and most Christians since, this woman performs a profoundly ministerial act, anointing Jesus with the precious commissioning oil of the Holy Spirit. "She has performed a good service for me," Jesus says, "she has anointed my body beforehand for its burial." [14] (14, 1-9)

After Judas has made his plans to betray Jesus the rest of the disciples went to make preparations for the Passover in the upstairs room. They were familiar with the way

Jesus broke the bread and gave it to them. "Take," he said, "this is my body". This is my bodiliness, the person I am, eat this bread so that you may become incorporate with me, I in you and you in me. Then he took the cup of wine to mark the new covenant of love he was forging between God and humankind, representative human bodiliness and God's Son at one in a determination to bring both persons and God into communion. Jesus urged the disciples to give thanks regularly by remembering God's loving act of sacrifice in him and their subsequent empowering by the Holy Spirit. They were to do it until the final grand celebration in the established kingdom. (Mark 14, 10-25)

All of them would now fall away, Christ predicted as they walked towards the Mount of Olives. The disciples all supported Peter in his assurance to Jesus that even if they were to die with him they would not disown him. They walked across the Kidron valley towards Gethsemane and into the olive tree garden. There, Jesus invited his three close companions to share his sorrow with him as he contemplated the onset of affliction.

They for their part were too tired after an exhausting angst ridden night and could not keep awake. Three times he walked over to them to find them asleep,
    Soon, now, the torches, the kiss:
    Soon the grey of dawn
    In the judgement Hall [15]
His passion was about to begin,

Essentially after the apocalypse there are three main events: the anointing, the last supper and the prayer in Gethsemane. In terms of the dynamic, after the desolation the anointing is the address, the great thanksgiving is the celebration and the prayer in the garden of Gethsemane is the time of engagement with the anointed way. Those Churches, which observe the Holy Week ceremonies each year contemplate these events from Wednesday in Holy Week until the evening of Maundy Thursday, the anointing at the meal in Simon's house some time on the Wednesday, which is usually remembered at the blessing of the oils on Maundy Thursday morning, the final supper on the evening of Maundy Thursday and then the vigil to mark the prayer in Gethsemane. These three events also give the major symbols of the anointed way; anointing itself, Eucharist, so powerfully developed in the exposition of the mandate to love of John 13, verses 13-35, and Jesus's participation in the affliction of humanity in the agony of his prayer in the garden. In the four histories which follow, each had reached a certain point in their exacting struggle on the way of the cross.

Iulia de Beausobre had been condemned to five years hard labour. She was 39, had been arrested nine months before and was now seriously ill in the Temniki woods camp hospital, apparently dying. She told Doctor Zassov about her son, Dimitri, and of the time when he had died, how she and Nicolay and Sasha had almost died at the same time and of how she too now felt that her time had come. The doctor felt she was saying no more than the truth. That evening she listened to a story told by Galeena, the prostitute she had met in the Boutyrki who was in the same ward. It was about the Maiden of the Holy Woods and as Iulia heard it in her delirium, she began to think of how her love for Nicolay had become 'too rarefied to be expressed in any earthly formula.' When that happens to a couple, she reflected, 'then their earthly aspect vanishes and they become pure spirit. This has come about with us.'[16] As she lay dying, imagining herself to be the dying maiden of Galeena's story she saw Nicolay 'swathed in shimmering gold' floating towards her and taking her right hand in his. She heard him say to her "'Let us now appear before the high altar of Him whose decisions are binding and final.'"[17]

It was in fact the evening of the actual day on which Nicolay had been shot, though she was not to discover this until much later. Next morning she woke up asking for food and she began to recover. "'When the Almighty performs His miracles,'" Dr Zassov commented, "'man can but second Him.'"[18] Somehow she knew that something momentous had changed within her and that her way, now that she was restored to life was going to be different. She had 'died' with Nicolay and in the abandonment of her life, she had become truly offered.

She made a good enough recovery and was returned to the camp, only to be readmitted some months later, this time with such severe frostbite that it was feared she might have to have both her hands and her feet amputated. It was not in the end to be necessary but she was declared too ill for prison and told that once she was well she would be released. Another patient on the ward was Mother Theodosia, an elderly nun who was dying from the severe effects of malnutrition. Mother Theodosia told her "'Even if Nicolay should go too, you must always remember … those of us who die in Him now, join Him at once. There is no pain for us, only rejoicing. Rebuild your heart into an eternal tabernacle for thanksgiving." "Yes, Mother,'" she replied.[19]

Later they had another conversation. '"Be comforted,'" Theodosia counselled her, "'for we are in the care of Serafim of the Holy Woods, the Intercessor for all who suffer here. Infinite is our joy …'", and she went on to reflect about Iulia's responsibility to tell people "'that they should see the light that bears our burden with us.'" Iulia protested that she would be looking for Nicolay in Siberia, but

Theodosia looked gravely at her and said: "'Of your wanderings in Siberia I know nothing, but I say to you, tell them. Tell our brothers beyond the distant border, it is their prayers we want, their prayers and understanding.'"[20]

On her release some time later she was conscious of a blessing from St Serafim as she boarded a train for Moscow. She visited the Brunis when she reached the city; Lev had flu and they remembered Iulia, swollen from hunger and frostbite sitting beside his bed and telling them about her life in prison. "They were both flooded with tears." They were never to see her again[21]

She went to the Political Prisoners' Relief organization, which undertook to find out what had happened to Nicolay. A few days later she received their report; "'The news is old, quite old. Sad news. Very sad. I'm afraid quite the saddest."
"Shot?"
He bows his head silently. Then:
"On the ninth of January nineteen-thirty-three"'[22]
It was the day she herself had 'died'. She was conscious that somewhere in her spirit she had known that Nicolay had died; but it had not been confirmed. She had been able to hope. Now she knew the truth.

She had met her friend Sofia of the Boutyrki the day before and had been invited to share a secret cabin Sofia had in the woods. As a released prisoner she was not legally permitted to live in or near Moscow but Iulia risked going with her. On one of her forays into Moscow to raise money for food she met Olga, a relative of Nicolay. Olga told Iulia that friends had paid for her to leave for America and she recommended that Iulia should try the same. Iulia gave her the address of her former nanny Isabel Paxton and Olga memorised it so that she could contact her when she reached the West. A short time later, a letter from Pussy arrived to say that she would try to raise the £300 ransom required by the Soviet Government.[23]

Several friends, Boris Pasternak who liked her poetry among them, urged her not to go. Sofia wanted Iulia to move with her to the Urals. The choice was stark, either to sever her roots or, as she saw it, to die. She felt she was at the end of her strength and nearing madness. There was too the mystery of Mother Theodosia's prophecy. As the train drew out of Moscow station for London, Sofia watched her, unsmiling, from the platform. Four years later she wrote a poem about it which she called 'Cross Ways.'
> I stood within that crucifix in time
> Which men have called the parting of the ways. [24]

Isabel's daughter Renée met her in London, expecting a disabled Iulia. Instead she saw an elegant woman walking towards her with her customary grace and dignity. The damage was primarily inward, together with utter physical and emotional exhaustion.

As she slowly recovered, she reflected that she had little idea what she, a vagrant as she described herself, an asylum seeker as we would say today, was to do. She had no money, no home and few friends. She felt increasingly that the mystery of her survival was related in some way to Mother Theodosia's words which echoed in her spirit. She somehow was to tell the West about the sufferings of her people.

Through friends of Isabel Paxton, who was an anthroposophist, Iulia was offered an administrative post in a **Rudolf Steiner home for children in the Clent Hills** near Birmingham. She was assured she would have time for writing. She was grateful for a place to live but found the atmosphere and the belief system debilitating. Once more she fell ill and spent a long 10 months struggling to allow grace to mend her damaged person. She painted again, 'strange' pictures a friend called them, bold colourful canvasses in which she exposed for her own consumption her wounded liveliness. The friend was Prue Barrington, a woman in some need who came to Clent to learn about anthroposophy. Prue's mother invited Iulia to their country home on the Suffolk coast and in the eleven weeks there, she at last found time to write. She wrote there almost all of *The Woman who could not die.*

Later in the year (1938), as Prue's mother had hoped, Iulia and Prue moved into **60 the Grampians, a flat bought for them in Shepherd's Bush Road in London.** The Grampians is an art deco apartment block with a splendid entrance flanked on either side by shops. Number 60 was reached by an outside gallery and, facing south was filled with sun. It was to be her home for more than 30 years.

Iulia had not been regularly to church since her sad experience as a young girl. Joining in liturgical worship and receiving the sacraments again was a rediscovery of joy. *The Woman who could not die* was published by Chatto and Windus in the spring of 1940 and she gave a more theological account of her sufferings to the students of Lincoln Theological College in her paper *Creative Suffering* described in the last chapter. [25]

In 1941, Russia joined the war and she suddenly found herself in demand as a person who knew about Russia and could both speak and write about it. Her next writing paved the way for her own development as a starets. She translated and edited the letters of the 19th century spiritual master, Macarius of Optino where she had stayed so memorably with Nicolay in the 1920s. Next came a life of St Serafim of Sarov. She told the story rather as she must have heard it, as part of the oral tradition, the facts of the saint's life woven into the legends and stories which had grown up around him, especially about his thirty-year withdrawal to a life of absolute silence. The presence in the Temniki woods, which had illumined her path and vocation while she had been there, had become clearer as she studied creative suffering in the life of St Serafim.

One of those who had been impressed by her *Creative Suffering* was the Jewish writer. Walter Zander. Through him she joined a group to discuss the similarities between the Jewish faith and Russian Orthodoxy. It was at one such meeting on October 25th 1942 that she first met Lewis Namier, the formidable Professor of Modern History at Manchester University. As Walter Zander who was speaking at the occasion observed, Namier fell in love with her the moment he saw her. She was aware of a tall, thickset man, who listened intently to all she said. He came round to see her almost immediately to discuss an article he had written for the *Manchester Guardian* and she showed him some of her own writing. He visited the Grampians increasingly finding he could talk and share his anguish and fears with her including the trauma of his failed marriage to Clara.

AJP Taylor, who was a fellow historian at Manchester and a great admirer of Namier says that in his early days 'he was fun and not the gloomy introspective Slav soul that Julia' – as she came to be known in the West – 'makes him out to be.' Friends nicknamed him 'CB – Clumsy boy. He was clumsy in personal relations and trampled on the toes of others without realizing what he was doing.'[26] For his part, Lewis recognized Iulia to be a woman of spiritual integrity who could guide him through the inner difficulties which had tortured him all his life. Taylor preferred Clara, whom he thought whimsical and he looked after her on Lewis's behalf when Lewis was at a loss what to do about her.

One evening in 1945, Lewis told Iulia that they should marry. Iulia was not so certain, whereupon in a frenzy of feeling, compelling her to pray, he flung himself to his knees, and clasping her legs, demanded of God that he should make them both of his mind. Iulia was astonished to learn from Lewis that on his return home there was a letter from Clara to tell him she was dying. There were still considerable barriers to their union. Iulia did not think she could contemplate marriage after being so physically and psychologically damaged by Stalin's men; and she certainly could not consider marrying a non-Christian. But she was also a woman to whom relationship was important, who had loved Nicolay deeply. Her vocation, she learnt from what she had suffered, was to intercede for the suffering. Often those called to a particular ministry of intercession perhaps for one person find the prayer for the one incorporates their concern for the whole. She also liked Lewis. She was in her fifties, a widow for whom spirituality was not detached from the physical; she could love a man who loved her. She valued Lewis's lack of sentimentality and the vigour of his conversation.

Julia did not want him to make a merely formal acceptance of the Christian faith but he had in fact been considering becoming a Christian for some years. He felt increasingly that baptism into Christ was a proper development for a Jew. He was baptized in the Anglican Church in Westminster Abbey on March 16th, 1947.

A little time before this, Lewis and Julia had been on holiday in Anglesey and had shared together the 'torn out pages' of their lives. For Julia it had been the anguish of leaving Russia, a decision which still distressed her. She had had to turn away not only from participating in the struggle with the evil of the situation there but also from her burgeoning promise as a poet. She did not expect him to understand the pain of her decision, 'but I was doing L a grave injustice', she wrote. 'The moral support he at once gave me was bestowed with the simplicity of perfect understanding.'[27]

They married in the chapel of the Russian Orthodox Church shortly afterwards, on June 4th, 1947. She was 53. The couple used 60 the Grampians as their London base, Julia occasionally making forays north to join him during term time; but mainly she remained in the South and received a growing number of visitors seeking spiritual guidance.

She presided over a home once more, entertaining at parties and accompanying her husband to the official functions which were the fruit of his illustrious career. Namier's deafness and his capacity for upsetting people often made social occasions difficult so her grace and social skills were a great asset. In 1952 Namier was knighted. He was delighted for Julia who would now have a title worthy of the distinction he felt she deserved.

Lewis had started work on the history of parliament before he retired from his professorial chair in 1953 and Julia drove him round the country, 'two old things in our jalopy' on a cross-country paper-chase to study the lives of 17th century MPs.[28] Travel became as much a part of her life as it had been in her late teens but this time of an infinitely more exhausting kind.

She was still struggling with the meaning of suffering, the suffering in Lewis being about as much as she could comprehend. At times he was so overwhelmed by guilt and self-hatred for not making amends to his father, for his further failure with Clara and indeed with all with whom he had been close. He almost took his life but resisted the temptation by reminding himself what it would do to Julia. As a child he had felt his attachment to his horse had amounted to idolatry and he feared he was beginning to feel the same degree of attachment to Julia. When he tried to explain this to her, he was distressed that she did not immediately grasp how serious and appalling this danger was for him. Sometimes she feared deeply for him and indeed towards the end wondered whether she could stand the strain.

Yet he was growing in serenity. Julia was about to go to church for the feast of the Transfiguration, August 18th in the Old Russian calendar, when he suddenly became ill. As they waited for the ambulance she saw to her joy that there was an interior transfiguration taking place within him. He died the following day, on August 19th, 1960. She told Brian Frost some years later that they had been right for each other. She knew that would not have been so if they had met earlier and though she was glad it was over she wept tears of grief. Julia had lived out her concern for Lewis within the physical bond of an intimate relationship to the point when he was finally at peace. Her concept of what it was to intercede had expanded and grown in their life together.

Lewis had asked Julia to write his biography and had prepared her by relating his life. Over the next nine years it was to be her major task. She had finished about three chapters when she met the Indian writer Ved Mehta, who was gathering material for articles about the British intelligentsia. He found her manner of speech 'overwhelming; she emphasized practically every word, and everything she said, no matter how matter-of-fact, had a deep emotional content.'[29] Namier's fellow-historians had spoken of her to Mehta 'with awe and affection' and he made his meeting with her the climax of his book.

She steadily wrote the biography, building up the picture of a great and inwardly tortured man slowly moving towards his fulfilment. It was finally published on May 13th, 1971 by Oxford University Press, Max Beloff describing it as 'one of the most extraordinary. moving and revealing biographies ever written.'[30] It is indeed a remarkable book, which won two prizes. It is quite unlike her other writing, full of human detail and beautifully written.

She was now free for her many seekers after spiritual help and advice. She says of Serafim shortly before he emerged from his final thirteen years silence that he could see 'the fabric of particular human lives' and could discern 'the pattern that every one of these lives should follow ...'[31] So it was with her, as the fruits of her struggle came to full maturity. Her room at the Grampians was a place of stillness, where alert and relaxed she dwelt in constant prayer, upheld by her own unique dialogue with God. She practised what she observed in Macarius of Optino, faithfulness to her tradition, coloured by her own fresh, unsentimental observations and interpretations.

Underneath she continued to struggle. Her ankles and hands had been damaged in the camp and her psychological strength had been severely stretched. EL Mascall, who met her at the end of the Thirties, said there was something sealed up inside her[32] and to others she seemed aloof and distant. While she had triumphed creatively over much of her experience she had still had to protect a part of her vulnerability by 'not feeling the pain.' She thought that some of her reactions, the need to be quiet, sometimes to hide away, were just her own weaknesses and she was immensely helped by Nadezhda Mandelstam and Alexander Solzhenitsyn when they described their similar experiences in *Hope against Hope* and *The Gulag Archipelago*.[33] It was at this point that she decided to move into a retirement home.

She had emerged from a time of terrible desolation and she was to spend the rest of her life, like Julian of Norwich contemplating the revelations she had had when she was 30, reflecting on and growing into what had happened. She had lost Nicolay, a second massive loss after the death of Dimitri, her hope of finding him had been crushed and she thought genuinely and reasonably that she herself was about to die. In a profound and baptismal sense, she spiritually did die. She thought the title of her first book *The Woman who could not die* was trite but her publishers saw that with all she had gone through she 'ought' to have died and that there was something spiritual in the fact that she had not. She had had a real encounter with death and although very early – she was still in her thirties – she was from that moment a survivor of an attempt to eliminate her. The concentration camps of Germany, Russia and elsewhere were the most appalling spiritual devastation of the 20th century and those who survived were either driven to despair or became men and women of spirit. She herself rose to hear the words of Christ through Mother Theodosia calling her to tell people of Russia's suffering. Then, like Serafim, after years of writing, her second marriage and as an intercessor and woman of prayer, she became a spiritual director to all who sought guidance from her.

After his Caesarea Philippi experience, **Angelo Roncalli** remained five years in Bulgaria before moving to Turkey where he was during the war. In 1944 he had become Apostolic Nuncio in Parish and when he was 71, Cardinal Archbishop of Venice. Now and another five years on and not long before his 77th birthday he was at the conclave to elect a new Pope. He will have realized that there was a possibility he might be chosen as the next Holy Father, because he was *papabile*, one of three considered to have the capacity for the position - though this was not known to the world at large – and he must have prayed that one of the others might be preferred. When he came to see that his election was imminent he became silent. He and Fr Capovilla ate their lunch in almost total silence. He had a twenty-minute rest, prepared some notes for his acceptance speech and at 4-50pm on October 26th, 1958 he was chosen. He took the name of John because it was his father's name, his new Lateran Cathedral's dedication and not least, because predecessors of the same name had 'nearly all had a brief pontificate.'[34]

Once elected, he became peaceful. Obedience to his fathers in God learnt throughout his ministry demanded that the Lord's will should be done and the two virtues, obedience and peace, had been the motto of his pilgrimage. He saw his election as one of the two surprises of his final years the idea for the Council being the other and that he should receive them from the Holy Spirit with simplicity. At his coronation he was anointed for this new stage of the way of the cross.

On moving into **the Vatican** he abandoned himself to God in the simplicity of faith. He was now himself the Holy Father which enabled him to relax and become his own person. That Christmas he set a new tone for the papacy by visiting a hospital and a prison.

The idea of calling a Council occurred to him early, if he did not bring the seed of it from before the conclave. Capovilla said Pope John first mooted the idea two days after his election and that he had counselled him rather to use the "charism of paternity that you undoubtedly possess." Pope John, after praying about this advice, commented, "the trouble is, Don Loris, that you're still not detached enough from self – you're still concerned with having a good reputation. Only when the ego has been trampled underfoot can one be fully and truly free."[35] At the end of his first month he told Capovilla, "I have in mind a programme of work and I'm not fussing about it any more. In fact I am pretty well decided."[36]

In January he met Cardinal Tardini to tell him of his ideas. He felt 'hesitant and uncertain' [37] because Tardini's response was crucial. In the event Tardini described them as splendid initiatives. Writing later about the meeting[38] Pope John implied that the inspiration had occurred to him at that very moment and that he was as surprised as everyone else; but 'surprise' was a word he always used to describe 'the presence of grace.' Excited by the vision, he was aware that January 20th, 1959 was the day when he was irrevocably committed to the Council.[39]

The day to announce his intention came in the midst of the week of prayer for Christian Unity and he was visibly nervous as he marked the week's end with a celebration in St Paul's-without-the-walls. After the service he told the assembled cardinals about the Council, adding an invitation to 'the separated Christian Churches to share with us in this banquet of grace and brotherhood.' The speech was received, he reflected, in 'a devout and impressive silence;'[40] some commentators have thought they were simply too stunned.

During the summer of 1959 he published his first encyclical *Ad Petri Cathedrum*, a traditional document urging Christians to find unity by returning to the embrace of Rome. Although his prayer and experience had jostled his views, he still regularly referred in his journal to unhappy Orthodox and sad Protestants. But he was about to appoint Augustin Bea, his predecessor's confessor, as head of a new Secretariat for Christian Unity. Bea was to guide the Catholic Church to understand other Christians as having an underlying unity with Catholics through baptism.

By the end of the year visitors of all kinds were queuing up to meet Pope John, because as Peter Hebblethwaite put it, 'Meeting John was ... like chatting with one's favourite grandfather.'[41] Archbishop Geoffrey Fisher of Canterbury was the first 'Protestant' to visit, greatly distressing the curia who coped with the crisis by pretending he was not there, the meeting beginning a dialogue between the Anglican and Roman Communions which has continued despite problems to this day.

The first of his ideas, a Synod of Rome opened on January 24th, 1960 and he was pleased with it, though it was a very formal occasion. After two years in Rome, he reviewed and revised the notes he had made of his first twenty years as a priest. He prayed that he might humble and lose himself in the Lord as he entered his eightieth year (from November 1960). The French bishops' view that Pope John had been 'pas sérieux' when he had first announced the Council was looking increasingly doubtful as preliminary papers and an agenda were prepared.

Mater et Magistra was published shortly after the seventieth anniversary of *Rerum Novarum* on July 15th 1961. It gave a welcome to the modern world, to the Welfare State and to the technology which was bringing people into new social relationships. It maintained that freedom for persons would be assured if there were enough independent 'intermediate bodies and corporate enterprises' to limit the power of central authority, and if the latter in its turn held a healthy view of the public good.[42]

He began his 1961 retreat on St Laurence's day, the anniversary of his ordination as priest. 'Here I am,' he reflected, 'already on the eve of the fourth year of my pontificate, with an immense program of work in front of me to be carried out before the eyes of the whole world ...'[43] He understood his role to be one of sacrifice of himself as '"priest and victim"'[44] for the work of God in the coming council and for peace in the world. During the retreat, the East German Communists in a major challenge to the peace of the world began to build the Berlin wall to halt escapers to the West. On the 14th he broadcast a message inviting Catholics throughout the world to join him in praying for peace with Mary on her feast day on the 15th. He counselled himself to be "filled with the love of Jesus ... for individual souls and for the whole world"[45] He reflected on the nature of sanctity, that he must be 'willing to be opposed and humiliated, rightly or wrongly.'[46] He found it very helpful to look at the pieta by Luigi Simone in his private chapel.

In the next few days he made a detailed confession, reviewed his spiritual life and summarized all that he had held dear, his desire for virtue and holiness, his readiness to direct everything to the well-being of the Church, his prayer that he might remain serene in service, and he entrusted it all to God, acknowledging his own nothingness, being ready to do what he had to do intelligently. He prayed that like Peter he too might be allowed to follow Jesus 'to sacrifice, to mortification, to death.'[47]

In December 1961 he noted 'the beginning of some trouble that must be natural for an old man,'[48] possibly an early sign of the cancer which was to afflict him. The invitations to the Council went out on Christmas Day, despite opposition, especially from some in the curia. Their attitude was an astonishment to him, but he struggled on with the support of people like Cardinal Montini (his successor, Pope Paul VI) to encourage a new hope and openness to the Spirit and for peace in a world which already in the 20th century had been torn apart by two terrible wars. His role, he told a Shinto delegation from Japan, was to suffer for the Council. Both of his sisters had died. He was an old man conscious that he was drawing near to his end and he felt in his spirit that some suffering awaited him. Desolation is not a word that comes naturally to mind when thinking of Pope John but he was undoubtedly by this time of his life, despite the people constantly around him, very much alone in the solitude of his great office.

On being elected the Holy Father he had received his new vocation in silence and it was in simplicity and obedience and peace that he had abandoned himself to his new calling. His life had had a disciplined beat to it so far, each experience building on the one before in a harmony of spiritual development as he had faithfully recorded in his *Journal of a Soul.* Anointed, he was now in thanksgiving ready to make his new life a sacrifice.

It is interesting to compare in what way the crises of the spiritual way of Pope John and Iulia de Beausobre actually differed, why this crisis was so early in the one and so much later in the other. It was early in Iulia de Beausobre's life because she was arrested and as so often happens to persons in similar circumstances, so seriously abused that she thought reasonably enough that she was about to die. In fact she survived, utterly changed by her experiences. Primo Levi [49] has written movingly of this in his books about the holocaust and of his own survival. If such oppressed victims do manage to survive, the fact that they do leaves them with a knowledge of abuse by persons trying to annihilate their spirit, of guilt about their survival especially if there is not some awareness of spiritual purpose in their still being alive. So many witnesses speak of this, even those who were young at the time of their affliction who were unable to process and comprehend it until very much later. Life has changed for them and they have an experience of a level of consciousness which never really leaves them. If they are to maintain life afterwards on a creative basis, or to put it the other way round, if spiritual death is to be avoided, as it was by Iulia de Beausobre, they will only advance if they adopt some form of spiritual exercise and prayer in relationship with God.

Bishop Roncalli's experience at an equivalent time in his life was different. When he was on retreat at Rustchuk he had been frustrated by the difficulties of his mission in Bulgaria but he was not in danger of his life. He was learning who Christ was and what travelling on the way of the cross meant and that the way of love was to be his calling.

It is necessary at this stage in the discussion to rehearse some of the points about the transitions. The first is that levels can be interwoven. In this particular transition and way for example, at the same time as Iulia de Beausobre was coming to life again in the Gulag she was hearing about her new vocation to become a witness to Russia and an intercessor for the afflicted and Angelo Roncalli when he was being ushered onto his way of the Cross was also at the same time being anointed by the Spirit. Similar points could be made about the other transitions. The baptismal possibilities of each transition make many gifts possible.

Secondly, at whatever level of consciousness persons are, the challenges that are primary at earlier or later levels in their lives are also active in the current one. They remain human, sinners coping with normal day-to-day stress. They are penitents, needing acceptance, healing and forgiveness, they continue to live out their vocation, contemplate the Lord and know themselves anointed, while they live primarily through whatever are the challenges of one particular stage.

Thirdly, there is a temptation, especially at the beginning of the way, for persons to try and assess how much personal progress they are making. The only possible value of doing this might be to make sense of something perplexing but too often it hides an agenda to do with being better or further on the way than others. Thinking that one Christian or group of Christians might be more advanced than another – Iulia de Beausobre further on than Angelo Roncalli for example because she had an earlier transition to the anointed way – and therefore more holy has been prevalent among Christians from the New Testament Philippian Church to the present day and it is not helpful. In the New Testament Church Christians were known as the holy ones because they were baptized and had received the Holy Spirit. They were holy because the Holy Spirit was present within them not because they had achieved any personal merit. In the later stages the need to prove anything becomes irrelevant as the desire to respond in love to God is enough in itself. Rather souls mourn just how separate they still are from God the more they learn how much their personhood rests in God alone.

It is this truth which Catherine of Siena shares in the colloquy she had with the Lord. She was not as a person short on psychological identity, but she did have a clear understanding that her personhood depended wholly on the love of God. Without God she was nothing. "If you know these two things," God said to her, "you have beatitude in your grasp. You are she who is not and I AM WHO IS."[50]

So fourthly, is there a reason for studying these transitions and stages? Yes, both because they happen and because they can be alarming. Souls experience desolation, aridity, the absence of God, other problems and they become frightened and especially today think that if all is going as wrong as it seems to be that there can be no alternative but to abandon the way. In any relationship things can become badly confused. It is worth learning about them.

Dag Hammarskjöld had now been Secretary-General of the United Nations for seven years. By June 1960 he was nearing his 55th birthday and was about to face the enormity of the 1960 Congo crisis. To comprehend this it is necessary to give something of the complicated history of the events in the Congo after Belgium suddenly granted its colony independence in June of 1960. Ralph Bunche, representing the United Nations, attended the independence celebrations which took place only six days after Patrice Lumumba, the first Prime Minister, had been able to form a new government. Something of the chaos of the period is described in Conor Cruise O'Brien's play *Murderous Angels*[51] written after O'Brien had served as the UN representative in Katanga. He took Hammarskjöld and Lumumba as symbols, the one as an ice man of Messianic pretensions representing the white West's quest for peace and the other, the warmly human black man representing the Third World's search for freedom. The play argues that at heart Hammarskjöld was the white man's tool, prepared to stop at nothing to keep the peace between the Soviet Union and the States. It was a harsh judgement as Hammarskjöld was indeed caught in an impossible conflict between Russia and the States but it illustrates well how entwining politics can be and how people are enmeshed in what happens.

Within a week of independence there was trouble, chiefly because the army, disappointed that independence had made so little difference to their conditions, went on the rampage. On the same day, July 7th, the Congo was admitted to the United Nations. Two days later there were riots in Elizabethville (now Lubumbashi) the Katanga capital on the Copper Belt and Moise Tshombe, the province's president invited Belgian troops to come back, ostensibly to protect the whites, but it was feared in order to allow Belgium to recover its former colony's wealth. Two days after that Tshombe announced that Katanga would secede from the Congo, and as the Congolese government appealed to the United States for military help, Hammarskjöld brought the matter before the Security Council.

With the situation in the Congo deteriorating by the hour the United States finally decided it should be a UN concern. By the 13th, the United Nations had decided to send its own international force, Hammarskjöld and his team working until dawn to prepare the details. After one brief meeting with Lumumba who was in New York, Hammarskjöld left for Leopoldville (now Kinshasa) to ease the arrival of the UN force. All went well except in Katanga and Hammarskjöld had to return to New York for a strengthening of the mandate to move in there. Back he went to Kinshasa and then flew on to Lubumbashi with four planes of Swedish troops, only to find on arrival that Tshombe had changed his mind about receiving them. Hammarskjöld parleyed from the air for 25 minutes before feeling it was safe to land. Success was short-lived; Lumumba was now angry that he had not been included in the mission and abandoning the UN turned for help to the Soviet Union. Hammarskjöld tried to meet with Lumumba, but failed, and returned to New York greatly fearing that the cold war would now extend to Africa. What the Congo needed was a basic administrative and national infrastructure, what it got was chaos and a mutinous army.

The crisis worsened on September 5th when the Congo president, Joseph Kasavubu summoned Bunche's successor, Andrew Cordier to tell him that he was dismissing Lumumba. Nothing could dissuade him and the country was divested of its prime minister and thrust into a constitutional crisis. In effect Kasavubu's action had delivered the country into the hands of the army – unpaid at that point and to avert worse crisis, paid through the UN – and its commander Joseph-Désiré Mobutu. Mobutu was to remain the increasingly corrupt ruler until 1997.

The United Nations General Assembly, which followed all this, was a vivid affair with leaders of many of the world's countries attending. On September 24th, 1960, Khrushchev of Russia proposed that the Secretary-General should be replaced by a troika representing the three 'worlds'. Hammarskjöld, realizing that this would introduce the veto into the very heart of the Secretariat, rose to the occasion. As an orator he was not usually impressive. He spoke a monotonous English with a pronounced accent but this time with a vigour which conveyed the passion of his feeling. He feared he had overdone it when the assembly responded with an ovation.

Meanwhile Lumumba was living under UN protection. On November 18th his daughter, who had been in Switzerland for an operation, had died and Lumumba was anxious to fly to Stanleyville (now Kisangani) to arrange her funeral. He asked the UN to sanction it, but the UN representative, Rajeshwar Dayal refused on the grounds that he could not guarantee Lumumba's safety. On November 27th Lumumba decided he would go anyway and on escaping was abducted by the army.

That Christmas Hammarskjöld felt acutely alone. He spent the evening of Christmas with his security officer, Bill Ranallo and his wife, who were continually solicitous of his needs. On the same evening he thought of 'the Manger ... situated on Golgotha, and the Cross ... already ... raised in Bethlehem,'⁵² and committed himself into the hands of the Lord. He had refused an invitation to spend Christmas with the Wieschoffs but loneliness made him ring up during the day to ask if he might change his mind.

He then wrote a series of haikus, dated in the November and December before, in Advent in fact but actually placed in *Markings* after the Christmas writing so that he could return to his meditation on the adamant young man in Gethsemane. He had written any number of haikus in 1959, which suggest that a new peace had come to him, but now he had come to understand that it was not the love the disciples had for Jesus which was the important thing, but the love that Christ had for them and that he had been prepared to give himself for them in a sacrifice of no significance:

Morning mist,
Chirping of early birds.
Who recalled the night's sacrifice? [53]

In looking back to his earlier crisis when he had been thinking about Christ and his obedience to the way of the cross, he recognized that then he had been thinking of it in theory, now he was actually experiencing it. In a rhymed poem he reflected on the darkness of the way of the cross and of his discovery that it was a road of pain and truth that simply had to be followed to the end

Hammarskjöld had come under increasing pressure during 1960 to dismiss some of his most trusted advisers because so many of them were American. "There are no neutral men,"[54] Khrushchev told Walter Lippmann after his fierce attack on Hammarskjöld in the Assembly, to which Hammarskjöld had responded that while UN officials might have their personal loyalties, they put their international obligations first. He had always depended on a few loyal and devoted colleagues like Dayal, Bunche, Cordier and Heinz Wieschoff and it was distressing to have to ask Andrew Cordier to cease as his Executive Assistant.

Mobutu still held Lumumba, but embarrassed by demonstrations in Lumumba's favour, arranged for his transfer to Katanga. On the journey Lumumba was seriously abused and probably killed, though his death was kept secret for a further month. The furore throughout the world when Lumumba's death was announced on February 13th, 1961, was intense and Hammarskjöld was the one who was blamed and vilified for it.

As it happened, February 13th was two days before Ash Wednesday and before the beginning of a UN General Assembly which was to be notorious for the unrelenting hostility of the Soviet Union towards Hammarskjöld. He felt, as he prayed about it that he was being made to stand naked before God, like Hercules wrapped in the 'burning shirt of Nessus' longing for relief on the funeral pyre, that he had become his own 'dark measure in the vein,' a human being who was not only an object of derision but one who still must try to retain a sense of being within the existential darkness of existence. He turned to Psalm 109 which speaks of becoming a reproach. The climax of his struggle came on Maundy Thursday that year. He wrote about the fate of Brand in Ibsen's play, falling to his death under an avalanche. Through the roar of the snow as it filled the valley, a voice was heard echoing through the din, "God is love," it said. 'Then thought I to understand this', he wrote, quoting psalm 73, 'but it was too hard for me; until I went into the sanctuary of God.'[55]

On Whit Sunday later that same year (1961) he looked back to the day when he had emerged from his Caesarea Philippi three-year crisis to find that his life had become meaningful. He had then said '*Yes* to Someone - or Something.' He remembered that, 'led by the Ariadne's thread of my answer through the labyrinth of life,' he came to a time and place where he realized 'that the Way leads to a triumph which is a catastrophe ... and that the only elevation possible to man lies in the depth of humiliation. After that, the word 'courage' lost its meaning,' since nothing could be taken from him. The more he journeyed on the Way, the more he discovered that behind 'every saying in the Gospels, stands *one* man and *one* man's experience.'[56] Tomorrow we shall meet, death and I, he had written at the beginning of *Markings*. Now he saw himself once more contemplating sacrifice:

> I have watched the others;
> Now I am the victim
> Strapped fast to the altar
> For sacrifice.[57]

Despite the political turmoil caused by the end of the colonial era, his Whit retrospection strikes a surprisingly peaceful note. It is as though life had been both opening up and closing down at the same time, Hammarskjöld always reverting to the expectation of coming sacrifice after an expression of faith and certainty.

In fact Hammarskjöld was within months of his death, so that this was a transition to his death as much as to his new way. Persons do not know when they will die, even those who are old and think that their death must come soon. It is always, to use Pope John's word and in his sense, a 'surprise', but very much more so when the person is comparatively young and healthy. The deaths of Hammarskjöld and King were unexpected, certainly premature, possibly arbitrary and yet not a complete surprise.

Dag Hammarskjöld felt that his vocation was to travel a way of sacrifice and Martin Luther King had always feared that he might be killed. Dag Hammarskjöld had become personally and politically isolated. He had come to know what desolation felt like and to understand what a vocation to sacrifice in the midst of a worsening political struggle could actually mean. He linked the darkness of suffering that was enveloping Africa, and was also so much a part of his own loneliness, to the Christian festivals and saw in the paradox of Brand's death the extent of the love of God in the midst of all affliction. He felt that in his living through Holy Week he was discovering the meaning of this in his own person. He had been greatly moved once to hear a scientist say that as far as he was concerned the universe could only be explained by love. This was hard to understand, he reflected, but he could discern it within the sanctuary of God. As he explained in his Whit retrospection he had found a new way.

In a strange way, both in the premature death of Dag Hammarskjöld, as in that of Martin Luther King, although both deaths were an outrage and a terrible loss, there was also a sense of completion about them. Even though they were so young, particularly Luther King, prior to the moment there were signs of coming passion and certainly after they had died meaning was not difficult to discern. Monica Furlong [58] writing about the last days of the mystic and prophet Thomas Merton on his final journey, described his death in an accident with a bedside lamp in an Asian hotel as in some sense a natural completion of his spiritual journey. Even tragic and early deaths acquire meaning within the mystery of life.

In contrast to the hidden nature of Hammarskjöld's pain, friends close to **Martin Luther King** knew all too well how exhausted he was and how depressed he had become. For the past twelve years, since December 1955 and the beginning of the Montgomery bus boycott, he had been working continuously in the Human Rights movement as Chair of SCLC, - major campaigns in Albany, Birmingham, St Augustine, Selma, Chicago plus everything else he was involved in – and it was taking its toll. Despite his distress, he was not deflected from his interior conviction that he must speak out about Vietnam. Reading of the effects of napalm attacks on children had especially disturbed him and after praying about it, and feeling that the fight for equality and the Vietnam war were connected, he felt he had no choice. '"A time comes,"' he said, quoting the words of those who had invited him to preach '"when silence is betrayal".'[59]

Three thousand people assembled in the great non-denominational Riverside church in New York to hear him deliver his most impassioned attack yet on the Vietnam War. The sermon is a devastating exposé of American foreign policy of the time and although his opinions now seem unexceptional, especially to a European ear, in the States then they were thought to verge on the treacherous. He told the congregation the war was draining the country of money which should be used for the poor, was taking poor blacks from their homes where they had few enough rights to join the whites in terrorizing the Vietnamese. The war was immoral, he said, and wrong. The sermon caused uproar and almost everyone was offended. '"I am giving most of my time to civil rights,"' he told one critic, '"The press gives all the publicity to what I say on Vietnam."'[60] There were very few, even friends, who had a good word to say to him. The best were that he had been unwise. The rest regarded him as a traitor. He began to doubt his beliefs and his depression became worse. By nature he was a lively soul and fun to be with, he liked bawdy jokes in the company of his friends and he had a gift for mimicry which made people roar with laughter. But now he was in torment. Had his work been effective? Was non-violence in fact the way forward? Was he on the right path? As it happened he preached the sermon on April 4th, 1967, which was precisely one year to the day before his assassination. Despite his fears he was ready to carry on in the face of his depression because it was his vocation and responsibility to do so.

He was still only 38 when he preached his Riverside sermon so that it was not surprising that he was still struggling with the temptations which he had found so hard to resist. 'When I delve into the inner chambers of my own being, I end up saying, "Lord, be merciful unto me, a sinner."'[61] he said in one of his sermons. He deplored people seeing him as a saint when he thought he was not.

Emotionally and physically he was by now fast approaching what many would describe today as burn out. His marriage was under severe strain, Coretta and he were hardly communicating and angrily when they were, he was desperately worried about the campaign and generally not far short of collapse; yet at the same time he was finding courage and strength to articulate his prophesies.

During this final year he came to Newcastle upon Tyne to receive an honorary degree from the University and the occasion was remembered by an international conference held here in 1993. He had been assured several times that he would not be required to speak but he was prevailed upon and the occasion was filmed, his quiet mellifluous words rolling out seriously and memorably to his delighted audience. But it is as if he was hardly there, as though his body was speaking while he was elsewhere. The event symbolized his predicament. He continued to preach his central message about love and non-violence and somehow found strength on each occasion to do so even when asked by his English North Eastern hosts, but he was drained.

His hope now was to compel the nation to consider the poor. He wanted to convict the United States of sin, by disrupting Washington by a huge pilgrimage of the poor. His vision had by now grown beyond political praxis and had become religious, a prophetic word from God to the world and in particular to achieve a spiritual goal in America. April 22nd was to be the day. "Now they may not respond. I can't promise that. But I do think we've got to go for broke this time,"[62] he argued to his unenthusiastic SCLC colleagues.

He served a short time in prison at the end of October for violating the Birmingham injunction, some of it in bed with a virus. Early in 1968 he holidayed in Acapulco with Ralph Abernathy. He felt very low. Seeing a rock by itself in the sea he began to sing *Rock of Ages cleft for me* as an act of faith in the midst of his dread of abandonment. Abernathy was thoroughly alarmed. Deenie Drew said that she thought of him as '"very, very lonely ..."'[63] Bayard Rustin and others of his friends, despite the reality of the dangers he faced felt he was deteriorating psychologically.

The next challenge was in Memphis. 22 black sewer workers had been sacked; could Dr King come and support their proposed strike? He arrived for March 18th, 1968, and again on March 28th, some of the marchers on this second occasion becoming violent. '"... Maybe we have to just give up and let violence take its course ... maybe it'll heed the voice of violence,"'[64] King was heard to say. He made arrangements to return later for a properly organized non-violent march.

On March 30th, King held a frank meeting with his staff about the Washington plans. '"Look,"' he told them, '"I'm not just getting *your* full support,"'[65] He left them to visit one of his women, while they thought about what he had said. They decided they must rally behind him.

On Passion Sunday (March 31st, 1968), only four days before he died, he preached in the Episcopalian (Anglican) Cathedral in Washington about his dream of a march on the city. He urged the congregation to open their eyes and see the enormity of the poverty around them, and then, drawing their attention to the Vietnam war said, 'This day we are spending five hundred thousand dollars to kill every Vietcong soldier - ... while we spend only fifty-three dollars a year for every person characterized as poverty-stricken in the so-called poverty program'. He added, 'which is not even a good skirmish against poverty.'[66] His vision at this point, growing while his physical and psychological strength was diminishing, was a universal one, of a nation which needed to be convicted by the radical problem of the poverty in its midst. His goal had at this point overtaken the means of bringing it about, the breadth of his vision taking leave of the practical end he was hoping to achieve, and this was part of the difficulty his team was having in supporting it. The anguish he suffered, the existential pain of prophesying to a world about injustice, which most people did not want to hear, was acute. Despite his youth, despite his problems, he held on through the affliction to a vision of a world coming together in justice.

Martin Luther King did fear that he might at any time be killed and as a sensitive soul was often very frightened. He was young, he still had personal issues to resolve, he had become depressed, partly through exhaustion and the sheer weight of his task, but more importantly, he still had much living to do. Yet there are these surprising signs of an end time, symbolized by his sermons and by his isolation and by his vision of a world become one in justice. The campaign he had led for so long had cost him dear but his vision had matured into a compassionate and universal vision and concern for the poor.

He too, like Dag Hammarskjöld, had aroused fierce opposition. Both their ways had led them to places where their vision of the goal had crossed with the almost impossible practicalities of the politics they grappled with. They were trying to steer reluctant communities towards a greater justice and righteousness and there were many who were stirred up to protest. The discreet and courageous way, and why the vocation of the politician is such a high one, leads eventually to a day when there is only one option left, the way forward being to remain faithful to the good vision however endangering it may be.

*   *   *

The three central features of the anointed way are anointing, thanksgiving and affliction. Each of the four persons – to start with anointing - lived in the strength of the Holy Spirit and as each contemplated the wonder of the love of God, his presence became more transparent within them. There is a greater peace, a stillness and serenity certainly in Iulia de Beausobre and Pope John, towards the end in Dag Hammarskjöld and even as his feelings of desolation grew, in the vision of unity of Martin Luther King. They had become persons with a greater insight and awareness and were alarmingly in touch with reality and the pain of others. Above all and in the Holy Spirit they were practising the twin fruits of love and humility.

Thanksgiving was very much at the heart of the older souls, Pope John and Iulia de Beausobre. They both knew themselves incorporate in Christ with the Eucharist as the centre of their prayer and Pope John would have warmed to Mother Theodosia's direction to Iulia on the nature of thanksgiving. Here was a woman in prison, her work as a superior of a community of sisters, in the normal sense of that word - she remained a mother to those around her in the prison - at an end and yet despite this inward and outward darkness she was still able to urge Iulia to build her heart into a tabernacle for thanksgiving. Thanksgiving is perhaps the single most important grace at the heart of Christian prayer.

In thinking of the third mark, the identification with affliction, all four, perhaps especially Martin Luther King were in touch with the pain of the world. Simone Weil used the word *malheur* to signify a suffering that 'takes possession of the soul and marks it through and through with ... the mark of slavery.' She said further that it was 'an uprooting of life, a more or less attenuated equivalent of death, made irresistibly present to the soul by the attack or immediate apprehension of physical pain,' and finally she said that it attacks the soul 'in all its parts, social, psychological and physical.'[67] Affliction is at the heart of the prayer which Jesus prayed in Gethsemane, an affliction which infused by a deep empathetic concern for the human condition reached out to the corporate distress and agitation of the world and yearned for its redemption. Physical fear is severe but far more terrifying is the exposure to mental pain, the cruelty and wretchedness of comprehending the mental anguish of the world which pierces like a sword to the heart. When the body is subjected to appalling physical pain it goes into shock to defend itself and basically shuts down. When the spirit is exposed to the bitterness of mental cruelty, the final defence is the mental disintegration of psychosis. Afflicted persons are those who expose their souls to the mental pain of others despite the risk of insanity. And this perhaps takes us to the heart of the spiritual vocation, that in Christ persons are invited to watch with him as he through them empathizes with the afflicted.

These then are the three marks of the anointed way from its harsh beginnings to the actual journey itself. To summarize the journeys of the four at the end of this chapter, for Iulia de Beausobre her transition to the anointed way had occurred in the Temniki woods camp hospital from which she was released into an alien world, living in various temporary places of accommodation in the environs of Moscow before she was able to escape to England. Some years later she was able to make her home at 60 the Grampians, in London. Angelo Roncalli had been in Venice and just as in his youth he had been summoned to Rome so he was again. After the Conclave he was never to leave Rome – apart from a visit to Assisi - again. Dag Hammarskjöld was in his later years at the UN in New York and his crisis took place between New York and Africa, New York remaining his base while he toured the world. Martin Luther King was also in New York, preaching his anti-Vietnam sermon there, continuing his constant travelling round the States, augmented by working holidays in the Caribbean and Mexico. He and his family continued to live in Atlanta.

This chapter has been about the penultimate crisis, which occurs towards the end of the way of the cross, usually but not always, as life draws towards its close. The crisis is inaugurated by a singular experience of desolation which only ends as souls become aware of the light of Christ enlightening their person with an anointing by the Holy Spirit. This gift of the Holy Spirit, together with thanksgiving and participation in affliction, which deepens empathy, are the marks of this final anointed way of the cross

Some years ago I was with a group of students considering whether it was possible to give thanks in the midst of suffering caused by bad and wicked events. Evil happenings are evil, however persons look at them, as is the cross and the bad things that led up to it. Nonetheless Christ inaugurated the Eucharist in the midst of such pain and whenever Christians gather they too give thanks whatever the circumstances. It is because God was active in Christ in the midst of evil and continues to be active through the Holy Spirit. The light shines in the darkness and God's love continues to reach out to anoint souls to be and to act within the wretchedness of evil and suffering. Only so may others come to know the full extent of his love and concern for his world.

The two piers at the mouth of the Tyne at Tynemouth. .

CHAPTER 8

THE FINAL ASCENT

Death and Resurrection

'See we are going to Jerusalem, and the Son of Man will be handed over to the chief priests and the scribes, and they will condemn him to death; then they will hand him over to the Gentiles; they will mock him, and spit upon him, and flog him, and kill him; and after three days he will rise again.' (Mark 10, 33-34)

> 'Tomorrow we shall meet,
> Death and I -,' Dag Hammarskjöld wrote
> 'And he shall thrust his sword
> Into one who is wide awake.' [1]

Like Isaac awaiting the strike of Abraham, Hammarskjöld was travelling a way which he expected to end in sacrifice, the natural conclusion he felt to the adamant young man's life of commitment. Similarly, but with less of a masochistic edge, Martin Luther King also thought he would die young. Once he was talking with the film director Abby Mann about a possible film of his life and Mann had asked him how it should end. '"It ends with me getting killed,"'[2] King had said, smiling.

The final crisis of the way is passion and death, passion being the passive events of the lead up to the moment of death and what lies beyond. 'Passion' is used here of this final stage advisedly because persons follow Christ in his passion, because it has several meanings to do with passivity before devastating events, intense self-giving in the act of making love as well as the acute suffering associated with the final days of life.

When I was working as a hospital chaplain, in 1970 I visited the comparatively new St Christopher's Hospice founded by the nurse and doctor, Cicely Saunders.[3] It was not a large building but inside it was spacious and airy, the nurses dressed in light Cambridge blue uniforms, children scampering about the corridors and in and out of wards, which was amazing to a chaplain coming from a traditional hospital. It bore out the words of another pioneer, Elizabeth Kübler-Ross who taught that those who care for the terminally ill should help them by encouraging them to live.[4] The hospices, which are now everywhere in the United Kingdom have not only provided high standards of care while pioneering new methods of palliative care, they have also had a powerful influence on the Health Service as a whole. The tragedy of the 'not telling' culture, which was so prevalent in the Sixties and still persists, was that the dying were afraid to voice their fears in case they distressed their carers while carers for their part were nervous of unsettling the sick person by sharing their grief. Loneliness and separation for both was the result, loved ones who had shared everything finding themselves unable to communicate, each person forced to bear their pain on their own. The hospice movement has restored a dignity to the process of dying which has done much to help Society adopt a new approach.

Passion begins as all the other crises have done after a preparation, this time on the way of the cross and beyond with an address, which alerts the soul to the fact, that he or she is approaching their death. Death is the 'liturgical' moment and resurrection beyond death is the new life. Of the four, only Pope John knew that he had a terminal illness. Martin Luther King and Dag Hammarskjöld both died suddenly, while Iulia de Beausobre suffered a series of multiple little strokes, which came after she had moved herself into a retirement home in Coulsdon. She knew as she became increasingly frail that she was nearing the end of her life. Pope John too was an old man, who had already had some twinges, which he feared might be serious, so that hearing the diagnosis did not disturb his peace too much.

It is different with younger people who learn that they are dying. Their coping with it has been well studied by Elizabeth Kübler Ross and others - their research, together with studies of bereavement, is illuminating also about the nature of human crisis in general.[5] Persons tend initially to disbelieve what they are being told, they become numbed or mentally anaesthetized by its enormity so that they cannot hear. It is like the initial absence of pain when a person is seriously injured. It gives persons time to gather themselves so that they might be a little more able to grasp what they are being told. Even then, many only cope by denying that there can be anything really wrong.

As things continue to get worse, the truth becomes increasingly hard to deny. Anger to others is a first response, such interior – or spoken – phrases as "Why is this happening to me?" "Why is there not a cure?" "What have I done to deserve this?" followed sometimes by an attempt at a bargain. "Is there anything I can do which will allow me a reprieve?" Increasing sadness leads to feelings of depression as the person struggles to come to terms with the dreadful reality.

It is usually the process of dying – for someone dying in the extended passion of Alzheimer's disease or one of the dementias especially, or the thought of agonizing physical discomfort - more than the actual prospect of death which frightens most though it varies from person to person. The need to talk about it is paramount.

There is always a moment in the midst of a crisis when both the dying person and the near relative – or whoever – both know intuitively through non-verbally listening that each needs to share with the other the important truth of a situation. It is similar in a therapeutic encounter, when there is a right time to speak and a right time to be silent, so listeners acquire a sensitive touch, a delicacy in relationship to know when it is appropriate to verbalize what needs to be spoken. This makes of the painful moment a creative and spiritual exchange[6] and with such loving support persons can embrace their truth and accept it in peace.

Medieval observers would have envied both Pope John and Iulia de Beausobre the time they had to prepare for their deaths. Both had time to ease themselves into their final preparation, the latter giving herself a long time to review her life and to work through those areas of suffering in the camps she had yet to integrate into her person. To die suddenly like Dag Hammarskjöld and Martin Luther King, without any time to prepare would have struck them as intolerably cruel, a contrast to the modern attitude, which views it as a mercy. This in itself shows how much persons dread the process and the actuality of death and how reluctant they are to prepare properly for it, though this could not be said of Dag Hammarskjöld and Martin Luther King both of whom had thought much about their death as an immediate possibility.

Returning to the allegory of the river Tyne, after it has reached the greater conurbation of Newcastle and Gateshead, representing here the new Jerusalem, the Saxons following their usual pattern of building where smaller burns (or streams) enter the main river, built a church where the Don enters the Tyne. There stands the remains of the great monastery of St Benedict Biscop and the Venerable Bede [7] – or at least St Paul's church does and it still has a window from the original date and some of the walls. It is not far from the mouth of the Tyne and the Tynemouth monastery which protects the headland. The symbolism here is of the place where souls begin their journey of passion before passing through the arms of the piers into the love of God beyond.

Ladislaus Boros[8] spoke of death as the moment of truth; the significant baptismal hour when what had been symbolized at baptism becomes a reality in the act of dying to the old life. The actual passing from death to life usually lasts about 24 hours, the soul lying naked before God as a ripe bodiliness ready to lose its materiality. The bodiliness reaches its zenith of physical fitness in the twenties, mental functions usually in the fifties or sixties depending on the type of mental thought, the spiritual climax is at the point of death, the moment of pure awareness of God. It is a profoundly moving liturgical moment, in my experience a meeting with angels ready both to receive and accompany the soul at 'this frontier of the unheard-of.'

*   *   *

When Christ invited each of his disciples to take up the cross and follow his way creatively regardless of the outcome the road does eventually reach its final end. Then the soul becomes passive in the last days or hours before the actual moment when life concludes. It was while Jesus was speaking on the third occasion in Gethsemane that Judas arrived with a party to arrest him. He was taken off for a hurried trial while all his friends and supporters fled, naked like the young man who ran away, leaving Jesus totally alone. The pretence of a political trial was about to begin and while Peter plucked up courage to come into the courtyard, it failed him when people began to identify who he was. (Mark 14,26-end)

Once convicted, Jesus was mocked and abused as a usurper, who had presumed to achieve power and had failed. After the abuse he was displayed to the people of Jerusalem, led through the streets to a place outside the town, 'a young man, adamant in his commitment', who had walked 'the road of possibility to the end without self-pity or demand for sympathy, fulfilling the destiny he has chosen. ... '[9]

He was crucified by hanging on a cross for three hours, a bodiliness tortured beyond feeling into affliction and disintegration, a spiritual being no longer able to comprehend that he had a Father; "My God, my God," Jesus cried out in the midst of his dereliction, "why have you forsaken me?" Mark simply says that there was a group of women watching from a distance. They watched too as he died and as his body was taken down from the cross and placed in Joseph's tomb. They thought it was the end. (Mark 15)

St Mark's description of the resurrection is spare. He says of the women who went to anoint Jesus's body that they were terrified to the point of catatonic stupor. It was not only that they were awed, but also that they were rendered speechless by a person telling them that Jesus had risen and they feared that they had seen God and that they would die. Life as they had known it had, so far as they could understand, ceased to be viable. It had not yet dawned upon them that something extraordinary might have occurred within the ordinary, that what Christ had promised might have become real, that they might be at the frontier of the unheard-of and beyond it, in a place where love and life were in actuality stronger than death. (Mark 16, 1-8)

When the passion which leads to death comes, the question put to every person is Jesus's response to the one put by the mother of the Boanerges brothers, Could her sons sit at his right hand and his reply, "Are you willing to be baptized with the baptism I am baptized with?"

Some 35 years after her imprisonment and 13 years since her second husband died, as she reached her 80th birthday (April 18th, 1973) **Iulia de Beausobre**, Lady Namier as she was by then, moved to a rest home for the elderly in Coulsdon on the Surrey North Downs. Two years before she had decided she must move somewhere where she would be cared for. She took with her a few books, mainly poetry, and settled into a sunny room equipped with a good mirror in which she could check her dress and makeup. She was now in the right place to prepare for her death, the only frontier which as she used to say, no one could avoid.[10] The depth of upheaval in her 30s meant that she did not need anything more than a quiet transition to a 'safe house' for her preparation for death.

As Lady Namier became weaker in the home at Coulsdon, the experiences she had suffered in her thirties surfaced once again in the stillness of her last years. She had to battle once more with the evil nightmares and flashbacks which she must have hoped had finally left her. She knew once again the fear she and Nicolay had felt as they lay together and talked in low voices in Samarkand. She lived again her fear-filled days in the silent corridors of the Lubyanka, seeing her jailors salivating at her door as they contemplated her abuse, and she felt again the terror of going mad in the Temniki woods camp, a victim of objectless cruelty and of how she had grabbed at prayer to calm herself and had been given peace in the presence of the Christ. She would have thought of that terrible night in the hospital when Nicolay was shot. Her life after that night and after Theodosia's words to her, as for so many such traumatized sensitive souls who have survived intense terror, was to live a resurrection life cast over by an afflictive shadow, terribly aware of the nature of crucifixion as she lived her resurrection.

When Una Kroll visited her, she found her "radiantly serene, despite considerable suffering from physical and I guess, mental weakness. Both she and I knew that she was "handing on something precious ... a capacity to use ... suffering as a prayer for the liberation of those under any kind of oppression be it physical sickness or societal imprisonment or constraint.""[11] Brian Frost remembers her as lonely, with a vital toughness. He recalls "an unrepeatable hour and a half with the 80-year-old saint who has so influenced me."[12]

She loved walking in the gardens where she would sit and be still and contemplate the symbolic significance of each flower. She remained the woman who could not die until the very end. Spiritually she was vibrantly alive for prayer and intercession, psychologically she still had to work through some of her unfinished suffering, physically she broke bones and as the years progressed had heart attacks or strokes, all of which slowly sapped her strength. She felt herself God's cripple whose body was disintegrating before her eyes, the various chemicals preparing to separate from her bodiliness as her person, growing into an ever deepening wisdom and wholeness, was prepared for life in God. 'When asked what she was doing, she replied, "walking forth to and fro in the world scouring it of evil." Una Kroll adds, "I believe that is what she did in union with Christ's continuing work of atonement until the eschaton comes – she did it by prayer which released her from the bondage of her physical state into the perfect freedom of the Body of Christ." She died quietly, as she felt persons should, 'like a ripe apple falling to the ground.'[13]

Angelo Roncalli, Pope John XXIII, was also nearing his 80th birthday in 1961. He made his retreat that year at Castel Gandalfo. He said he felt 'like St Martin, who "neither feared to die, nor refused to live,"' and that he was being called to a final obedience to drink from the chalice of Christ in the passion of his final days.[14] Fifteen months later, as part of his final preparations for the Vatican Council he withdrew to pray in the Torre San Giovanni, a tower he had had restored in the Vatican. The altar there, given by the Church in China, reminded him of the missionary calling of the Church. As he concluded his retreat on September 23rd, 1962 he learnt that he had cancer and that he probably had only about six months to live.

Pope John opened the Council on October 11th, 1962, some 2449 bishops attending together with observers from non-Catholic Churches in the front rows under the care of Cardinal Bea. In his opening speech Pope John spoke of his hope that the Council would be a celebration of faith and an opportunity to leap forward in understanding and proclaiming the faith. The Council, he declared, must not be a forum for condemnation.

Battle lines between traditionalists and radicals had scarcely been drawn when the world was suddenly shaken by the Cuba crisis and the possibility of nuclear war. Pope John was asked if he would help as an intermediary and his appeal, which seemed to stir Khrushchev, reached the pages of *Pravda*. Khrushchev announced his withdrawal on October 28th, the fourth anniversary of Pope John's election and followed it by presenting him with the Balzan prize for peace.

Pope John kept in the background of the Council, encouraging and intervening only when necessary. It was clear, as he closed the final session that he was not well. It was as if the pains of the world and the Church were tearing at his inside and it became especially painful when the critics rounded on him for publishing *Pacem in Terris*[15] the week before the Italian General Election. He had chosen the day of Christ's mandate to the disciples, Maundy Thursday (April 11th, 1963), because he wished to address the world, everyone of good will as he put it, as well as the Church and not just one Italian political party. The encyclical is a call to people to respect each other and to be sensitive to the rights of both men and women. It celebrates freedom wherever it is found and applauds the founding of the United Nations as an international forum for reconciling peoples in a world in which war can no longer be tolerated. As he introduced the encyclical he was in great physical pain, which became worse over Easter. It eased towards the end of Easter week and he was able to maintain his usual round of activities. He received the Balzan Peace prize in May in his private quarters, visited the President of Italy in the Quirinale Palace and spent long hours in prayer. His final Mass was on May 17th after which he was confined to bed. One of his last acts was to commend the beatification of Luigi Palazzola

On the feast of Pentecost the crowds gathered in St Peter's Square to pray as he lay dying. He rallied for another night, woke early on Whit Monday (June 23rd 1963) to say "Lord you know that I love you,"[16] and then towards the evening, as Cardinal Traglia was saying the final words of the mass – "Go, it is finished" – Angelo Roncalli died.

Things were much quieter now in the Congo for **Dag Hammarskjöld**, though the Katanga secession continued. Some Belgians had been sent home but little more had been achieved and officials in the field wanted some action. Hammarskjöld counselled caution, but unknown to him and while he was travelling to the Congo, an operation had been authorized and launched to end the Katanga secession. Militarily, Operation Morthor as it was called was a fiasco. Tshombe was allowed to escape; the official explanation that the UN had been responding to a fire was, so O'Brien insisted, a fabrication on Hammarskjöld's part to put a good explanation on a blatant act of aggression. Urquhart maintains that the UN in New York certainly had reports of a fire, but whatever the case, the UN's reaction had been imprudent. Hammarskjöld was in an awkward position but he was determined somehow to meet Tshombe, who was now in neighbouring Zambia, Northern Rhodesia as it was then. Arrangements were made for a meeting in Ndola.

Markings in its later pages is prayer and poetry. Hammarskjöld was tired and conscious that his work as Secretary-General was almost done. Close associates knew of his plans to resign as soon as the Congo crisis was resolved. Personally, he was finding relationships easier and translating Martin Buber's *Ich und du* [17] on his final journey was a symbol of this. He had met Buber in New York and then again in Jerusalem and both had been moved by the encounter. Loneliness was still integral to his vocation, but through his communion with God and his friendship with a few, he was feeling himself more whole. In his final entry in *Markings* he asked,

> 'Is it a new country? ...
> ... I begin to know the map
> And to get my bearings.' [18]

He boarded the plane at Kinshasa and travelled a very roundabout route to Ndola to avoid any danger of an attack by Katanga forces. There are those who thought he might have been the victim of a conspiracy, some papers coming to light at the South Africa Truth Commission in support of this in 1998, but the evidence is not strong. Many would have liked him dead, but the mundane truth is probably that the pilot misjudged the landing path to Ndola airport and tried to land too soon. He was not killed instantly. He died a few minutes later, his expression one of peace and fulfilment. The manner of Hammarskjöld's death fulfilled his deepest wish for a sacrificial death without any trace of self-aggrandisement. He had followed the adamant Christ to the end.

Martin Luther King was in contrast in considerable fear of being killed. Once, he had felt so low that he had missed a plane to give a talk in Louisiana. '"I get tired of going and not having any answers,"' he had told Coretta and she had replied: '"You mustn't believe that people are losing faith in you"' she said, '"there are millions of people who have faith in you and believe in you and feel that you are our best hope."' [19]

The threats on his life never stopped. The FBI still kept a close watch and some have suggested that the Bureau itself was responsible for his death. There were often times when he reflected with congregations what people might say after his death. 'I'd like for someone to mention that day,' he said, 'that Martin Luther King, Jr., tried to give his life serving others. I'd like for somebody to say that day that Martin Luther King, Jr., tried to love somebody.' [20]

On April 2nd, Martin and Ralph, together with Coretta and Juanita, had a quiet evening meal together before the men flew to Memphis the following day. He decided not to go to church for the evening meeting and had rung Coretta to say how pleased he had been with the day, but Ralph called to urge him to come. He had given his sermon about going to the mountaintop many times, but on this evening he preached it with a new intensity. 'Well, I don't know what will happen now ... I just want to do God's will. And he's allowed me to go up to the mountain. And I've looked over. And I've seen the Promised Land. ... I want you to know tonight', he said as he drew to his conclusion 'that we, as a people will get to the Promised Land. And I'm happy, tonight. I'm not worried about anything. I'm not fearing any man. Mine eyes have seen the glory of the coming of the Lord.'[21]

He returned to the hotel and slept well, though Abernathy disputes this[22] causing a frizzle of excitement with his last book, in which he wanted to emphasize that King was a human being with failings. On any account, the next morning he felt much better, cheerfully receiving his colleagues' reports on the day. It was as he was standing on the hotel balcony that a crack was heard. Martin Luther King had been shot. The time was 7.05pm on April 4th, 1968. The suddenness of his death meant that he had not had time to experience fear, which given his dread of it, was merciful.

The journeys of all four were now done. They had been baptized into the silent finality of death.

*   *   *

There was then a pause. After the initial shock of a death there is a space between the moment and the burial, in the West usually of a few days, in many other countries of less than a day. It allows people time to tell the story, to recall the memories, to contemplate the significance of what has happened before the completion of burial. Dag Hammarskjöld was buried in a grave in Uppsala, Martin Luther King in a catafalque in the middle of a lake next to Ebenezer Church in Atlanta, Pope John in St Peter's, Rome, where his embalmed body is still on view, and Julia Namier in London.

When Christ was buried the tradition has it that he went to rescue the souls of those who were bound in situations of hell, a theme picked up by Iulia de Beausobre in a paper she wrote on intercession.[23] She recalls the Christian tradition that Christ visited hell between his descent from the cross and the resurrection and sees him engaging there with the full extent of human horror – concentration camps, the Holocaust, the Gulag and the more recent genocides in Cambodia and Rwanda and Darfur, among forgotten persons, the mentally ill, those cut off from human relationship, souls in modern oubliettes. Christ blazed a trail, which Christian intercessors are to follow so that they can help when they know there is nothing practical that they can do. Intercession, she taught, begins with the descent into each person's personal hell, souls trusting that as Christ leads persons out of darkness so he will lead out those for whom they intercede. They are to watch and pray with them, to be a praying presence among them, to witness their anguish, giving their support by the level of their understanding; that each for whom they pray may find their own personal solutions within a corporate interdependence.

*   *   *

Then there is the mystery of Easter. Life and love are stronger than death and evil. As Martin Luther King, reflecting with the Ebenezer congregation about life beyond death said, 'Yes, Jesus, I want to be on your right side or your left side, not for any selfish reasons. ... I just want to be there in love and in justice and in truth and in commitment to others, so that we can make of this old world a new world.'[24]

Iulia de Beausobre had been released from prison to give a resurrection witness to the sufferings of many. There is something richly symbolic in Pope John's living through the entire Easter season until the day of the birth of the Church in the Holy Spirit before he was allowed to leave. Some years before his death, Dag Hammarskjöld had said that while he felt alone he had found 'the hard straight brutal answer' to be that 'in the One you are never alone, in the One you are always at home.'[25]

Angelo Roncalli, Dag Hammarskjöld and Martin Luther King were international figures and their deaths made international news. Iulia de Beausobre as befits a spiritual guide had a quieter parting. It may seem, when we have been thinking about such remarkable people that their example is far beyond what the rest of us can contribute. Some do live out their vocations on the international stage, others on the national, and others again in the local arena. In my last parish some of the people were large in the community, a former head teacher, a foreman in the Water Company, a St John's Ambulance chief officer, the local taxi driver, for all of them the church was packed to the doors for their funerals. Other lives were more hidden, a young boy battling courageously with a terminal illness, a dying mother worried about her child, a policeman dying in a swimming accident abroad, a woman taking five years to die from Alzheimer's disease, each of their vocations was no less important because they were played out on a local stage. Both groups of persons had the same type of funeral. At the end of the service we used to say together the *Nunc Dimittis,* Now Lord you let your servant go in peace. A Saxon nave – our church in Ovingham was Saxon - is short and as the priest leading the procession I always found I was just emerging from the open church doors as we reached the Gloria:

> Glory to the Father and to the Son and to the Holy Spirit,
> As it was in the beginning, is now and shall be for ever. Amen.

A moment of adoration with a soul at the threshold of the mystery of resurrection!

EPILOGUE

The Holy Spirit, the Lord and Giver of Life[1], who breathes fire into the heart, is the guide on the way of Christ. Nonetheless, personal difficulties do get in the way of discernment. It is the experience of the Church that the presence of Christ in another pilgrim is an invaluable help to persons who are struggling to find their way.

This book was written for such other pilgrims on the principle that souls who live and reflect on their own personal journeys are likely to be the best to help others on theirs. It will not be their task to prescribe a way even if they think they know what it is. They are there to listen, especially to the Holy Spirit, that the other may be able to discern his or her own particular path.

The temptation of any companion is to talk too much. You can observe the effect by looking for the bemused expression which settles like a veil over the face of the other. The work is to listen, to empathize, to attend to the presence of the Holy Spirit loving and guiding the other towards holiness and righteousness, to be present before the mystery of the other.

All this occurs whenever there is a meeting for spiritual conversation; the companion in Christ with the other in Christ together reflecting on what they might of the spiritual agenda. Sometimes such conversations happen spontaneously, like Martin Luther King talking with Harry Wachtel on a plane journey to London.[2] At other times it is by arrangement with someone especially called to the ministry like Iulia de Beausobre, who out of her experience and knowledge of persons could guide them to discern the way.

Knowledge of God opens the soul to knowledge of the self as Angelo Roncalli found in Bulgaria, when penitently confronting his truth before discerning his way of the cross. Knowledge of the self prepares the soul for knowledge of God as Dag Hammarskjöld also found when he was probing the deep springs of his soul to lay bare his truth and discovered he was at the frontier of the unheard-of.

The 21st century spiritual companion is a person of the way, disciplined by the parameters of his or her spiritual tradition, who prays and knows persons and is skilled in the art of being with them in their vulnerability. Formed by the Holy Spirit, spiritual companions and those they help will discern the way and in communion journey towards the ultimate goal.

GLOSSARY
FURTHER READING
NOTES
INDEX

GLOSSARY

Scientific words describing the human being are precise and analytical, theological and spiritual words tend to be metaphorical. 'Soul', 'spirit, 'person' are all metaphors of the human being in terms of different parts of the human body. In the course of the book these words are used fairly synonymously according to context.

Soul. (In Greek *psyche*, in Hebrew *nephesh*). It is a metaphor, like 'spirit' below, from an old Anglo-Saxon word for breath and it refers both to the whole being as a unity and to the core of the being. The soul is the life-breath, the self. In English 'soul' carries an undertow of meaning to do with transcendence; someone has 'soul'; is a person of spiritual character, is someone of depth especially in the arts. Note that St Paul contrasts persons who are *psychichos* (merely breathing beings) with those who are *pneumatichos* (spiritual beings) filled with Spirit as a result of their relationship with God.[1]

Heart.
(In Greek *cardia*, in Hebrew *leb) leb* occurs as many times in the Old Testament as *nephesh* (soul). Since the physical heart is more or less in the centre of the body it symbolizes the core or organizing centre of the soul, its mystery, its warmth; the inner life-blood as it were and character of the soul.

Person
(Latin, *persona*, Greek equivalent, *prosopon*) *persona*, 'per sonare' means to sound through. Both the Latin and Greek originals refer to the mask worn by actors on the classical stage and so to the underlying metaphor of the hidden soul behind the human face.. The Swiss doctor and psychologist Paul Tournier[2] used the word 'personage' to speak of the mask of the face protecting the inner person or heart from exposure. It is at moments of inner truth and prayer that the real person shines through the outer mask of the face.

A 'Person' of the Trinity translates a different Greek word *hypostasis* meaning something unique. The substance of the one God is referred to as *homoousios,* meaning much the same: three Persons and one God, the first word emphasizing the distinctions, the second what they hold in common.[3]

The concept of the person is first of all a theological idea, that God is personal. Personhood derives from the personhood of God.

Bodiliness

Body and Soul in their physical oneness; the Biblical writers speak of the person as a unity of body and soul. (The Greek word for body is *Soma*.. *Sarx* Greek *basar* Hebrew are usually translated 'flesh' meaning the physiological, animal body, see John 1,14) *Soma* refers to the human body in its oneness as a physical organism, hence Paul's description of the Church as 'the body of Christ.'[4] James Nelson[5] speaks of the soul as *embodied*, the Dutch philosopher C A Van Peursen[6] of *bodiliness*. Van Peursen's word, even though cumbersome, is preferred in the book because it expresses more completely the inherent oneness of body and soul. The soul is only apprehended through the body but to speak of the body as no more than a body is to say too little. The soul adds something more. The bodiliness is body and soul together.

Mind

(*nous* in the Greek The Greek Old Testament (LXX) sometimes translates the Hebrew *leb* by *nous*.). The word means 'mind', the intellectual, rational, reasoning faculty of the person.

Spirit

(*ruach* in Hebrew, *pneuma* in Greek) Literally, breath, the breath of life, spirit and breath being analogous words in both Hebrew and Greek and also in English. When the Lord God observed the inert body he had made[7] he breathed into its 'nostrils the breath of life (*ruach*); and the man became a living being (*nephesh*)', alive and conscious as a result of the address of God. Spirit is the heart of the soul, by which the person relates. From preconscious servitude to the instincts the bodiliness becomes personal through the Holy Spirit, capable of relationship with God and persons.

Emotions and Feelings

(Latin, *emovere*) Literally, to move; the person is moved to pleasure or pain by something which happens. The emotions register whether the happening is 'good' or 'bad', the metaphor referring to the physical sensations moving within which cause the feeling. Hormones are distributed round the body either by engaging the parasympathetic system, which affects the gut so that he or she feels the inwardly 'moved', churned up ('his bowels did yearn upon his brother' as the Revised version of the Bible has it, 'overcome with affection' in the New Revised Standard version[8]) or the sympathetic system that prepares the body for fight or flight. The word 'feeling' refers to the sense of touch, the touch of the hand for example.

A few psychoanalytic words:

Ego

Freud's word in the German was 'Ich', 'I', which when it was first translated into English was 'ego'[9] Freud meant the subject acting rationally and sensibly.

Id

'Das es' in the German, literally 'the it.' Freud thought of this 'it' or 'id' as the mass of disorganized instincts and passions which the child starts with at birth, the source of energy, of sexual libido. Some modern psychoanalysts have dispensed with 'id' on the grounds that human beings endow everything that concerns them however instinctive or chaotic with personal meaning.

Super-ego

Inner parental supervisors of the 'I' or ego. The child, according to analytic theory, introjects (takes into the self) the values and concerns it assumes are the parents' views and uses them unconsciously to control and civilize the wavering ego and indeed all else within.

One picture of the relationship of ego, super-ego and id is to compare them to a house, a sex mad crazed ape dwelling in the cellar (the id), a timid clerk on the ground floor (the ego) with a prim, proper and thoroughly correct aged relative in the attic (the super-ego) [10]

Object--Relations

The English psychoanalytic world is strongly influenced by the object-relations school of Freudian analysis - The London Tavistock clinic, the Scottish Institute of Human Relations etc.- which was developed by Melanie Klein, Ronald Fairbairn, Donald Winnicott, Harry Guntrip and their successors. Psychological research originally referred to both researcher and researched as 'subjects' so 'object' was introduced to refer to the other, the one related to. Originally it referred to the child as subject relating to the mother as object. 'Objects' usually refers to persons, or part persons or symbols of persons who as it were dwell within or outside the person to whom the subject relates consciously and unconsciously.[11]

Self

Psychoanalysis studies the person from the point of view of his or her individuality or self relating to others. Self is therefore the word of choice of analysts and psychologists when describing the whole being. It refers also to the capacity of the bodiliness to organize the different parts and aspects of the being into a coherent whole or 'self'. The self is subject (an 'I' when speaking of the self) and object ('me' - when studying the self.) The whole being is the self.[12]

Narcissism/Schizoid.

(*schizein* –Greek meaning to split, *oidos* – shape or form) a splitting or cleaving apart of the heart. It describes such a severe experience of being out of relationship that the person withdraws into isolation and loneliness, like the mythical Narcissus.[13] Narcissus was so absorbed by his own reflection he could not hear the woman who was trying to communicate with him so that she eventually became a mere Echo. Narcissism is a metaphor for the person who is cut off from relationship with God and anyone else.

Container/Contained

The capacity a mother or mother substitute to know her child's feelings and to 'hold' or 'contain' them whatever they are without being overwhelmed by them W.R. Bion was the first to use the word in this sense.[14]

When a child is hurt and runs to mother, she hears and feels and suffers the pain and anxiety without herself becoming distressed. She contains the chaos of feelings and by her calm understanding transforms them so that they can be borne and thought about and reflected upon A therapist similarly contains the pain of a disturbed person.

FURTHER READING

IULIA de BEAUSOBRE (Iulia Mikhailovna Kazarin, Lady Julia Namier)

The only biography that I know of is **Iulia de Beausobre, a Russian Christian in the West** (DLT 1983) by Constance Babington-Smith, who kindly invited me to tea in her Cambridge home when this study was in its infancy. There is also a chapter (pages 238 - end) in Ved Mehta's account in **Fly and the Fly-Bottle** (Columbia University Press 1963). She features of course in her own biography of her second husband **Lewis Namier** (Oxford University Press 1971), which she wrote as Julia Namier. **Namier** (Weidenfeld & Nicolson 1989) by Linda Colley has a few references to her.

Iulia de Beausobre's own account of her imprisonment, **The Woman who could not die,** was one of the first books written about the Russian terror. The first edition was published by Chatto and Windus in 1938, a second by Gollancz (1948). **Creative Suffering** was first published by Dacre Press in 1940, by SLG Press in 1984. Her book on Serafim of Sarov, **Flame in the Snow** was originally published by Constable in 1945 and was reissued in a Fount edition in 1979. **Macarius, Starets of Optino, Russian Letters of Direction 1834-1869** was published by Dacre Press in 1944 and then by Vladimir Seminary Press, Cassell in 1975. At the end of her life she was working on a final book about the kingdom, based on Dostoievski's Aliosha from 'The Brothers Karamazov'. Some notes entitled **Alyosha's Way** are included in the Babington-Smith biography, 153-171. She published a number of articles. Her important 1967 paper on intercession, **The Expanding Universe of Intercession** appeared in *Theoria to Theory*. Some of her articles for *Time and Tide* are listed in Constance Babington-Smith's book. At the time of Russia's entry into the Second World War she wrote three articles for *Sobornost*, **The New Catacombs** (June 1941, 4-11), **The Other Russia** (June 1942, 3-8) and **Prayer and Personality** (December 1942, 14-16). She was a friend of Sir John Lawrence and contributed to his journal *Frontier*: **A letter from the Only Frontier** is in Volume 17, No 4 (Winter 1974/5) pp217-220.

To read her story as a continuous narrative the pages are as follows:

Childhood & Adolescence	25-28
Young adulthood	63-66
Caesarea Philippi	87-88
Way of the Cross	125-127
Anointing	138-144
Passion and Death	165-166

DAG HAMMARSKJOLD

The major and official biography is **Hammarskjöld** (Bodley Head 1973) by Brian Urquhart, Under-Secretary at the United Nations with Dag Hammarskjöld. Sir Brian Urquhart's study is re-visited in his autobiography **A Life in Peace and War** (Weidenfeld & Nicolson 1987). **Dag Hammarskjöld, a Biographical Interpretation of Markings** (Faber 1967) was written by the former President of Union Theological Seminary, New York, Henry P Van Dusen and includes charts at the end, which relate the events of Hammarskjöld's life to different sections of **Markings** (Faber 1964). There is a useful chapter (152-171) on Hammarskjöld's friendship with Martin Buber in **Encounter with Martin Buber** (Penguin 1972) by Aubrey Hodes. A collection of photographs is **Hammarskjöld, a pictorial biography** (Thames & Hudson 1962) by Sten Söderberg.

Hammarskjöld describes **Markings** as a sort of 'White Book' concerning my negotiations with myself – and with God.' It was translated by W H Auden and Leif Sjöberg with an introduction by Auden. Auden did not know Swedish, so the commentary, **Dag Hammarskjöld's White Book, an analysis of Markings** (SPCK 1970) by the Swedish theologian and bishop, Gustaf Aulén is invaluable. Wilder Foote collected a selection of Hammarskjöld's lectures and writings in **Dag Hammarskjöld, Servant of Peace** (Harper & Row 1962) and there is an account of Hammarskjöld's visit to Nepal and his photographs in National Geographic (January 1961, 87-93), **New Look at Everest.**

To read his story as a continuous narrative the pages are as follows:

Childhood & Adolescence	31-33
Young adulthood	70-72
Caesarea Philippi	89-93
Way of the Cross	114-119
Anointing	149-154
Passion and Death	167-168

MARTIN LUTHER KING Jr

The outstanding biography, and account of the Human Rights movement, is **Bearing the Cross, Martin Luther King Jr, and the Southern Christian Leadership Conference** (Jonathan Cape 1988) by David Garrow. A more popular biography is **Let the Trumpet Sound** (Search Press 1982) by Stephen Oates. Coretta Scott King's reflections are in **My Life with Martin Luther King Jr** (Holt, Rinehart & Winston 1969). There is even a new comic book biography, **King** by Ho Che Anderson (Fantagraphics Book 2005). **The Life of Rosa Parks, Mine Eyes have seen the Glory** (Weidenfeld & Nicolson 2000) by Douglas Brinkley, is illuminating about Montgomery at the time of the boycott and what it incidentally reveals about Dr King. **Martin & Malcolm & America** (Fount 1991) is an interesting comparison and appreciation of Malcolm X and Martin Luther King by James H Cone. A recent study of the influences on Martin Luther King's theology, with a foreword by Coretta King, is **Martin Luther King Jr, Spirit-led Prophet** (New City 1999) by Richard Deats. On Afro-Caribbean spirituality, see **The Negro Church in America** (Shocken Books 1974, 1st published 1963).

An invaluable compendium of King's writings is **A Testament of Hope** (Harper & Row 1986) by James Melvin Washington. It is in two parts, part 1 the philosophical writings and part 2 his sermons, addresses and extracts from his books. The first of these latter was his account of the Montgomery boycott, **Stride Towards Freedom, a leader of his people tells the Montgomery Story** (Harper & Row 1958). This was followed by a collection of sermons, **Strength to Love** (Hodder 1963). **Why we can't wait** (Harper & Row 1963) is an argument for human rights built around the Birmingham campaign and includes his letter from Birmingham jail. **Where do we go from here: Chaos or Community?** (Harper & Row 1967) is a polemic arguing for the value of non-violent methods in the face of the rise of black power. **The Trumpet of Conscience** (Hodder 1967) is a collection of sermons given in the last year of his life on Canadian Radio.

To read his story as a continuous narrative the pages are as follows:

Childhood & Adolescence	34-38
Young adulthood	66-67
Caesarea Philippi	84-87
Way of the Cross	104-114
Anointing	154-157
Passion and Death	168-170

ANGELO GUISEPPE RONCALLI (Pope John XXIII)

The major biography in English is **John XXIII, Pope of the Council** (Geoffrey Chapman 1984) by Peter Hebblethwaite. Of early works there is **The Heart and Mind of John XXIII** (Corgi 1964) by his secretary from Venice days, Loris Capovilla. The most useful early biography is Meriel Trevor's **Pope John** (Macmillan 1967). A popular work is Lawrence Elliott's **I will be called John** (Collins, Fontana 1976) and there is also Paul Johnson's **Pope John XXIII** (Hutchinson 1975). **John XXIII, a pictorial biography** by Eric Pecher (Thames and Hudson 1969) is a useful collection of photographs and there is an anthology of stories in **The wit and wisdom of Good Pope John** (Harvill Press 1964) collected by Henri Fesquet.

Peter Hebblethwaite includes a comprehensive and annotated bibliography with details of the Italian editions of Roncalli's life study of St Charles Borromeo's visitation of his diocese. **Journal of a Soul,** translated by Dorothy White (as are all the books mentioned in this paragraph), was originally published by Geoffrey Chapman in 1965. A revised edition, to which the notes refer, was published with a new introduction in 1980. Roncalli wrote an appreciation of his bishop. **My Bishop, a portrait of Mgr G M Radini Tedeschi** (Geoffrey Chapman 1969) after Radini's premature death and there are also collections of Roncalli's papers, **Mission to France** and more personally, **Letters to his Family 1900-1963** (Geoffrey Chapman 1970)

To read his story as a continuous narrative the pages are as follows:

Childhood & Adolescence	38-41
Young adulthood	67-70
Caesarea Philippi	93-95
Way of the Cross	119-125
Anointing	144-148
Passion and Death	166-167

NOTES

After a first mention references are by author and date. Russian spellings are those of Iulia de Beausobre. Biblical references are to the New Revised Standard Version.

Preface

1   Frost, Brian 2002 *Poems of Grief and Glory* 27 Sliphatch Road, Reigate, Surrey: New World Publications. 71.

2   Washington, James M ed. 1986. *A Testament of Hope, the essential writings of Martin Luther King Jr.* San Francisco: Harper & Row.

3   Beeson, Trevor 1963. *New Area Mission.* London: A R Mowbray.   The book describes the work of the parish of St Chad and St James, Stockton-on-Tees.

4   Hammarskjöld, Dag. 1964 *Markings.* London: Faber & Faber

5   Pope John XXIII. 1980. *Journal of a Soul.* 2nd ed. London: Geoffrey Chapman.

6   Portsmouth, William, 1954 *Healing Prayer with daily prayers for a month.* Evesham: Arthur James

7   Lake, Frank. 1966 *Clinical* Theology. London: Darton, Longman & Todd   For a shorter, reduced edition see Yeomans, Martin 1986 *Clinical Theology – Frank Lake abridged.* London: Darton, Longman & Todd . and Christian, Carol., ed. 1991 *In the Spirit of Truth, a reader in the work of Frank Lake,*. London: Darton, Longman & Todd.   The Clinical Theology Association is now called the Bridge Pastoral Foundation.

8   Hazell, Jeremy. 1996. *H J S Guntrip, a psychoanalytical biography.* London: Free Association Books. The biography is built round the detailed notes Guntrip kept of his analyses with W R D Fairbairn and D Winnicott. See also Hazell, Jeremy., ed. 1994 *Personal Relations Therapy: The Collected Papers of H J S Guntrip.* New Jersey: Jason Aronson.   Guntrip, H J S. 1949. *Psychology for Ministers and Social Workers.* London: Independent Press and Guntrip, H J S 1970 *Your Mind and your Health.* London: Allen & Unwin

9   Lambourne, R A. 1963. *Community Church and Healing.*   London: Darton, Longman & Todd.   Wilson, Michael 1960 *The Church is Healing.*   London: SCM.

Chapter 1 – Summons to the way

1   Galatians 6, 2

2   Hooker, Morna D, 1991. *The Gospel According to St Mark.*   London: A & C Black.   Reference is also made to Nineham, D E, 1965. *The Gospel of St Mark.* London: Pelican Gospel Commentaries.

3   Address - Mark, 1, 1-8 cp Matthew 3, 1-12 Luke 3, 1-17 and John 1,19-28. Baptism - Mark 1, 9-11 cp Matthew 3, 13-17 Luke 3, 21-22 and John 1, 29-34. Engagement - Mark 1, 12-13 cp Matthew 4, 1-11 Luke 4, 1-13.

4   Hooker, Morna D, 1991. 51

5   Mark 1,35 Jesus prays in a solitary place. 2, 23-28 the incident in the cornfield, 6,31 & 6,31-44 the disciples and Jesus go to a solitary place and the 5000 are fed. 6,46 Jesus goes up the mountain to pray. 8,4 & 8,1-9 The disciples are in a deserted place & the feeding of the 4000. 8, 14-21 discussion about the significance of the feedings. Cp also 5, 1-20, the healing of the man who lived among the graves.

6   Mark 2, 26. See I Samuel 21,26. Mark has the name of the priest wrong. Abiathar was the son of Ahimelech. Hooker 1991. 103

7   John 1, 35-end.

8   Hooker, Morna D, 1991. 8

9   De Beausobre, Iulia, 1977, *Flame in the Snow* London, Collins 126-127

10 Rowan, John, 2004   *Three Levels of Therapy* Counselling and Psychotherapy Journal (CPJ) November. 20-22.

11 Pseudo-Dionysius 1987. The Ecclesiastical Hierarchy *In* Luibheid, Colin, 1987. *Pseudo-Dionysius, the Complete Works.* New York: Paulist.   235 paragraphs 504B & C.

12 Bloom, Anthony, 1966. *Living Prayer.* London: Darton, Longman & Todd). Chapter 2

13 Archer, David 1992 *Land of Singing Waters* Stocksfield, Northumberland: Spredden Press & Archer, David, 2003 *Tyne and Ride, a Celebration of the River Tyne,* Ovingham, Northumberland: Daryan Press. See also Thornton, Ron 2002, *The River Tyne, from sea to source* Newcastle upon Tyne: Zymurgy Publishing.

Chapter 2 – The child addressed

1   Psalm 139, parts of verses 13, 14 and 16.

2   See Winnicott, D W, 1964. *The Child, the Family and the Outside World.* London: Penguin. 20-21. The mother and her infant have knowledge of each other before birth. See also *Life before Birth* 2005, TV Channel 4, April 7.

3   Erikson, Erik H, 1965. *Childhood and Society.* London: Pelican. Chapter 7, 239-266

4   Fowler, James W, 1981. *Stages of Faith: the Psychology of Human Development and the Quest for Meaning.* New York: Harper & Row. Ch. 16, 122-134. See also Astley, Jeff & Francis, Leslie, ed. 1992. *Perspectives on Faith Development.* s.l. Eerdmann   See also Jacobs, Michael, 1988. *Towards the Fullness of Christ, Pastoral Care and Christian Maturity..* London: Darton, Longman & Todd.   Jacobs quotes L Kohlberg's summary of Fowler's understanding of faith as 'people's orientation to the ultimate environment in terms of what they value as being most relevant and important to their entire lives.' 58.

5   Wilber, Ken, 2nd ed. 1996 *The Atman Project, a transpersonal view of Human Development* Wheaton, Illinois: Quest Books. See also West, William, 2000. *Psychotherapy & Spirituality* London: Sage. Chapter 6, 75-99.

6   Christian, Carol ed 1991. 43-50

7   Heard, Dorothy, Lake Brian, 1997. *The Challenge of Attachment for Caregiving.* London: Routledge, 27. For attachment theory see 'Bowlby, John, 1979. *The*

Making and Breaking of Affectional Bonds. London: Tavistock and Bowlby, John 1988. *Our Secure Base: Clinical Application of Attachment Theory.* London: Routledge. See also *Attachment, three educational videos.* By Richard Bowlby, free with s.a.e. from Boundary House, London NW11 7JB.

8 Heard, D & Lake B, 1997. 27

9 Berger, Peter, 1963 *Invitation to Sociology* London, Penguin 117.

10 Brian Lake and Murray Leishman, two psychotherapists confirmed this story but were unable to supply a reference. See also Newton, Michael, 2002. *Savage Girls and Wild Boys, a history of Feral Children.* London: Faber and Faber & Gregory, Richard L., ed. 1987. *The Oxford Companion to the Mind* Oxford: Oxford University Press. 57-58. See article on 'attachment, which discusses the relevant studies of K Lorenz and Harlow.

11 Song of Songs 2, 8-9

12 Song of Songs 2,16

13 Erikson, Erik H, 1958. *Young Man Luther.* London: Faber & Faber. See also Osborne, John, 1961. *Luther.* London: Faber & Faber. The play is based on Erikson's study. See also Erikson, Erik H, 1968. *Identity, Youth and Crisis.* London: Faber & Faber.

14 Picken, Gerda, 1992, Away with the Fairies *The Observer* Feb 16,

15 Erikson, Erik H. 1965. 254

16 Babington Smith, Constance, 1983. *Iulia de Beausobre, a Russian Christian in the West.* London: Darton, Longman & Todd. 7-8

17 Hosking Geoffrey, 2001. *Russia and the Russians, a history from Rus to the Russian Federation.* London: Allen Lane, the Penguin Press. 366

18 Babington-Smith, C, 1983. 11

19 Babington-Smith, C 1983. Photograph 13 between 132 & 133

20 Tournier, Paul, 1983. *A Doctor's Case Book in the Light of the Bible..* London: Highland Books.57. The book was originally published by SCM in 1954.

21 Siirala, Martti, 1969. *Medicine in Metamorphosis.'* London: Tavistock and Siirala, Aarne, 1964. *The Voice of Illness* s.l.: Fortress Press. They were brothers, the first a doctor specializing in speech disorders, the second a theologian.

22 CIBA Foundation, 1972. *Physiology, Emotions and Psychosomatic Illness.* London: Associated Scientific Publishers. Symposium No.8 (New Series).

23 Foote, Wilder, ed. 1962. Servant of Peace, A Selection of the Speeches and Statements of Dag Hammarskjöld, Servant of Peace, Secretary-General of the United Nations 1953-1961. New York: Harper & Row. 23.

24 Van Dusen, Henry P, 1967. *Dag Hammarskjöld, a Biographical Interpretation of 'Markings'.* London: Faber & Faber. 16-17.

25 Hammarskjöld, Dag, 1964. 152

26 Hammarskjöld, Dag, 1964. 150

27 Urquhart, Brian, 1973. *Hammarskjöld.* London: Bodley Head. 36

28 Aulén, Gustaf, 1970. *Dag Hammarskjöld's White Book, an analysis of 'Markings'.* London: SPCK. 140 Bishop Aulén (see page vi) sometimes gives an alternative reading for W H Auden's translations of particular markings - noted at the relevant points.

29 Hammarskjöld, Dag, 1964. 7
30 Hammarskjöld, Dag, 1964. 7
31 Hammarskjöld, Dag, 1964. 31
32 Söderbeg, Sten, 1962. *Hammarskjöld, a pictorial biography.* London: Thames & Hudson. 28-30
33 Van Dusen , Henry P, 1967. 55
34 Christian, Carol. ed. 1991. 50-62.
35 King Jr, Martin Luther, 1958. *Stride Towards Freedom, a leader of his people tells the Montgomery Story.* New York: Harper & Row. 19
36 Oates, Stephen B, 1982. *Let the Trumpet Sound, The Life of Martin Luther King, Jr.* London: Search Press. 12
37 Oates, Stephen B, 1982. 12
38 On the first occasion Martin thought he had killed his grandmother when he slid down the banisters and hit her at the bottom of the stairs, see Oates, Stephen B, 1982. 8-9. The second occasion was after she died See Garrow, David J. 1988. 35
39 Garrow, David J, 1988. *Bearing the Cross, Martin Luther King Jr. and the Southern Christian Leadership Conference.* London: Jonathan Cape 39
40 Garrow, David J, 1988. 40-41
41 King, Coretta Scott, 1969. *My Life with Martin Luther King, Jr.* New York: Holt, Rinehart and Winston. 50-55. The quotation is from 55.
42 Hebblethwaite, Peter 1984. *John XXIII, Pope of the Council* London: Geoffrey Chapman. 10
43 The practice of carrying popes on a raised papal chair was abandoned by Pope John Paul I
44 Trevor, Meriel, 1967. *Pope John.* London: MacMillan. 10
45 Pope John XXIII, 1980. 4-12.
46 Pope John XXIII, 1980. 40
47 Pope John XXIII, 1980. 47
48 Pope John XXIII, 1980. 44
49 Pope John XXIII, 1980. 25-26
50 Pope John XXIII, 1980. 28
51 Pope John XXIII, 1980. 49
52 Pope John XXIII, 1980. 59 & 60
53 Pope John XXIII, 1980. 82
54 See Hebblethwaite, Peter, 1984. 23-24
55 Pope John XXIII, 1980. 88
56 Pope John XXIII, 1980. 113
57 Pope John XXIII, 1980. 157
58 Pope John XXIII, 1980. 157
59 Pope John XXIII, 1980. 170
60 Pope John XXIII, 1980. 172

Chapter 3 – Discipline and Training

1 Methodist Conference Office 1974. *The Covenant Service.* D1

2 Ganss SJ, George E, 1992. *The Spiritual Exercises of Saint Ignatius, a translation and commentary.* Chicago: Loyola Press. 32, section 23, Principle and Foundation.

3 Methodist Conference Office 1974. *The Covenant Service.* D10. See also Central Board of Finance of the Church of England, 1991. *The Promise of his Glory.* London: Church House Publishing & Mowbray. 220. This Anglican adaptation refers particularly to baptism.

4 Nineham, D E, 1965. 73ff

5 1 Corinthians 7,5. See also Cervantes, Ferdinando, 2002. The Lost Art of Leisure. *The Tablet* July 13.

6 Von Hügel, Friedrich, 1927. *The Life of Prayer.* London: Dent 30-33.

7 Kirk, Kenneth Escott 1955. *Beauty and Bands and other papers prepared by E W Kemp, a collection of addresses given by the Bishop of Oxford.* London: Hodder & Stoughton..

8 Hammarskjöld, Dag, 1964. 31

9 Pope John XXIII, 1980. 4-12. The 'Little Rules' of Ascetic Life, as they were given to students, are in Appendix 1, 427-434

10 Pope John XXIII, 1980. 7.

11 Pope John XXIII, 1980. 182

12 Pope John XXIII, 1970. *Letters to his Family 1901-1963.* London: Geoffrey Chapman. 768-769

13 Hammarskjöld, Dag, 1964. 24. From the foreword by W H Auden

14 Garrow, David J, 1988. 241-242

15 The Jesus Prayer is a compilation of the prayer of Bartimaeus (Mark 10, 47) and the Publican's prayer (Luke 18, 13). See also French, R M, 1954. *The Way of a Pilgrim The Pilgrim continues his way.* London: SPCK.

16 Babington Smith, Constance1983. 166ff.

17 Hawkins, David G, 1982 *In* Burnout – Occupational Hazard: Description and Prescription, quoting from Evans, R W, 1842. *The Bishoprick of Souls.* London: Hospital Chaplains Magazine, Church House.

18 Hebblethwaite, Peter, 1984. 240. See also the note in the bibliography. 506

19 Hebblethwaite, Peter, 1984. 108. See also Trevor, Meriel 1967. 147

20 De Beausobre, Iulia, 1940. 13-14.

21 Pope John XXIII, 1970. 381

22 Pope John XXIII 1980. 255. see also Pope John XXIII, 1970. 385

23 Namier, Julia, 1971. *Lewis Namier, a biography* Oxford: Oxford University Press 320

24 Taizé, 1965. *The Rule of Taizé in French and English.* London: Faith Press, Les Presses de Taizé. 132-134.

25 Ind, Jo, 2003. *Memories of Bliss: God, sex and us.* London: SCM Press

26 Hebblethwaite, Peter, 1984. 182

27 Pope John XXIII, 1970.

28 Ind, Jo, 2003. 56

29 Anderson, Digby, 2002. *Losing Friends.* London: Social Affairs Unit. 19 and 25.

30 Aelred of Rievaulx, 1977. *Spiritual Friendship.* Michigan: Cistercian Publications. See also Carmichael, E D H (Liz) 2004. *Friendship, Interpreting Christian Love.* London: T & T Clark International. Ch 3.

31 Namier, Julia, 1971. 131

32 Garrow, David J, 1988. 375

33 Oates, Stephen B, 1982. 283

34 See Garrow, David J, 1988. 617

35 Dicks, H V, 1967. *Marital Tensions.* London: Routledge & Kegan Paul.

36 Garrow, David J, 1988. 374. The FBI letter 373 Issue discussed 373-378. The Willard Hotel incident 310.

37 Garrow, David J, 1988. 375

38 King Jr, Martin Luther, 1969. *Strength to Love.* London: Collins/Fontana. 115

39 Philippians 3, 13-14

40 Health & Healing Summer 1984. 1 & 4. The doctor was Dr Peter Nixon of the Charing Cross Hospital.

41 See Deuteronomy 6, 4-9. The Jewish confession of faith

42 Townroe, John 1992 *Somerset Ward Memorial Lecture to mark the 30th anniversary of his death.'* Guildford: Cathedral Office. 6. There is a relief sculpture of Reginald Somerset Ward on the West Front of Guildford Cathedral. See also Goodacre, Kathleen, 2003, *NWG, Priest, Counsellor, Friend.* Newcastle: Leighton Counselling Services. 36-38.

Chapter 4 – Clambering in the foothills

1 Chatwin, Bruce, 1998. *The Songlines* Vintage: London 180.

2 King Jr, Martin Luther, 1969. 37

3 Mark 1,13

4 Pope John XXIII, 1980. 262

5 De Beausobre, Iulia, 1979. 93

6 The psychotherapist was Elizabeth Templeton, who spoke about it in a lecture noted in *The* Tablet, the date of which has proved untraceable.

7 'Contain' – the word is used technically, see Glossary.

8 Babington Smith, C, 1983. 20

9 Babington Smith, C. 1983. 182-183

10 Irina Prehn, a Russian emigré living in Edinburgh, who had been a friend of both the Brunis and Iulia de Beausobre, told me this and other stories.

11 Babington Smith, C, 1983. 24

12 A story from Irina Prehn.

13 King, Coretta Scott, 1969. 50

14 Deuteronomy 24,5

15 See for example, Harper, Lee 1960. *To Kill a Mocking Bird.* London: Heinemann

16 Pope John XXIII, 1969. *My Bishop a portrait of Mgr Giacomo Maria Radini Tedeschi.* London: Geoffrey Chapman. 82

17 Pope John XXIII, 1980, 189

18 Roncalli, Angelo Guiseppe (Pope John XXIII), 1966. *Mission to France 1944-1953.* London: Geoffrey Chapman. 178. Roncalli spoke of his debt to Radini

Tedeschi in his speech of thanks to President Auriol of France on receiving the cardinal's biretta from him. 178-180.

19 Pope John XXIII, 1980. 206
20 Pope John XXIII, 1980. 209
21 Hebblethwaite, Peter, 1984.101
22 Pope John XXIII, 1970. 53
23 Pope John XXIII, 1980. 212
24 Pope John XXIII, 1970. 70
25 Pope John XXIII, 1980. 218
26 Pope John XXIII, 1980. 220
27 Hammarskjöld, Dag, 1964. 85
28 Hammarskjöld, Dag, 1964. 127-128
29 Hammarskjöld, Dag, 1964. 34
30 Hammarskjöld, Dag, 1964. 37
31 Hammarskjöld, Dag, 1964. 35
32 Hammarskjöld, Dag, 1964. 38
33 Hammarskjöld, Dag, 1964. 39-48
34 Hammarskjöld, Dag, 1964. 40
35 Hammarskjöld, Dag, 1964. 36
36 Balint, Michael, 1968. *The Basic Fault, therapeutic aspects of regression.* London: Tavistock. For information about Pavlov's study of the behaviour of dogs, which underlies the modern understanding of hearts breaking and the aetiology of narcissism. see Gregory, Richard L., ed. 1987. 574-576
37 Hammarskjöld, Dag, 1964.54
38 Foster, Kenelm, Ronayne, Mary John, ed. 1980. *I Catherine, Selected Writings of Catherine of Siena* London: Collins 151.
39 King Jr, Martin Luther, 1969. 126
40 King Jr, Martin Luther, 1969. 136
41 Pope John XXIII, 1980. 262
42 Brown, Peter, 1967. *Augustine of Hippo.* London: Faber & Faber. 200
43 Pope John XXIII, 1980 294
44 King Jr, Martin Luther, 1969. 48
45 Hammarskjöld, Dag, 1964. 110
46 Namier, Julia, 1971. 251. See also De Beausobre, Iulia, 1967. The Expanding Universe of Intercession. *Theoria to Theory.* 50-51.
47 King Jr., Martin Luther, 1969. 125-126
48 Pope John XXIII, 1980. 259
49 Pseudo-Dionysius 1987
50 Mark 2, 17
51 Hazell, Jeremy 1996. See also Hazel, Jeremy 1994, 351-369.

Chapter 5 – Cairn encounters.

1 Erikson, Erik H. 1965. 258. See also Erikson, Erik H. 1969, *Gandhi's Truth.* London: W W Norton . A study of mid-life crisis in the life of Gandhi.
2 Fowler, James W, 1981.

3   Wilber, Ken, 1996, 38.

4   Wilber, Ken 1996, Chapter 7, 53-72

5   Wilber, Ken, 1996, Chapter 6, 43-52

6   Burkin, Nancy, 1989. The Discovery of the Astonishing in the Common. *The Way*. Volume 29, July No.3 207ff

7   Koestler, Arthur 1966 *The Act of Creation*. London: Pan Books.

8   See From Robert Louis Stevenson to Mendeleev; Sleeping on it does make a difference. *The Independent*. Jan 22, 2004. 3

9   See Ramsey, Ian T. 1957. *Religious Language* London: SCM

10 Bede, tr. Sherley-Price, Leo 1955. *A History of the English Church and People*. London: Penguin. Volume V.2. 266-268. The story of the healing of the boy. Aelred, later Abbot of Rievaulx was born in Hexham. See Tristram SSF, ed. 1997. *Exciting Holiness, Collects and Readings for the Festivals and Lesser Festivals of the Church of England.* Norwich: Canterbury Press.28.The recent vicar of Warden was Jim Gledhill..

11 Brinkley, Douglas, 2000. *Mine Eyes Have Seen the Glory, the Life of Rosa Parks*. London: Weidenfeld & Nicolson 98ff

12 Garrow, David J, 1988. 22

13 King Jr, Martin Luther, 1958. 61. A summary of the speech 61-63

14 Garrow, David J, 1988. 58. The description of his experience in the kitchen is in King Jr, Martin Luther, 1958. 133-5. See also Oates, Stephen B, 1982. 88-89.

15 King Jr, Martin Luther, 1969. 154

16 Garrow, David J, 1988. 60. The event is described 59-62.

17 De Beausobre, Iulia, ed. 1975. *Russian Letters of Direction 1834-1860, Macarius, Starets of Optino*. USA: St Vladimir's Seminary Press. 14-16

18 Babington Smith, C, 1983. 26-27

19 Trungpa, Chögyam , 1973. *Cutting through Spiritual Materialism*. London: Robinson & Watkins Books Ltd. The lives of the Tibetan Gurus, Marpa 31-38 and Milarepa 39-40 have this story if I remember correctly.

20 Babington Smith, C, 1983. 27

21 Babington Smith, C, 1983. 27

22 Van Dusen, Henry P, 1967. 69-70

23 Hammarskjöld, Dag, 1964. 50

24 Aulén, Gustaf, 1970. 58

25 Hammarskjöld, Dag, 1964. 62

26 Hammarskjöld, Dag, 1964. 65

27 Hammarskjöld, Dag, 1964. 79. See also 76

28 Hammarskjöld, Dag, 1964. 53

29 Hammarskjöld, Dag, 1964. 59

30 Hammarskjöld, Dag, 1964. 52

31 Hammarskjöld, Dag, 1964. 52-53. The quotation is on 53.

32 Hammarskjöld, Dag, 1964. See 51 and 54-55

33 Hammarskjöld, Dag, 1964. 61

34 Hammarskjöld, Dag, 1964. 52

35 Hammarskjöld, Dag, 1964. 54, the subject of the paragraph.

36 Hammarskjöld, Dag, 1964. 68

37 Hammarskjöld, Dag, 1964. 56
38 Hammarskjöld, Dag, 1964. 67
39 Hammarskjöld, Dag, 1964. 70
40 Hammarskjöld, Dag, 1964. 71
41 Hammarskjöld, Dag, 1964. 72-73
42 Hammarskjöld, Dag, 1964. 74, 75. 'Morning Star' is one of the titles of Christ.
43 Hammarskjöld, Dag, 1964. 77
44 Hammarskjöld, Dag, 1964. 78
45 Hammarskjöld, Dag, 1964. 77
46 Hammarskjöld, Dag, 1964. 83
47 Hammarskjöld, Dag, 1964. 82
48 Hammarskjöld, Dag, 1964. 84
49 Hammarskjöld, Dag, 1964. 86
50 Hammarskjöld, Dag, 1964. 73
51 Hammarskjöld, Dag, 1964. 87
52 Hammarskjöld, Dag, 1964. 169
53 Urquhart, Brian, 1973. 15
54 Hammarskjöld, Dag, 1964. 87
55 Urquhart, Brian, 1973. 13
56 Hammarskjöld, Dag, 1964. 88
57 Pope John XXIII, 1980 232
58 Pope John XXIII, 1970. 164
59 Pope John XXIII, 1980. 229.
60 Pope John XXIII, 1980. all the quotations in this paragraph 229
61 Pope John XXIII, 1980. 230-231
62 Pope John XXIII, 1980. 231
63 Pope John XXIII, 1980. 232
64 Pope John XXIII, 1980. 232-233
65 Thomas, Keri, 2004. A Vision for the Dying. *The Tablet* Jan 17th, 19
66 Dewar, Francis, 1988. *Live for a Change: Discovering and Using your Gifts.*
    London: Darton, Longman & Todd. See also Dewar, Francis 1991 *Called or
    Collared? An Alternative Approach to Vocation* London: SPCK and Dewar,
    Francis 1996 *Invitations: God's Calling for Everyone.* London: SPCK.
67 1 Corinthians 12, 10

Chapter 6 – The path is steeper

1   Hodes, Aubrey 1975. *Encounter with Martin Buber* London: Penguin 187
2   Washington, J M, ed.1986. 220. These words conclude the sermon.
3   Niebuhr, Reinhold, 1963. *Moral Man and Immoral Society.* London: SCM. The
    book was first published in 1932.
4   Halmos, Paul, 1978. *The Personal and the Political, Social Work and Political
    Action.* London: Hutchinson 123
5   Bonhoeffer, Dietrich, 1971, *Letters and Papers from Prison,* the Enlarged edition.
    London: SCM Press 5. Quoted in Halmos, Paul, 1978, 174.
6   Niebuhr, Reinhold, 1963. 81.

7   Garrow, David J, 1988. 65
8   Garrow, David J, 1988. 87
9   Garrow, David J, 1988. 89
10 Washington, J M, ed. 1986. 197. The full address is 197-200
11 Washington, J.M. ed. 1988. 285. For the incident see Garrow, David J, 1988 109-110.
12 Washington, J M, ed. 1986 23-30. The article appeared in the July 1959 issue of *Ebony.*
13 Garrow, David J, 1988. 125
14 Garrow, David J, 1988. 128
15 Garrow, David J, 1988. 148
16 Garrow, David J, 1988. 158.
17 Garrow, David J, 1988. 171   See *Face to Face.* 1961. BBC TV. Oct 29th.
18 Garrow, David J, 1988. 331
19 Garrow, David J, 1988. 200
20 See chapter 3, 48
21 Oates, Stephen B, 1982. 220
22 Garrow, David J, 1988, 242
23 Oates, Stephen B, 1982, 220 & 221
24 Garrow, David J, 1988. 243
25 King Jr, Martin Luther, 1964. *Why we can't Wait* .New York: Signet Books, Harper & Row. 80. The Letter from Birmingham Jail forms chapter 5, 76-95
26 Washington, J M, ed. 1986. 220. The full address is 217-220
27 See chapter 3, 55-56
28 Garrow, David J, 1988. 354
29 Oates, Stephen B, 1982. 322
30 See chapter 3, 55f
31 Washington, J M, ed.1986. 230. The full address is 227-230
32 Garrow, David J, 1988. 443
33 Garrow, David J, 1988. 501
34 Garrow, David J, 1988. 455
35 Garrow, David J, 1988. 483. One of the murderers was only convicted in 2005.
36 Garrow, David J, 1988. 496
37 Garrow, David J, 1988. 503-514.
38 Garrow, David J, 1988. 533
39 Garrow, David J, 1988. 532
40 Niebuhr, Reinhold, 1963. 252-254. Niebuhr's prophetic reflections about the plight of Afro-Americans and how they might emulate the example of Gandhi.
41 Washington, J M, ed. 1986, 38
42 Washington J M, ed. 1986. 13. The address to the YMCA and YWCA, Berkeley, California given in June 1957. 12-15
43 Washington, J.M. ed. 1986. 19. The full address,, an Experiment in Love, 16-20
44 Washington, J.M. ed. 1986. 12
45 King, Coretta Scott, 1969. 186
46 Foote. Wilder, ed. 1962. 28
47 Foote, Wilder, ed. 1962. 40-48. The New 'Santa Maria' address.

48 Foote, Wilder, ed. 1962. 23-24
49 Hammarskjöld, Dag, 1964. 94, quoting *The Book of Common Prayer,* Psalm 62,11.
50 Urquhart, Brian, 1973. 102
51 Hammarskjöld, Dag, 1964. 94
52 Hammarskjöld, Dag, 1964. 98-99
53 Hammarskjöld, Dag, 1964. 99
54 Hammarskjöld, Dag, 1964. 104-105
55 Hammarskjöld, Dag, 1964, 108.   See also Aulén, Gustaf, 1970, 99. 'Sanctification' replaces 'holiness' and 'the world of' is omitted.
56 Hammarskjöld, Dag, 1964. See 110-111.
57 Hammarskjöld, Dag, 1964. 111
58 Foote, Wilder, ed. 1962. 123-124. See also Hammarskjöld, Dag, 1964. 121.
59 Urquhart, Brian 1973. 218
60 Hammarskjöld, Dag, 1964. 126
61 Hammarskjöld, Dag, 1964. 128
62 Hammarskjöld, Dag, 1964. 133. April 7th, 1957 was Passion Sunday – see 129.
63 Urquhart, Brian, 1973. 252-253
64 Hammarskjöld, Dag, 1964. 134
65 Urquhart, Brian, 1973. 294
66 Hammarskjöld, Dag, 1964. 156
67 Hammarskjöld, Dag, 1964. 148
68 Foote, Wilder, ed.1962. 265
69 Hammarskjöld, Dag, 1964. 102
70 Pope John XXIII, 1980. 239
71 Pope John XXIII, 1980. 252
72 Trevor, Meriel, 1967. 177 & 174.
73 Hebblethwaite, Peter, 1984. 174
74 Hebblethwaite, Peter, 1984. 186. For the figure of 24,000 mentioned at the end of the paragraph, see 186-188.
75 Hebblethwaite, Peter, 1984. 201
76 Pope John XXIII, 1970. 491
77 Hebblethwaite, Peter, 1984. 181, quoting from Vittore Righi's account of Roncalli's work in Turkey. See Pope John XXIII, 1966. 28-34 for Roncalli's sermon in Lyons on June 24, 1945. .
78 Pope John XXIII, 1980. 291
79 Story told me by Archbishop Bruno Heim
80 Pope John XXIII, 1980. The first quotation is 297, the second 298.
81 Pope John XXIII, 1980. 299
82 Pope John XXIII, 1966. 162
83 Pope John XXIII, 1970, 725
84 Hebblethwaite, Peter, 1984. 227
85 Pope John XXIII, 1980. 305. He was 71 at the time but in his 72nd year. For his address to the people of Venice see Trevor, Meriel, 1967. 235-6.
86 Pope John XXIII, 1970. 747
87 Hebblethwaite, Peter, 1984. 245-246

88 Capovilla, Loris, 1992. Pope John and his Council. *The Tablet* Nov 7th. 1391. See website address: http://www.thetablet.co.uk

89 Hebblethwaite, Peter, 1984 264

90 Pope John XXIII, 1980. 313 and 314

91 Pope John XXIII, 1980. 293

92 Babngton Smith, C, 1983. 154

93 De Beausobre, Iulia, 1938. *The Woman who could not die.* London: Chatto & Windus.

94 Irina Prehn told me that Iulia de Beausobre had not referred to her physical torture because she thought that people would not believe her. Compare and see Report from Amnesty International, U K. February 2004. Get It Right, How Home Office Decision Making Fails Refugees. Chapter 5.

95 De Beausobre, Iulia 1948. 21

96 De Beausobre, Iulia 1948. 19

97 De Beausobre, Iulia 1948. 76

98 De Beausobre, Iulia 1948. 151

99 De Beausobre, Iulia 1948. 158

100 De Beausobre, Iulia 1948. 174

101 De Beausobre, Iulia 1940. *Creative Suffering* London: Dacre Press, A & C Black.

102 De Beausobre, Iulia 1940. 36.

103 De Beausobre, Iulia 1940. 43

104 Washington, J M, ed. 1986 378

105 Hammarskjöld, Dag, 1964. 138

106 Dunnant, Sarah, 2003. *The Birth of Venus.* London: Little Brown. 408.

Chapter 7 – Fire wind playing the strings

1 Hammarskjöld, Dag, 1964. 31

2 Jacobs, Michael, 1988. 127.

3 Wilber, Ken, 1996. Chapter 9, 83-91

4 Burton, Naomi, Hare, Brother Patrick & Loughlin, James Ed. 1974 *The Asian Journal of Thomas Merton* London: Sheldon. 312

5 Athanasius, 1980 *The Life of Antony and the Letter to Marcellinus.* London: SPCK 42. St Antony of Egypt spent 20 years living a solitary life of prayer in a tomb like building. Athanasius gives a vivid account of his coming out to be greeted by those who had come to see him.

6 Clément, Olivier, 1993 *The Roots of Christian Mysticism* London, New City 213. See also the final chapter, 'The Difficult Love, 270ff

7 Wolters, Clifton, tr.& intro.1978 *The Cloud of Unknowing and Other Works* London: Penguin.

8 Wilber, Ken 1991. *Grace and Grit* Dublin: Gill & Macmillan 188.

9 Pseudo-Dionysius 1987. 224f

10 Psalm 133,3

11 Babington Smith, C, 1983. 169-170. It comes in an outline for 'Alyosha's Way', a book Iulia de Beausobre drafted, based on the character of Aliosha in Dostoievski's 'The Brothers Karamazov'. 153-171.

12 Teresa of Avila, 1957. 123
13 John of the Cross *In* Peers, E Allison, ed. 1964. *Dark Night of the Soul.* Volume 1, Book 2, Ch 10. 403.
14 Hooker, Morna, 1991 314. See Mark 13, 14
15 Mark 14, 6 and 8
16 Hammarskjöld, Dag, 1964. 165
17 De Beausobre, Iulia, 1948. 141
18 De Beausobre, Iulia, 1948. 180
19 De Beausobre, Iulia, 1948. 181
20 De Beausobre, Iulia, 1948. 209
21 De Beausobre, Iulia, 1948. 219 & 220
22 Told me by Irina Prehn
23 De Beausobre, Iulia, 1948. 238
24 £300 is the figure given by Irina Prehn, about £10,000 in today's money. See Babington Smith, C 1983, 46. She gives it as 'not certain, but it was probably less than £500'
25 Babington Smith, C, 1983. 58
26 See Chapter 6, 127
27 Taylor, A J P, 1983. The Struggle for the Chair. *The Observer.* London. May 22nd. 25 in the Review section.
28 Namier, Julia, 1971. 265
29 Namier, Julia, 1971. 304
30 Mehta, Ved, 1963. *Fly and the Fly Bottle.* New York: Columbia University Press. 261-2
31 Babington Smith, C, 1983. 93
32 De Beausobre, Iulia, 1979. 117.
33 Babington Smith, C, 1983. 70
34 Mandelstam, Nadezhda, 1975. *Hope Against Hope.* London: Penguin. See also Solzhenitsyn, Alexander, 1974 (Volumes 1 and 2), 1975 (Volumes 3 & 4) 1978 (Volumes 6 &7). *The Gulag Archipelago, 1918-1956, an experiment in literary investigation.* London & New York: Collins and Harvill Press.
35 Hebblethwaite, Peter, 1984 286
36 Hebblethwaite, Peter, 1984. 308
37 Hebblethwaite, Peter, 1984. 302
38 Hebblethwaite, Peter, 1984. 315
39 Pope John XXIII, 1980. 349
40 See Hebblethwaite, Peter, 1984. 317-318
41 Trevor, Meriel 1967. 274
42 Hebblethwaite, Peter, 1984. 300
43 Hebblethwaite, Peter, 1984. 362
44 Pope John XXIII, 1980. 325
45 Pope John XXIII, 1980. 338
46 Pope John XXIII, 1980. 340
47 Pope John XXIII, 1980. 325
48 Pope John XXIII, 1980. 341
49 Pope John XXIII, 1980. 342

50 Levi, Primo 1987. *If this is a Man* and *The Truce* London: Abacus, Sphere Books. See also his other writings. See also Matthew 10, 28.
51 Fatula, Mary Ann, 1987.*Catherine of Siena's Way*. London: Darton, Longman & Todd. 79
52 O'Brien, Conor Cruise, (date*) Murderous Angels*. London: Faber & Faber. See also O'Brien, Conor Cruise, 1998. *Memoir, my life and themes*. s.l. Profile Books. 207 and 258-264. For O'Brien's work in Katanga and his assessment of Hammarskjöld see chapters 9 and 10, 201-264.
53 Hammarskjöld, Dag, 1964. 163
54 Hammarskjöld, Dag, 1964. 166
55 Urquhart, Brian, 1973. Note on 462. See also Foote, Wilder, ed. 1962. for Hammarskjöld's lecture in response to the criticism, 'The International Civil Servant in Law and in Fact' given at Oxford on 30th May 1961. 329-349
56 Hammarskjöld, Dag, 1964. 168. All references in this paragraph are from this page
57 Hammarskjöld, Dag, 1964. 169
58 Hammarskjöld, Dag, 1964. 170
59 Furlong, Monica, 1980. *Merton, a biography*. London: Collins.
60 Washington, J M, ed. 1986. 231. From his address, 'A time to break silence', 231-244
61 Garrow, David J, 1988. 566
62 Garrow, David J, 1988. 587
63 Garrow, David J, 1988. 582
64 Garrow, David J, 1988. 603
65 Garrow, David J, 1988. 611-612
66 Garrow, David J, 1988. 616
67 Washington, J M, ed. 1986. 275 from his sermon 'Remaining awake through a Great Revolution.' 268-278
68 Weil, Simone, 1959. *Waiting on God* London: Fontana. 76, 77 & 78. See pp76-94.

Chapter 8 – The Final Ascent.

1 Hammarskjöld, Dag, 1964. 31
2 Garrow, David J, 1988. 469.
3 See Boulay, Shirley du, 2001 *Changing the Face of Death: the story of Cicely Saunders*. Norfolk, RMEP. A Hospice Info Service is at St Christopher's Hospice, 51-53 Lawrie Park Road, Sydenham, London SE26 7DZ.
4 Kübler-Ross, Elizabeth 1970. *On Death and Dying* London: Tavistock. 19.
5 For books on dying see Kubler-Ross, Elizabeth 1970 and Hinton, J, 1967 *Dying* London: Penguin. On Bereavement see Parkes, C Murray, 1975. *Bereavement, Studies of Grief in Adult Life* London: Penguin, Worden, J W. 1983. *Grief Counselling and Grief Therapy* London: Tavistock and Lendrum, Susan & Syme, Gabrielle, 1992, *Gift of Tears, a practical approach to loss and bereavement counselling.* London: Routledge..

6   See Glaser, Barney & Strauss, Anselm, 1966 *Awareness of Dying.* London: Weidenfeld & Nicolson.

7   Bede, 1955. 328-329.

8   Boros, Laidislaus, 1965*The Moment of Truth* London: Burns & Oates.

9   Hammarskjöld, Dag, 1964. 72 & 73

10 De Beausobre, Iulia, 1974. A letter from the only frontier. *Frontier,* Volume 17, No.4, Winter 217-220

11 Kroll, Una, personal letter to Brian Frost

12 Frost, Brian. 1973. An extract from his personal diary for January 6th-13th.

13 Babington Smith, C, 1983. 167

14 Pope John XXIII, 1980. 325

15 Pope John XXIII, 1964. *Peace on Earth.* London: Magnum, Paul Hamlyn. The encyclical was published on Maundy Thursday, 1963, this edition with pictures.

16 Hebblethwaite, Peter, 1984. 503

17 Buber, Martin, tr. Gregor Smith, Ronald, 1937 *I and Thou* Edinburgh: T & T Clark..

18 Hammarskjöld, Dag, 1964. 181

19 Garrow, David J, 1988. 571

20 Washington, J M, ed.1986. 267. The quotation comes from 'The Drum Major Instinct', 259-267.

21 Washington, J M, ed.1986. 286. The final words of 'I see the promised land.' 279-286

22 Hoggart, Simon, 1989. Black anger as King disciple reveals a sexy last night. *The Observer,* Oct 15th.

23 De Beausobre, Iulia, 1967. The Expanding Universe of Intercession *Theoria to Theory.* 47-54

24 Washington, J M, ed. 1986, 267

25 Hammarskjöld, Dag, 1964, 132. See also Aulén, Gustaf, 1970. 94 Aulén puts 'severe' instead of 'brutal'.

Epilogue

1   'The Lord and Giver of Life' from the Nicene Creed. See also Symington, Neville 1993 *Narcissism, a New Theory* London: Karnac Books 40-41 and his concept of the Life Giver throughout the book.

2   Garrow, David J 1988, 364

Glossary

1   1 Corinthians 2, 14-15

2   Tournier, Paul, 1968 *The Meaning of Persons* London: SCM

3   Clément, Olivier, 2000 *On Human Being* London: New City 28. See also Chapter 2.

4   1 Corinthians 12, esp. v.27

5   Nelson, James B, 1979 *Embodiment, an approach to sexuality and Christian Theology* London: SPCK.

6   Peursen, C A Van, 1966 *Body, Soul, Spirit: a survey of the body-mind problem.*
    London: Oxford University Press.

7   Genesis 2, 7

8   Genesis 43, 30

9   see Lee, Alison, 2003. Translating Freud again? *The Scottish Institute of Human
    Relations Newsletter* 12, Sept. 14-15

10 I am grateful to Derek Raffaelli of Glasgow for this picture.

11 See Malan, David H, 2nd edition, 2001. *Individual Psychotherapy and the Science
    of Psychodynamics* London: Arnold.

12 See also Scharff, Jill Savege, ed. 1994. *The Autonomous Self, the work of John T
    D Sutherland.* New Jersey: Jacob Aronson. 304.

13 For the myth see Golding, Arthur tr. 2002 *Ovid's Metamorphoses* London:
    Penguin. 105-111.

14 Bion, W.R., 1962. *Learning From Experience,* London: Maresfield Reprints.
    Bion, W R, 1967. *Second Thoughts.* London: Heinemann. 140-1 & 150 and Gray,
    Anne, 1994. *An Introduction to the Therapeutic Frame.* London: Routledge. 7.

INDEX